Praise for
Your Best Just Got Better

"In these pages Jason Womack takes you through a process of assessing and reapplying the vital aspects of success and achievement in any field. Take the short road to improvement; let Jason Womack be your guide."

—Jim Cathcart
Author of 16 books including the upcoming *Make It Better*

"Jason has a remarkable ability to get your attention—it's like putting a mirror up in front of yourself and suddenly realizing you are due for a major makeover!"

—David Fink
Vice President, Human Resources EADS North America

"Jason Womack owns the personal productivity category in the training community. His workshops incorporate activities that create tangible learning by asking participants to make small changes that, when practiced over time, produce big results."

—John Robinson
Federal Agency Field Training Consultant

"*Your Best Just Got Better* helps you work smarter so that you have the time and energy to live your optimal life. Jason Womack shows you how to get out of your own way, eliminating both external and internal roadblocks and illuminating a path forward with easy-to-implement actions that make big differences."

—Michael Deutch
Product Director, Mindjet

"Jason Womack helps people realize their high productivity potential in *Your Best Just Got Better*."

—Michael Guarnieri
Sr. Marketing Manager, Citrix Online

"Jason Womack is an inspired and visionary business leader. His concepts and ideas for creating best business practices are based on deep insight and understanding of the psychology of human performance. *Your Best Just Got Better* is exactly the kind of tool we need to help us work most effectively—in life and at work."

—Frances Hesselbein
President and CEO, Leader to Leader Institute

YOUR
BEST
JUST GOT
BETTER

YOUR BEST JUST GOT *BETTER*

work SMARTER

think BIGGER

make MORE

JASON W. WOMACK

WILEY

John Wiley & Sons, Inc.

Published by John Wiley & Sons, Inc., Hoboken, New Jersey.
Published simultaneously in Canada.

For general information on our other products and services or for technical support, please contact our Customer Care Department within the United States at (800) 762-2974, outside the United States at (317) 572-3993 or fax (317) 572-4002.

Wiley publishes in a variety of print and electronic formats and by print-on-demand. Some material included with standard print versions of this book may not be included in e-books or in print-on-demand. If this book refers to media such as a CD or DVD that is not included in the version you purchased, you may download this material at http://booksupport.wiley.com. For more information about Wiley products, visit www.wiley.com.

Library of Congress Cataloging-in-Publication Data:

Womack, Jason W., 1972-
  Your best just got better : work smarter, think bigger, make more / Jason W. Womack.
    p.   cm.
  Includes index.
  ISBN 978-1-118-12198-6 (hardback)
  ISBN: 978-1-118-22472-4 (ebk)
  ISBN: 978-1-118-23003-9 (ebk)
  ISBN: 978-1-118-23011-4 (ebk)
    1. Success in business.   2. Success.   3. Change (Psychology)   I. Title.
  HF5386.W83   2012
  650.1—dc23   2011037179

Printed in the United States of America

10 9 8 7 6 5 4 3 2 1

To you,
so you make your best even better

Contents

Foreword

THROUGHOUT MY CAREER as an executive coach, I have focused on helping successful people get even better. And, they do! They do get better but not without the help of extraordinary people like Jason Womack. Jason's experience as a workplace performance expert and executive coach shines through in *Your Best Just Got Better: Work Smarter, Think Bigger, Make More*. Following his advice will make you more productive; using his techniques and tools will help you to significantly improve your performance.

If you have any doubts about taking the time to read *Your Best Just Got Better*, I want to make it very easy for you to make up your mind to keep reading!

Three (of the Many) Reasons Why I Like This Book

First, Jason begins with the biggest obstacle to success and change— "Me." Most people, especially those who are already successful, believe that because they do a certain behavior that has led to success in the past, the same behavior will lead to success in the future. I call this the Success Delusion. Overcoming the delusion requires vigilance and introspection. It requires, as Jason puts it, "Identifying Our Individual Role in Making Our Best Better."

Second, Jason's chapter about the powers of positive *and* negative focus (Chapter 9) taps into a fundamental concept that is often overlooked. Dramatic performance improvement is not necessarily the byproduct of gaining new knowledge or doing more work; it is more often the result of getting rid of distractions and interruptions that take us away from working on our MITs (Most Important Things as Jason calls them).

And, finally, each chapter provides ideas you can begin experimenting with right away. Jason provides extraordinarily helpful tools for improving workplace performance. The exercises in each chapter help you focus on improving; that will help you maintain your momentum as you forge your path to more success.

The insight that *Your Best Just Got Better: Work Smarter, Think Bigger, Make More* is universally applicable. It provides a roadmap that any individual can use to improve performance. And, with Jason's positive approach and upbeat writing style, this blend of simple, doable actions and pragmatic ideas will take you far down the road to peak Workplace Performance!

Life is good.

—**Marshall Goldsmith**
Million-selling author of the *New York Times* bestsellers, *MOJO* and *What Got You Here Won't Get You There*

Prologue

I WAKE UP before the alarm clock goes off—again. Here at home, unlike at my office in the city, it is serenely quiet outside—no noisy cars, airplanes, or sirens; just the gentle sound of water splashing into the fountain that sits on the patio. Across the room, embers glow through the window of the airtight stove, remnants of the fire I built the night before. I gently step out of bed onto the carpeted floor, which I manage to do without waking my wife. The dog looks at me as I leave the room, as if to say, "Go back to sleep; the day will start later."

Moving down the short stairway, I make my way to my home office and review the list I wrote the day before of today's MITs—the Most Important Things. I elect to work on the article that is due in two weeks to the business magazine editor for whom I write a monthly column on management development.

I sit down at my writing desk with pen in hand and notebook spread open to the next blank page. I set the timer for 80 minutes, during which time I fill up page after page after page with ideas. I spend the time thinking, connecting, writing, making lists, drawing, and organizing thoughts around the topics of engagement, productivity, and purpose. Soon, I'm lost in thought, and before I know it, my morning writing time is up!

Next, less than 90 minutes after waking up, I'm reviewing my notes for a conference call with a client in Asia; I generally talk with them early morning, my time, about twice a month. I stand up to face the large whiteboard, dial in, and present my idea: a customized management development learning program. The call goes well, and we make plans to co-develop a series of videos to teach basic and advanced leadership, workplace performance, and personal productivity methodologies to their global workforce. The videos will be hosted on their intranet, where more than 80,000 employees will have access to what we name the Productivity TouchPoint Learning Program.

I look over my desk out the eastern window. The glow from the computer monitor is losing its prominence as the first of the day's sunshine begins to fill the room.

I get dressed in my late-spring running gear (which some would argue is enough for a winter run in Colorado), open the door, and step outside into the cool morning air. Since I'm running by myself, I decide to take the western route and chase my shadow for a while. It's a beautiful five-mile, single-tracked trail along the river; I return to the property in just under 65 minutes, a good time for that course! I'm hungry, wide awake, and ready for the day to continue getting even better.

I'm sure that my wife is up by now, dressed in her robe and sitting in the family room reading a book, with a homemade latte within arm's reach and our dog curled up at her feet. Walking up the last of the path to the deck, I look up and see her through the French doors, and for an instant my mind flashes back to the day we met . . .

Introduction

Hɪ! Mʏ ɴᴀᴍᴇ is Jason, and what you read in the Prologue is the beginning to what I call an "Ideal Day."

Not *the* Ideal Day, of course, just one of the many that I've sat down to imagine. I've been writing these for years, and, as a result, life for me continues to get better. The one I wrote about in the Prologue, featuring the mountain property, writing, client calls, and trail running, first appeared as a draft journal entry in 1995. Some time after that, I typed it, saved it and reviewed it from time to time. I always thought it'd be an amazing way to start a day.

Your Best Just Got Better: Work Smarter, Think Bigger, Make More will show you how to make your best even better, how to achieve more in work and in life, and how to sustain those changes over time.

I encourage you, before you even start reading Chapter 1, to write a first draft of one of *your* Ideal Days. Sit down, set a timer for 15 minutes, and write. Begin by writing about that portion of the day when you know you have a lot of energy and do your best work. Do you have more energy in the morning? Or, would you consider yourself a "night owl"? Pick the time of day when you *could be* at your best. (You'll notice I wrote about the early morning.)

The first time I wrote out an Ideal Day, I remember it was a challenge. Over the years, however, practicing this technique has gotten easier, and the time invested has paid huge dividends. For example, I couldn't imagine (a) living in the mountains, (b) being a published author, (c) raising a dog, or (d) getting married. I wrote that Ideal Day you just read after a mentor, Ron Kok, challenged me to do so. Ron was a graduate advisor at the University of California–Santa Barbara and he asked me the following incredibly thought-provoking question: "Would you know a great day if you saw one?"

Since then I've stopped from time to time to script out another Ideal Day; and over the years, I've imagined quite a few of them. They evolve over time, just as I do.

Let me make it very clear that I don't routinely experience Ideal Days exactly as I write them, *nor do I expect to*. I anticipate, however, that I will achieve parts of those days from time to time. And, over the past 15-plus years, I have! Since initiating the practice of imagining, designing, and anticipating Ideal Days, I've lived in the mountains, renting homes in Alaska and Lake Tahoe; and, I've taken off entire weeks from work, solely to write, in wonderful places like Costa Rica and Colorado. Thanks to these breaks, I've written dozens of speeches, many booklets and hundreds of articles. I've gone for trail runs in the morning, and I've read, sitting in the family room, sipping on a latte sitting next to my wife, Jodi, and our Labrador Retriever, Zuma.

For more than a decade, I have studied the mindset, skill-set and toolkits that global clients depend on to make their best even better as individual contributors, team members and managers. I've presented these principles in leadership development workshops in board rooms, conference rooms and via electronic means such as conference calls and webinars to audiences around the world. People from the Americas to China, from Argentina to Italy are using these practices, often new habits, to implement improved productivity behaviors and achieve more than they ever thought possible in their lives and their workplaces.

When you redirect your focus, your perspective changes, and when that happens, you have a significant option: You can begin to make things better. And, of course, if you change your direction, even a little bit, you could easily progress toward a new goal, achieve a big dream, or live a different life. Want to make your best even better? Focus on, write down, and review what that would look, sound, and feel like. That is, write out an Ideal Day scenario for yourself!

Look around and think about your work, life, community, family, and habits. The life you are currently experiencing is the result of accumulated thoughts, discussions, actions and experiences. If you would like your life to be different, then it's very important to get started. You can begin right where you are—right here, right now—to make things better.

Think deeply about what an Ideal Day would look, sound, and feel like. Take some time—right now—to draft your detailed description of one. Put it somewhere you can review it, daily or weekly. Again, you're not writing *the* Ideal Day; what you ultimately experience could be even better! Once you have that ready to go, you're prepared to begin your journey of working *smarter*, thinking *bigger*, and making *more*.

Your Best Just Got Better shows you how to gain clarity, develop structure, and build momentum as the Architect of Your Experience. It will lead, inspire, and motivate you to walk the path of persistence, moving you toward a better you. I am confident these experiences will support you along the way.

Open to Part 1, Chapters 1-3, and get started using ideas, practices, and systems that make it easy to work smart. I'll show you how to manage your ideas, think about your projects, and make the most out of the time you have so you can do more of what you'd like to do.

While reading Part 2, Chapters 4-7, you'll learn how to practice specific ways to think bigger. Here, I will present the tools and techniques people use to build leadership skills and get the most from their business and personal networks. I also will show you how you can study your current routines in order to improve your approaches to personal productivity and workplace performance.

And when it's time to assess your results at the end of a project, the end of the year, or when you retire (!), use the ideas and activities in Part 3, Chapters 8-10, to make more. What does "more" mean to you? While you're reading this book I ask you to keep that question in mind.

A bit about me: I am a workplace performance expert and executive coach. I have worked with thousands of clients over the past 11 years, and I've always told them, "I study this stuff so you don't have to!"

One more thing: I define *productivity* as: "Doing what I said I would do, within the time that I promised." The "more" that I want is to keep more of those promises. With that in mind, let me share the promise I am making to you:

As a result of reading this book, you'll know why, how and when you must make your best even better.

PART

1

Work Smarter

IN THE WORKPLACE, there is a constant feeling of pressure to do more and more...often with less. How many of you have less time and fewer resources while you're managing bigger goals and more complexity? New projects arrive, team members move on, and the organization's leadership sets bigger, or different, goals. Simultaneously, opportunities arise, surprises show up, and life changes on a personal level, as well. How smart you work depends on: how well you know yourself, how clear your next-level goals are, and how you're using that all-too-limited resource, time. These are the topics of the first three chapters of this book.

Successful people set a clear direction to move in, and work effectively utilizing all their strengths. By applying just a little focus to *when* you're at your best, you can improve the way you approach the things you need to get done, both on the job and off. Don't just wish things were different; set yourself up to engage and make new things possible. As business philosopher Jim Rohn said, "Instead of wishing things were easier, wish you were better."

Setting realistic goals does not mean you should understate what you think is possible. Instead, direct your focus toward the experience of completion and give ample attention to the next milestone of achievement. Build a series of bridges as you continually reach toward experiencing more of your Ideal Days.

With only 96 15-minute blocks in a 24-hour day, and more to do than we have time to do it in, we need to work smarter, getting more of the right things done. When you identify tasks that take too much time, and practice ways to work productively, effectively, and efficiently, you could easily net 1 to 3 *extra* 15-minute blocks of time each day. With 15 to 45 extra minutes tomorrow, and every day after that, imagine how you could make progress toward setting up and experiencing your own Ideal Days!

I promise, after reading and implementing the ideas in the next three chapters you'll have more time, energy, and focus to make progress and achieve more of your Most Important Things!

1

Improvement and You

Identifying Your Role in Making Your Best Better

In 1988, NIKE launched its Just Do It advertising campaign. Ever since, those three words have been used to motivate, inspire, encourage, and even demand people to take on all kinds of goals and work harder to make things happen—personally *and* professionally. What have you ever tried to "just do"? Of course, that slogan may resonate for *some* people, *some* of the time, for *some* of the things they work to achieve. But if you're anything like me (and I'm assuming you're at least a little like me since you're reading this book), you've occasionally found that "just doing it" can be hard.

When you take on something big, it can be daunting to think, "Okay, I'll just do it." How do you make it easier to achieve a goal, or even *begin* to move in a specific direction?

To identify your role in making your best better, you must know how you *work*, how you *think,* and how you *make things happen.* The better you understand yourself, the better able you will be to work effectively and efficiently to get the important things done.

When you think of changing the way you do things, how you can work smarter, think bigger, and make more, stop and ask yourself:

- Where do I begin?
- What if it's too much to take on?
- What if something doesn't work out?
- What if I'm not yet ready to start?

These kinds of "contingency" questions are extremely useful when you're project planning; you have the opportunity to bring up all kinds of possible scenarios. Unfortunately, for more creative people (you among them, perhaps?), these kinds of questions may actually slow you down; you may even stop and question that which you're planning to change (and hopefully) improve. These questions can force hesitation; even worse, prompts like this may make you feel so intimidated by the prospect of taking action that you end up just *not* doing it. (Sorry, Nike.)

What are you interested in making better? That is, "Why did you pick *this* book?" Of all the books on improving your performance, increasing your productivity, and getting more of what you want, you picked this one.

I know you can work *smarter*, think *bigger*, and make *more*. I, myself, have used all the techniques that I write about, and I coach clients around the world to test the very same principles, methods, and activities I outline for you here. As you can guess, the campaign that *I* promote is: "Just get started!"

Once you clarify your role in improvement, you'll use every chapter in this book as a rung on the ladder to success. Each chapter in each part adds another level of depth to the overall mission of professional and personal development.

Now, you must be wondering, "Okay, how do I do that? How do I 'just get started?'" Fortunately, the I.D.E.A. elements I teach will guide you in taking personal responsibility and achieving your goals. They are:

I: *Identify* a very specific area you want to improve. Focus your attention on making the best better in one area of your life, and clarify what that will look like when you get there.

D: *Develop* strategies to engage in specific actions and techniques to direct your professional improvement and personal development. Acknowledge the process—remember, you're just getting started! An important aspect is that the most sustainable changes people tend to make usually start small, are repeated with consistency, and often result in a payoff greater than anyone could have hoped.

E: *Experiment* by planning for and taking actions that generate bursts of momentum. Experimenting gives you the freedom to stop at any time to try something new. It also provides a more objective framework so that you can determine whether you should stop or continue moving forward. When you take specific actions to make your best better, it continues to get better.

A: *Assess* the value the effort has created. Here is the question I consistently ask myself, my friends, my family, even my clients: "Is what you're doing worth the effort?"

It All Starts with You

Begin at the beginning; tell your own story—the tale of you getting from where you *were* to where you *are* to where you are *going*. There's no time like the present; take the time right now to clarify your role in making your best better.

One of my favorite sayings comes from a high school math teacher who said, "If you wait long enough, the bell will ring!" There are several distinct factors and experiences that set me on this path of learning, experimentation, and achievement. Throughout the book, I will share them with you. My hope in doing so is that you will generate new ideas of what you can do. Read this book, talk about the ideas with your friends and colleagues, and practice with the ideas and exercises. Little by little, your best will get better.

Since before I started college, I've been interested in how people get from here to there. I distinctly remember having dinner one night while I was still in high school and living with my father, stepmother, and younger brother. One evening I asked my dad, "When did you know you were an executive?"

He was the president and COO of a store called The Sharper Image, and I wanted to know what he had done to get there. He talked

about the work he had done to figure out how he worked most effectively, and the goals he set for each three-year period of his life. He also
told me about the importance of patience and pacing, something that
I believe I've gotten better at over the past few decades.

Beginning in August 2000, and for the next six years, I worked
as a senior facilitator with David Allen, originator of Getting Things
Done (GTD), a work-life management system. I coached senior leaders
in effective workflow and organization strategies, and presented more
than 350 GTD seminars in Europe, South America, and throughout
the United States. During that same time, my wife Jodi (who was the
first full-time employee of David Allen Company) worked as an office
administrator, customer service liaison, and public seminar coordinator.

In 2006, I decided to set a new goal, and it was then that I launched
The Jason Womack Company. I had gained the experience of working
for someone else in presenting information; now it was my turn to create content, publish reports and articles, and work with clients focused
on their next level of success. I am dedicated to advising individual
leaders at small to large-sized companies, providing "Workplace Performance" seminars and coaching.

The company is now more than five years old, and I continue to take
my leadership role as a founder very seriously. I use all of the methods
and systems you'll read about in this book to manage the complexities,
surprises, and successes of our coaching and publishing company. How
do I do it? It's quite simple (though not always easy!); I continue to
return to the theme of this chapter: I just get started.

Let me share with you how some of my goal-setting and strategic planning sessions with mentors have changed things for the better for me.

Over lunch one day with my long-time mentor, executive coach
Marshall Goldsmith, I shared my dedication to a three-step process,
which I outline in detail a little later in the chapter: (1) Set a goal.
(2) Be consistent. (3) Take action. During that discussion and throughout subsequent e-mail conversations, he encouraged me to stay on
message. "What is it you want to do?" he asked. Though it sounds like
a simple question, it took us a couple of hours to discover the real core
goal I had set for my small company:

I teach principles of human psychology and sociology that make
it easier to get done what you *have to do*, so you have the time,
energy, and focus for what you really *want to do*.

That is the ultimate goal for my company—and, this book! The statement also acts as a filter while I'm interviewing a client, talking with a journalist, writing an article, or serving as an advisor to a board. It's the entire purpose of my work. If we ever get to share a conversation, and if what I am sharing with you can help you work smarter, think bigger, and make more, let's keep talking and figure out a way to work together!

I reflect often on that lunchtime conversation with Marshall. I know it was one of two best things I did when my wife and I were preparing to launch this company. A second memorable coaching session also took place over a meal some time later.

The next meeting Jodi and I scheduled was with another of our mentors, Jim Polk, here in our hometown of Ojai, California. We met for breakfast one morning to share the overarching goal of our company. He encouraged us to think about the overall strategy of our company—that is, what would *indicate* that we were living and working "on purpose"? His questions were intense, and the conversation was deep.

Subsequently, Jodi and I had several conversations about the prompts that Jim gave us; they were great business development questions we could come back to again and again. And, notably, they triggered our thinking beyond our new company. Later that week we spent another two hours together in his office identifying what became our four Most Important Things (MITs) for The Jason Womack Company. On a large whiteboard in my office, we transcribed the following critical success factors (along with objective goals, strategies, and measures) for the first 12 months of our business. Our four MITs were:

1. *Lifestyle*: We longed for a lifestyle that was more focused on contribution (what can we give) than on acquisition (what will we get). It's important to us, to this day, to work with people who do good work. We spend time sharing our guidance and knowledge with organizations and companies that promote a focus on sustainability—and I'm not talking only about our environment, but also about the larger picture of sustaining and building contribution, improvement, health, wellness, prosperity, happiness, and joy as a lifestyle.

2. *Revenue*: We had two reference points over the previous decade: From 1995 to 2000, I worked as a high school teacher (lower

annual salary) and from 2000 to 2006, as a seminar facilitator and executive coach (higher annual salary). We created a budget and planned for our savings, vacations, and monthly expenses. We defined "our nut," that sum of money we'd have to make each month to keep moving forward. We multiplied that by 12 months to come up with a goal for the first year of our business. It was as easy a goal-setting strategy as that! (In that first year, we did enough work to earn almost 15 percent more than our stated goal! Of course, we then used that as a metric for the next year's plan.)

3. *Client list*: This MIT was fun. I started by looking at my office supplies and visiting my favorite companies' websites. I reviewed my bookcase, and even walked through the garage. I made a master list of the companies and the products I thought were awesome, the things I used and would be willing to recommend. From the triathlon bike that I race on to the books in my bookcase, and from the technology on my desk to the clothes in my closet, I made a list of the companies I supported with my wallet.

I then decided to reach out to these companies to see if I could support their leadership development programs. In January 2007, I developed a Presentations course for managers of my favorite outdoor lifestyle company, Patagonia, based in Ventura, California. Later that same month I worked with a senior leadership team from one of my favorite not-for-profit organizations, the World Wildlife Fund (at an off-site meeting in Antigua, Guatemala). Later that year, I presented a speech to more than 1,500 small to medium-sized business owners at a business planning conference for Loan ToolBox (the founders were friends of mine from California), at the company's annual conference in Las Vegas, Nevada. Ever since that first year, I have continued to introduce myself to the people and companies I'd like to work with, and this effort continues to pay off!

4. *Products*: Our fourth MIT was to create products—books, ebooks, and audio and video recordings—that people could use to review and learn about ideas to make their best even better. We decided that first year we'd record an audio CD and build an ebook (in PDF format that we could e-mail) containing ideas on digital organization. Later on, we created more products, and even started drafting the outline of the book you're now holding in your hands.

If you agree that goal setting is a very powerful process (whether you *think* about your goals, *write* your goals, or *see yourself* in your goals), then your role in making your best better is clear to you. Every six months, Jodi and I return to our MITs and talk to, meet with, and e-mail our mentors with updates. We like to review and renew our short-, medium-, and long-term goals with each other, and then ask for ideas and feedback from our network. By doing so, we continually identify and clarify the focus of our consulting and advising work, and learn about the challenges our clients face so that we can develop newer strategies, better techniques, and more efficient processes they can use immediately.

Focus on Making Your Best Better

In this section, I outline in detail the three steps—concepts, really—I mentioned earlier, which I firmly believe are crucial to a focus on making your best better:

1. *Set a goal.* A goal goes a long way toward making more things possible. A clear outcome helps form a structure, clarifying the *destination* while making obvious the *direction* to go in. Once you have set a clear path to achieving a goal, it will be easier to say no to things that take you off-course.
2. *Be consistent.* Consistency is key to personal and career success. If you can repeat positive, valuable behaviors, develop routines that build upon each other and that generate and enhance momentum, you will demonstrate your trustworthiness to everyone you work with and around.
3. *Take action.* Action is necessary to achieve your goals. To get from where you are to where you want to be, you must plan *and* take specific action steps directly related to the goal.

Now it's time to stop and ask yourself, "How do I apply these three concepts to my own work and life experiences?" As you continue reading, make notes of how you think you identify your goals, how you plan for consistency, and how you take deliberate action toward achieving your desired outcomes.

Identifying Your Own MITs

It might seem intimidating at the beginning of the process, but there are small, very easy steps you can take to get started. Begin right now, while you're reading this book. Take a page from a notebook or pull out a blank piece of printer paper. On top of that page, write "MY MITs." Underneath, write down the kinds of things you already know are among your top three to five MITs. Blend them, mix them, and clarify them among the categories of work and life, professional and personal, big and little.

Here are two things you can do *this week* to take ownership of your role in making your best, better.

1. *Strike a deal: Ask a mentor, coach, or friend to serve as an accountability buddy.* Identify one very specific goal you have, either in your personal life or at work, and tell your accountability buddy about it in person, over a Skype call, or on the phone. Then, every 5 to 10 days, schedule time to talk. Ideally, you'll meet several times over the course of two months. Decide at the beginning of the process just how many meetings you'd like to have. This clarifies the beginning, middle, and end. Over the course of those few conversations, you'll share your goal and progress, and keep your ears open for the "feed-forward" (as Marshall Goldsmith calls it) that this person can share with you.

   This kind of a check-in process gives you a special opportunity: You get to see your progress through someone else's eyes and, as a result, notice some things that you might not see on your own. As fast as life happens, sometimes it's simply easier to think about and reflect on what needs to be done than to put the time, energy, and focus into reviewing what you've done and how it's leading to something better.

   As your accountability buddy reflects back to you what you are sharing, and asks you the kinds of questions you need to answer to continue improving on the situation, you will make more progress—faster than you thought possible.

2. *See yourself in your goals.* There are three kinds of goals: (1) goals you think about, (2) goals you write on paper, and (3) goals in which you actually *see yourself.*

I find the third group to be the most effective. Instead of thinking about what you'd like, or making yet another list of things you "need to do," try the following: Stand in front of a mirror holding a dry-erase pen (the kind you use on whiteboards). Look yourself directly in your eyes and ask, "What do I want to get *better* at? What do I want to make *more* of?" Write down the first couple of things that come to mind. Yes, write them on the mirror so that you actually *see* yourself and the goal at the same time, in the same space.

Start practicing this on small things. For example, early in the morning before you leave for work, stop and write what you'd like to make progress on during the day. Then you have an opportunity to check in with that goal two more times during the day: first, when you return home (or to your hotel room if you travel as much as I do!), and then right before you go to sleep. Again in front of the mirror, look yourself in the eyes and ask, "Based on what I wanted to have happen today, how did I do?" Listen to the answer(s) and use that information to help guide you toward the following day.

Acknowledge the Process of Iterative Improvement

Another author, speaker, and leader I have learned a lot from over the past decade is Frances Hesselbein. She is president and CEO of the Leader to Leader Institute and author of, *My Life in Leadership*. Over a conversation one morning in her New York City office, she offered me this slice of wisdom: "You get what you expect." I truly believe this to be true, and have found that what I think should happen, often does. Whether I'm coaching a corporate executive on the psychology of teamwork and accountability, or working with a friend who's preparing for a triathlon, we *always* focus on what we want to occur over the long term, and we acknowledge that it is always an incremental process to identify projects and milestones to make things happen.

Knowing where to expend your next effort is critical to working smarter, thinking bigger, and making more. Everything you read here will support this process:

Clarify where you *are*, get started toward where you're *going*, and regularly evaluate the *payoff(s)* of the effort.

When I taught high school (U.S. history, world history, and Spanish) from 1995 to 2000, I always shared the rules of the game with the students in my classroom. I didn't hide my teaching methods, personal objectives, or required standards. At the beginning of each term, I shared with students my scoring and grading strategies, and even provided a copy of the California State Standards (the guidelines of content I was to teach over the 10 months of the school year) to keep in their notebooks. When it was time to start a new unit, I asked them to review the state standards. "Here's where we're going," I'd always say.

By understanding my grading strategies and knowing the California content standards for each subject I taught, they could determine *exactly* where we were along the path to their ultimate goal: to complete the course. Throughout the year, I even held special monthly classes (always on Saturday mornings) to share what I thought were important student skills, such as note taking and backpack organization. One month I even presented a two-hour workshop titled "How to Talk So Adults Will Listen." It was one of the most popular weekend classes I ever taught!

Why Improve Iteratively?

Iterative improvement presupposes that small actions—identified, completed, and reviewed with consistency—can build positive momentum. When you review your day-to-day activities in the office, what do you remember about the day? Do you reflect on the actions you took toward the goals you said you wanted to reach? One of the most important, and time-saving, things you can do to speed the process of improvement is to *continually* define, clarify, and create the support structure you need to succeed.

Have *you* done this? If so, how? Does your team or your boss know where you are going? What about your friends and family members: Are they aware of the path you wish to be on? Do they see you taking steps each day, each week, each month, toward achieving your ultimate outcomes? How do you continue to make things possible?

Once you have identified even some of your MITs, it's time to do the work necessary to make progress toward achieving them. To do so, you're going to need and use more support. (I will talk much more extensively about building your social network in Chapter 5.)

Most professional and executive leadership or talent development programs promote the idea of accountability and teamwork. By identifying what you expect to happen, creating realistic and specific milestones, and asking for help when you need it, you put yourself on the way to a whole new level of success. Following is an iterative approach you can take to improve, one that will enable you to step more fully into your role in making your best even better!

Scripts for Success

WHO DO YOU KNOW WHO . . .?

This is a question I have used for years to ask people to introduce me to others who may share my interests. I find that when I reach out and ask for help, those around me—my friends, colleagues, and even clients—make an effort to do whatever they can (and sometimes more!) to assist me in my endeavors. As you continue on the path to making your best better, make the people around you aware of the kinds of things you're working on, and who you're looking to meet. One chance meeting and one extra conversation may wind up moving an entire project forward by leaps and bounds. And it may have started with one simple question, "Who do you know who?"

WHERE ARE YOU LOOKING TO EXPAND?

At a conference, meeting, or networking event, you're bound to meet someone and hear the question, "So, what do you do?" I have found that this question, more often than not, actually opens a chasm between two people. Despite the fact that it's intended to begin a conversation, it instead creates dissonance, as each person starts unconsciously to compare him- or herself to the other.

By instead asking a question like, "Where are you looking to expand?" you invite the other person to a different sort of conversation. As he or she is talking, you can even use a conversation script based loosely on the one above by saying something like, "Hey, I know someone who . . ." Being interested *and* interesting in conversation is another way to gently, simply, and positively take responsibility for your own improvement.

To Get Started, Just Get Started

Years ago, my business coach Tim Braheem said to me, "Jason, when you're at work, *work*." Very quickly, I came to understand that he did not distinguish between his personal and professional expression of work; his definition of the term was all-inclusive. It simply meant: "Anything you're doing right *now*." What he taught me in that one conversation—really, in just those six words—was, wherever I am, no matter what I am doing, I need focus on the task at hand. Whether I'm coaching an executive, pushing myself to the limit in a triathlon, reading a book, or taking a get-away-from-it-all weekend vacation, I have one intention: to engage completely and give as much of my focus as possible to the endeavor.

It is important to recognize, however, that it's not realistic to give 100 percent, all the time, to everything you do. For that reason, you must make important choices; in other words, you have to prioritize.

What's your current approach here? Do you try and do a little bit of everything? Or do you focus on a few important areas of your work life on a somewhat rotating basis?

When we fail to make our MITs a priority, we become overwhelmed trying to think about and remember all there is to do. The phrase "the stress of it all is killing me" comes to mind. What does it mean? It means that the anticipation of trying to get all of your MITs done can kill the motivation to even begin on a single task.

To begin, bring to mind just one of your MITs and *just get started*.

Understand the Impact of Your Style of Working

Your individual role in making your best better requires that you: (1) know the way you *work* and *get things done*, and (2) constantly *ensure that you are aligned with* the way you work and get things done.

There's a simple question you can ask to distinguish your own working style: Are you a verb person or a noun person?

To help you answer that, put down this book and find a to-do list you composed sometime in the past month or so. If you can't find one, make one. It's best to have a list with more than 30 things that need your attention. Now look at the first (or sometimes, only) word of each item on the list. Is it a noun or is it a verb?

There's no right or wrong way to write a list. If you get things done, you get things done. Here is what I know about these two kinds of work: I have had the valuable opportunity over the past decade to sit down with hundreds of people and their to-do lists. I have also sat in (as an observer) on scores of meetings (in person and via conference calls) with teams around the world. I find that although everyone will switch between nouns and verbs here and there, the very real data is there for you to see in your own hand; some people tend to choose nouns over verbs; others prefer verbs to nouns.

As you clarify the ways you can work smarter, consider the distinction between the two.

Working with Nouns

People who have a lot of nouns show up in their notes and to-do lists (and my own hand goes up here—I write down events, people's names, situations, article titles, and so on) tend to be known as visionary, big-picture thinkers. It's easy for them to talk in generalities, or want to discuss overarching aspects of the project before defining the details and actions necessary to get the work done.

At the *end* of a day, noun workers want to know which projects or events received attention, and that the people around them understand where they're going. During meetings, I frequently observe noun workers talk about what's going to happen, who will be involved, and/or how great it will be when they're done. Sometimes, I'll even hear them repeat something that was said previously (as if saying it for the first time), as they're still processing the idea mentally. Looking around my office, I have a list on my office whiteboard right now:

- Marketing Plan/Excel file
- Singularity University
- Book Launch
- Website Landing Page
- Mastering Workplace Performance Online
- June (D-Day) trip to Normandy, France

Note that these signify projects that no doubt have several actions (verbs) tied to them. The nouns act as bookmarks, or placeholders, for those things that I need to be thinking about, planning, and acting on in order to achieve some objective goal. I naturally surround myself with noun workers. I like them close by, as they are the ones to whom I can bring a new, crazy, big idea and who will make it *newer, crazier,* and *bigger!*

How do you work on the big things?

When it's time to think creatively, innovatively, or differently, invite your friends or mentors who are known to do just that. Don't worry just yet about figuring out *how to do* what it is you're thinking about. That comes later. As you bring your colleagues, friends, and mentors to mind, please keep in mind that being a noun worker is by no means a good or a bad thing. There is no right or wrong here. In fact, knowing which members of your team *are* the noun workers could add to the effectiveness and efficiency of meetings by designating a specific period of time for noun-only-focused discussions.

If you happen to work with (or for) someone who is a noun worker, try this five-day experiment: At the end of each day, bring to this individual a short list of the major accounts, issues, projects, or events you worked on. Resist telling them *what* you did on those accounts or projects, unless of course they ask for the details. If the noun worker is an especially efficient and astute manager, he or she will know exactly where and when to ask follow-up questions regarding the "verbs" of the day.

Working with Verbs

Now, look at the list of someone who is a verb worker and you will see he or she has clearly defined the things that need to be *done,* sooner rather than later! Every item on each line of that person's to-do list will start with an action verb (big or little). Verb workers manage their productivity in terms of action, delegation, and progress.

Generally, when I work with someone and we start talking "verbs," I advise him or her to write down tasks for the next one to four days. This time frame imposes urgency and lends effectiveness to the process of getting the important things done. When you do this, you will find it easier to get started, as you have already identified the "bookmark" for each project you're managing.

If I take the "things I'm thinking about" (those nouns from above) and filter them through what I call the "verbing process," here's what I come up with for the tasks I need to do in the next 24 to 96 hours:

- Draft six-week book promotion tour outline and objectives.
- Call Rao to discuss attending Singularity University Executive program.
- Find 10-plus bookstores in San Francisco, New York, and London for book promotion.
- Edit second draft of website landing page with pop-up for downloadable Chapter 1.
- Review (plus 60 minutes) current layout of MWPO website.
- E-mail Craig, Roel, and Pip re: next leadership trip to Normandy.

I will raise a caution flag here: If your to-do list has "big" verbs— by which I mean verbs that are mentally demanding or longer term in nature (such as *plan, discuss, create,* or *implement*)—you can help yourself (and may save time and reduce the sense of overwhelm) by deciding on the action step to *just get started.* That is, pick a "smaller" verb—by which I mean verbs describing tasks that are easier to start and faster to finish.

My own rule of thumb: I keep my defined "work" actions to 15 to 30 minutes each. These are the "chunks" of time I can use to stay focused, minimize interruptions, and work effectively.

Let's say you have items on your list like:

1. *Plan* HI-PO leadership development program scheduled for March 7 to 12.
2. *Discuss* org chart re: budgeting for next year.
3. *Handle* staffing issues.

Consider experimenting for the next week by breaking down those bigger lead-in verbs to smaller verbs, in this way:

1. *Review* last year's feedback comments from participants at leadership program.
2. *Collect* and *review* current org chart and this year's budget.
3. *Call* Sam in HR to schedule a 90-minute meeting on staffing.

I also like to surround myself with verb workers. Why? Because whether during a meeting, on a phone call, or in casual conversation, they are the ones who will pause and say, "You know Jason, that's a good idea. Now, what are going to *do* about it?" The book you are holding in your hand is a direct product of my mentor, Jim, asking me that very question quite some time ago.

For months, I discussed this book (a noun), which was only an idea in my head at the time. Finally, it got to the point where, one morning over a breakfast at the Ojai Café Emporium, Jim said, "Enough talk already; what are you going to *do* about this book idea?" This one question changed everything. *Your Best Just Got Better* is now available because I took my natural tendency to think in terms of nouns and matched them to verbs that, when acted upon, moved my mission forward.

If you happen to work with or for someone who is a verb worker, try this five-day experiment: At the end of each day, bring him or her a short list of what you *did*. Resist focusing on just the noun (the project or event) you worked on, and instead clearly identify and emphasize the *actions you took* to move those toward completion. For example, instead of saying, "I worked on the XYZ account," say something like, "I *met with* Pat from the XYZ account and *closed a sale* with her that we'd been working on for about a month."

Someone who is verb-oriented will appreciate the significance of the bigger picture, as well as the action taken and completion experienced each day.

Working with Nouns and Verbs: Your Turn

Ready for an experiment? Take out a piece of paper and begin to think about both kinds of work. Even though you may prefer one style over the other, it's absolutely critical—the more responsible you become, and as you develop your strengths and goals professionally *and* personally—that you be able to easily, effectively, and efficiently engage in both kinds of working.

Set a timer for 15 minutes and in those minutes fill that page with your handwriting. On one side of the page, write down a list of the many "things" you're thinking about—that is, just the nouns. Examples might be a meeting you're attending, the trip you're planning, a book you're reading, someone you need to talk to, and so on. Once you've filled the page, pause and reflect.

When the 15 minutes are up, turn the page over, and for each item you wrote, identify a single action you can take within the next 24 to 96 hours to just get started (as you can see, I'm going for something action-able here). Even if the "thing" on the other side is *big* (e.g., your next promotion, a life goal to vacation in the islands, your child's upcoming college choice), identify just one task you can absolutely, positively *do* in the next one to four days. If you identify your work at this level of action, by midweek next week you just may have moved some very important tasks forward well ahead of schedule! That's what it looks like when you take responsibility for working *smarter*, thinking *bigger*, and making *more*!

Maximizing Your Limited Resources

In Chapter 2, I describe the importance of pacing as it relates to goal setting. I caution people not to attempt to go too far, too fast, and I focus intently on identifying when progress is going too slowly. But right now it's time to clarify your "resources," the limitations you face while working to make your best better.

You may have read this brief conversation from Lewis Carroll's book *Alice's Adventures in Wonderland*, between Alice and the Cheshire Cat: "Would you tell me, please, which way I ought to go from here?" "That depends a good deal on where you want to get to," said the Cat. "I don't much care where—" said Alice. "Then it doesn't matter which way you go," said the Cat. "—so long as I get *somewhere*," Alice added as an explanation. "Oh, you're sure to do that," said the Cat, "if you only walk long enough."

Chances are, you aren't like Alice. You know the direction and already have an idea of the destination you'd like to reach. For specifi-cally those reasons, the more clearly you've identified where "there" is, the easier it will be to efficiently identify the decisions—the actions you can take now and in the near future—you need to make to get started. Once you make those decisions, it's time to maximize your limited resources. These are the four critical elements of productivity: *time, energy, focus,* and *tools.*

They are limited because you only have so much of each before you need to replenish them. How you use—and maximize—these four resources will directly and significantly affect what you get done over the course of a day at work.

No doubt you have tried managing *time* before. Whether you've made prioritized daily to-do lists or time-blocked your calendar, "time management" techniques are probably not new to you!

Chances are you already know when during the day your *energy* is highest (and lowest). Most people know when is the best time (i.e., the most productive) of the day for them—the morning, the afternoon, or the evening.

Next, let's assume you can *focus* on your MITs and not get distracted, so that you accomplish your priorities during the day.

Finally, you likely have productivity *tools* (or a system) that you utilize in order to make it easier to get the important things done in the time you've allotted for them.

Take the opportunity now, while reading this, to think about and to study all four of these elements, in the order I describe below, as you move toward a clearer definition of your role in making your best better, and specifically how you can work smarter. In my coaching programs, we always start with tools, as they constitute the basis of each person's professional productivity and workplace performance.

Tools: There are countless systems, apps, and tools available to help you. Are you a fan of the buy-it-now-and-see-if-it-helps-me-later methodology? Do you have binders on your shelves? Have you downloaded "most" of the productivity apps now available online? Have you attended seminars and workshops, hoping you'll find the "magic bullet" to time management and productivity?

Of course, knowing *how* you can use those tools to their full potential will make you even more effective and efficient. If you have a journal or a notepad nearby, open it to a fresh new page. If not, simply find a piece of paper and a pen. On the top of the sheet, write today's date. Under that, write: "As of right now, the tools, systems, and gear that I use/rely on to get my work done include: _____, _____, and _____." (Keep this list handy, as I will refer to it again.)

Later in this book I will show you how to save time and get the most out of the tools you have, whether they are paper-based, digital, or a combination of the two. Suffice it to say that, for now, if you can learn one or two new features of each of the tools you use, you can save time, by working smarter each day.

Focus: You have the ability to be interested *in* and concentrate *on* something specific as long as you can—until you get distracted. I'm talking about attention span here, and we all have different limits. What one person can sit down and focus on for hours at a time another person may get up and walk away from after just minutes.

Over the past 24 hours, think about how many times you were interrupted by others, distracted from what you were working on, or even forgot what you were just about to do. (Have you ever had this happen at home? You leave one room to get something in another room, and by the time you get there have completely forgotten why you went there in the first place? That's how fast our focus goes!)

In other words, your attention span will always affect what you get done. Consider the various areas of your life: personal interests, work, family, health, finances, career, leisure activities, and more. Let it all come in to your mind. When you think about the next 6 to 18 months (which, by the way, is a great place to start with goal setting; this span of time is short enough to begin experiencing momentum and long enough to realize significant change), where do you imagine you'll be? What do you picture yourself doing? With whom do you imagine you'll be spending more (or less) time? I devote Chapter 9 to the topic of focus, and how you can maximize yours to make your best better.

Energy: You may be a morning person; you may be an evening person. (Do you have a spouse or a boss who's your opposite?) No matter your preference, you are already aware that there are certain times during the day when you are more productive, as well as when you're not. One of the most effective things you can do is study the times of the day and the physical locations you work in to identify when and where you have the most energy to give to your important projects. Matching your tools, focus, and energy is always one of the most effective ways to save time while you're working.

Time: You may want to highlight this sentence: *There are only 96 15-minute blocks of time in a single day, and there are just 168 hours in a week.*

Was this fact as profound to you as it was to me when I first realized it? When I learned that our time is that limited, I started using mine very, very differently.

Here's a challenge: Set a timer for 15 minutes. Right now. Go ahead; do it. Then continue reading this chapter. When the time is up and you hear the beep-beep-beep or the buzz of the timer, think about this: That was about 1 percent of your day. How well did you focus during that time? Were you able to read page after page after page? (If you do, you will most likely be able to continue reading the next 15 to 20 pages of this book.)

For the next few days, keep that timer nearby. I maintain that time is the *most limited* resource of the four (time, energy, focus, and tools), and it's often the one we have the least control over. Therefore, you need to *objectify* your time, by which I mean you need to be able to watch as the minutes you have count down to 0:00. In Chapter 3, I will show you very specific tactics you can take to manage, control, and get more from your time each day.

Did you happen to notice that I originally listed the four limited resources in one order, and then outlined their impact on productivity in another? I have a very specific reason for doing this.

I have spent many years studying productivity and time management. I frequently meet people who say, "I wish I had more time," or, "I just need another hour in the day." When I first meet with my clients by phone, I ask the next four questions, in this order, to better understand the work they do and the areas we'll focus on during our coaching program.

1. What *tools and systems* do you use to get things done?
2. How do you *focus all of your attention* on the goal you have for each work session?
3. When do you have the *energy to be productive* and remain in a positive, proactive frame of mind?
4. When do you have the *time to consistently work* at a higher level of focus and motivation?

You see, when you study the four resources in this order, you can then more effectively utilize your blocks of time; perhaps even getting more done faster, and expending less energy and effort.

Oh, and the reason I asked you to set a timer for 15 minutes? That was about 1 percent of your day today. (Remember, there are 1,440 minutes in a day, so 15 minutes is about 1 percent.) I will go into much more detail on this in Chapter 3. The idea here is to demonstrate how little time it can take for you to make some significant progress on your important work. As a colleague of mine, Michael Bungay Stanier teaches, "Do More Great Work." Here's what I know: You will get important things done when you maximize your tools, focus, and energy effectively.

Just Keep Moving

When you clearly identify an objective goal (perhaps your Ideal Day!), you automatically begin to make things better, and you can continue moving in a positive direction. When you think about where you are going, talk about your dreams, write goals, and reflect on your efforts, you make significant progress. Focusing on a specific direction is important for two reasons: (1) You'll notice more opportunities, while (2) you narrow your focus. The more you can see the direction in which you are heading, the easier it will be to collect ideas and information to get you closer to achieving the results you're after. Remember the words of Abraham Lincoln: "A goal properly set is halfway reached."

But how do you pick, manage, and celebrate the "right" goals, whether they are personal or professional, short term or long term? Surely you have heard that one way to be effective is to set goals that are SMART: Specific, Meaningful, Actionable, Realistic, and Timely. However, that doesn't work for everyone. It's too easy to make excuses for, to "explain away," not reaching goals and objectives. Here are the "goal-stoppers" I hear all too often:

- *But, what if goal-setting doesn't work?* Do you know someone who has said this? Generally, it happens when people set the bar too high, taking on goals that are too big to begin with. They take something on, work on it, stress about it, think about it, work on it some more, only to realize that for some reason (and they usually have several to share with you!), they won't be able to "just do it." They won't be able to finish what they started.

- *Won't setting a goal limit my opportunities?* Other times, people claim they prefer the serendipity of achievement; that is, by not picking anything too specific to work toward, they keep themselves open to living life in the moment and taking advantage of what shows up, as it shows up. "Sure I'd like to know about that next promotion, if it's ever offered. If not, it's okay; something else will show up." That was a comment I heard from a participant in an open seminar I presented at a not-for-profit organization.

There *is* a middle ground, fortunately. For those of you who have set goals in the past and not achieved them, it's time to start anew. And for those of you who enjoy the surprises life has to offer, I encourage you to keep on working and living that way. Just realize that to make your best better there will be some things you'll want to do starting *now*.

Start Where You Are

One of the activities I ask people to undertake is to draft, by hand, a long, unprioritized, private list of the things to which they—and other people—have said yes to, and to acknowledge how many of those things are still outstanding. This inventory of open loops usually contains items such as promises, projects, reminders, tasks, ideas, and more. And, it's usually a fairly long list. (The longest one I've seen from a client had over 400 single-line items.) As in the previous exercise, start by giving yourself 15 minutes of uninterrupted focus time to answer this question: "What have I promised to do that I have not yet completed?"

As you gain more and more clarity about the work you have to do (I define "work" in a very general way, as I explained earlier in this chapter), I am confident you will realize the importance of improving your productivity and performance methodologies.

How Do You Start Your Day? So now what do you *do*? Here's my recommendation: Start right where you are. Chapter 1 is all about working smarter and making a commitment to taking personal responsibility for your own improvement. Now is the time to identify when you're at your best.

No doubt you know the kinds of things that can happen at the beginning of any day to set you off on the wrong foot. To turn 180 degrees, here's another day-day experiment: Ask the following questions at the beginning of each day.

- Did I wake up rested?
- Is my mind already on overdrive, thinking about all I have to get done today, this week, this year?
- Are there certain people who, just by thinking about them, cause me stress or overwhelm me?
- As I start the day, am I able to anticipate to any degree of clarity (or certainty) what I may be able to accomplish?

As you ask and answer these questions over the next five days, make a note of those mornings that start in an unproductive and potentially discouraging way. You don't have to track everything that happens to you; just notice those things that you can use to your advantage. Often, when we know what gets in the way of our having a good day, we can take steps to preempt them, so that they don't knock us as far off track as they have in the past.

The "I am at my best when . . ." activity I describe next is one that I introduce to everyone I work with, from high school students planning for college to retirees taking on a second career by volunteering in their communities. Most of my work is with senior executives, whom I coach as they move up in their organizations; I also work with startup founders as they grow their ideas into full-fledged businesses.

Take a cue from a lesson I offer to these individuals: Give yourself the gift of your own attention! Stop now to make an inventory of the kinds of things that could happen during a day that would get you working in a positive direction.

When Are You at Your Best? How Do You Find Out? It is human nature to return to some natural set point (often referred to as *homeostasis*) by doing what you normally do. Recognizing your habits and routines are very significant aspects of reaching your overall level of productivity and goal achievement. By focusing on that which is within your control, you give yourself one simple (though not always easy to implement, as you'll see in just a moment) key to success.

Knowing, focusing on, and practicing the actions you must take to be at your best requires initiative and discipline. True, working when you are at your best might require significant behavioral changes, but, I assure you, the process will produce significant and sustainable quality-of-life improvements.

Figuring Out When You Are at Your Best in Three Easy Steps

1. Take out a piece of paper.
2. At the top, write "I am at my best when . . ."
3. Underneath that phrase, write down 5 to 10 things you can do to support yourself in having a good day. Make sure they are items that you can control. For example, "When I eat a good breakfast," is something you can control, whereas "When my manager is in a good mood," is not. (See the list below for some examples to get you thinking.)

The practical application of starting your day with a focus on "me at my best" will result in a proactive, productive change. Some of my clients call it their recipe for a great day. Post this inventory where you can see it first thing in the morning and throughout the day.

Review your list at the beginning of each day, over the next five days. If you haven't done something on it that could significantly improve each of those days, take a moment now and make the effort to do so. Set yourself up for success.

For the first few days you experiment with this productivity tool, make a conscious attempt to *review the list each morning* and to do at least one thing on it as close to that moment as possible. Turning these practices into daily habits will often result in quicker reaction times, a better mood, and a reduction in both work- and life-related stress. Think about where in your daily routine you can easily incorporate simple, new, and better behaviors.

Here are a few samples from the "I am at my best when . . ." lists of other people. Feel free to use them and add your own.

I Am At My Best When . . .

- I get enough sleep and eat breakfast each morning.
- I arrive on time for my appointments.
- I reach out to clients in advance of meeting with them.
- I create a list of daily objectives and deliverables.

- I'm prepared for my meetings and presentations.
- I have all the updated travel logistics I'll need on my computer/in my smartphone.
- I acknowledge others on the team and let them know they made valuable contributions.
- My electronic gear (ereader, BlackBerry, laptop, etc.) is fully charged and ready to use.

Now, take some time to identify the habits you can repeat to be at your best. Once you begin to focus on the things that you can do to be at your best, you can magnify them, thus increasing the likelihood you'll experience a more productive day, every day. Now *that* is a way to work smarter.

2

Improvement and Pacing

Building and Sustaining Habits
That Lead to Productivity

By READING CHAPTER 1 you learned how to clarify the individual role you must play to make your best better. Now please ask yourself this very important question: "What does working smarter mean to *me?*"

In answering, consider the words: *sustainability*, *consistency*, and *pacing*. These are three significant characteristics of making lasting change. If you want to achieve a higher level of productivity and performance, you must understand how they work together.

When I meet with a client for the first time, I ask him or her: "Is the way you are working, working for you?" By this I mean, are you getting done what you need to get done? Are you putting things off until later, only to find that there's never a less busy time? "How is your system of working, *working?*" is a question I'd like you to reflect on a few times this week. Let it roll around in your mind for a while. You might find yourself coming up with more and more answers, some positive, some not. Eventually, you'll get to the point of wondering about purpose, priorities, and the personal and professional goals you still have on your list.

Sustainability relates directly to professional development and personal performance. For our purposes here, let's go beyond the traditional and environmental meanings of the term "sustainable" to arrive at a more textbook definition, to include: "able to be maintained at a certain rate or level."

Think about the sustainability of your workflow practices and behaviors. Will they last? Can you continue at the pace you're working at for much longer? For years or decades to come? During the past week have you arrived to the office early one day? Have you stayed late one evening? Is this becoming more and more common? Have you ever arrived early *and* stayed late on the same day?

Take a moment and reflect on the specific qualities of the most effective people you know—in life and at work. What are the people like who get the right things done, on time, effectively? What do they *do*? What can you count on them for? Before you read on, write down a few answers to these questions. Mentally go through the roster of the people you work with on a daily basis. How do the most effective people you know work?

Some of the common descriptors I've heard over the years are:

- They are effective, consistent.
- I know what's important to them.
- They have an "even keel."
- I know what to expect from them, day to day.
- They work smarter, not harder.

Think about what *you* do consistently. Identify the things that people around you can count on you to do during your workday.

Maintaining a Vision and Effort Over Time—That's Pacing

In long-distance running, holding pace makes the difference between a strong finish time and possibly not finishing at all. Over the last decade I have raced in more than 50 triathlons (a competition incorporating three events: a swim, a bike ride, and then a run, one right after the other). I compete in my age group in events ranging from sprint races, which last an hour or less, to Half Ironman events I finish in about six hours.

Each year, I build a new training program that corresponds directly to the goals I have identified early in the season. By February of each year I've already made my decision: If I'm racing the "short" sprint and Olympic distance races, I train at higher levels of intensity for shorter periods of time. Alternatively, the years I race "long" (a Half Ironman competition consists of a 1.2-mile swim, a 56-mile bike ride, and a 13.1-mile run), I spend much more time in the pool, out on long runs, and on the bike for hours at a time, at a lower intensity and less strenuous, but consistent, effort.

Is your work and life made up of actions and tasks that show up today and are finished by tomorrow? Or are you overseeing long-term projects for which you need to continually check status and recalibrate based on timelines, budgets, and product launches? Either way, it is absolutely essential, not to mention more effective and efficient, to know at the beginning of each day the level of pacing you need to set to finish your work on time, on budget, and "on purpose."

I travel around the world advising individuals and speaking in front of large groups of executives on the topics of productivity and pacing. I coach clients to manage their professional goals in a similar fashion. In this chapter I will share strategies and tips you can use to work more effectively, get things done more efficiently, and consistently make more progress, faster, than ever before. Let me begin by saying that for the mid- to long-term goals you set, it is critical that you plan for them with sustainability, consistency, and pacing in mind.

Slow Down to Speed Up and Create Lasting Change

Think of yourself as an athlete who must maintain a steady rate of speed in order to avoid hitting the wall before the finish line. At the end of a particularly stressful day, have you ever felt sudden fatigue and loss of energy? That's what athletes mean by "hitting the wall!" They simply have no energy left to do anymore, to go any farther.

I mentioned earlier that, for me, it is necessary to run at a different pace depending on whether I'm in a sprint triathlon or aiming to finish a Half Ironman event. Likewise, while you're working, you need to manage your goals, set expectations, and reach milestones by pacing your way to success. In other words, you have to "spend" your effort carefully in order to avoid burnout. You know yourself better than anyone else, so you are the one to determine the pace that works best for you and, conversely, that you work best *at*.

Choose a project you're working on now that is going to take 6 or even 12 months to complete. For example, in my case, projects like writing a book, rebuilding a website, or remodeling the garage at our house all take a lot of planning and pacing to accomplish effectively.

As a triathlete, I've experienced the difference between running a strong 13.1 miles (a half-marathon) and a fast 3.1 miles (a 5K race). As a writer, I've experienced the difference between writing a 1,200-word article and submitting a 55,000-word book. And I know what makes the difference: pacing.

Let me give you a more specific example. After the bike segment at a Wildflower Triathlon in Paso Robles, California, several years ago, I started the run portion feeling strong. At the 1-mile marker, I looked at my watch only to realize I had made a terrible mistake: I finished that first mile in 6 minutes 12 seconds. In my excitement and over-exuberance, I had abandoned my training and racing plan and pushed myself too hard (I had planned and trained for a pace of 8 minutes per mile for the first 7 miles and 7:15/miles for the last 6).

"Uh oh," I thought. "That's too fast." Sure enough, at mile 5 of that race I "hit the wall." I was hurting, running slowly, and didn't feel good. Eventually, I walked, sat down, and spent many minutes at each of the last few aid stations, taking in fluid and resting. But, by using all the techniques I describe in this chapter, I was able to come back the next year and run faster, feel better, and achieve the goal I had set. I had finally learned—in a real-time, physical setting—about the importance of pacing.

Whether you're racing on the field or in the office, this chapter will show you how to work smarter by finding and maintaining a sustainable pace.

No doubt you're looking for the habits, ideas, and skills to get better and go faster. Is this a new idea for you? Probably not. Surely, your friends and coworkers are not surprised you're reading a book titled: *Your Best Just Got Better: Work Smarter, Think Bigger, Make More.* Most likely you've been on this path for a while.

Right now, you need to slow down—*way* down. That's right, it's time to rededicate your focus, move in a positive direction, and hold your pace! When we go too fast, when we look for the one thing to do or the next shiny thing to buy to be more productive, we tend to lose sight of how much more we can accomplish if we stick to a plan of taking deliberate and focused actions toward clearly defined outcomes.

For the next five days, get yourself into this mind-set: "When I slow down, I can speed up." Imagine how this might apply to your productivity. When was the last time you double-booked yourself—to, say, attend two meetings at the same time? Have you been thinking lately that you've been saying yes to too much, in life or at work? Have you forgotten to do something you promised you would do? Did you end a phone call with someone, only to remember minutes later you forgot to ask him or her an important question?

Consider where and when you've been running purely on adrenaline. Sure, you're making things happen, but you may be working so quickly that you're outrunning your pace. Have you hit the wall recently? Are any of these statements true about you?

- You've ended a day completely exhausted.
- You wake up in the middle of the night, thinking about all the things you are responsible for.
- You're not able to rest or completely relax in between the pressures of work and life, it's as if you're always "on."
- People around you have hinted that you might not be able to maintain the pace you're on.

Because much of what you're already doing works (that is, everything you've done up to now has gotten you where you are today), it is often very, very difficult to change your pace, to institute new routines, to slow down. But in order to realize different, and better, results, you're most likely going to have to do things differently. To that end, I have two pieces of advice: (1) Identify what works, and do more of it. (2) Identify what does not work and stop holding yourself accountable to that.

Let's begin where you are (always a good idea in setting a pace). Think about the next 24 to 96 hours: What will you be doing? Where will you be going? What do you hope happens?

One way to get a clear sense of the pace you need to hold is to ask, "Who will expect me to have done what, by when?" Of course, if you ask that question and really listen to the answers, you will probably come up with a long list of things that need your attention. And this fact may be just the impetus you need to think about, fix, and commit to changing your pace.

Focus on these three important question words as you go about improving your productivity techniques: *who, what, when*. As you review each of the three groups below, ask yourself: "Can I keep on going the way I am and hold this pace for much longer?"

Who: This includes you, your team, your organization, your family, your friends, and your community. Write a list of the 20 to 30 people you expect to spend significant time with over the next week. These are the people who are counting on you. Use this list as a trigger to identify anything you need to do for them or with them, sooner than later. Also, think of anything you need to renegotiate with them, if you know now you're not going to be able to complete something when you said you would.

What: Clarifying tasks, projects, and roles is a significant aspect of productivity management and workplace performance. Hours can be saved *every month* when we are completely honest about what we say yes to, and say no (or "not now") to things we know we can't get done in the near future.

Next, list the 20 to 30 major projects, initiatives, or programs you anticipate spending time and other resources working on over the next 12 months. Remember, we're talking about pacing here, so we have to look into the future, as well as manage through today.

When: Deadlines, milestones, and meetings are other important aspects of achieving effective productivity and workplace performance. They are, in fact, the collective theme of this chapter. Pacing yourself, over time, increases the likelihood that you'll continue moving toward the outcomes you're aiming at.

Why do things go out of control? How does life get to the point at which feeling stressed and overwhelmed seem to be the norm for most of the people we work and live with? The answer, which I have always found interesting, is: It takes time.

Reset Your Pace

Consider where you are right now on the path of your career (or careers). You have probably spent hours thinking about the approaches to productivity you take, as well as the goals you plan, work toward, and achieve. Most likely, every day you begin by following the same habits and routines (i.e., your pace) that have become comfortable for you over the past few years. To reset the pace, you need to look at three areas:

1. *What do you do to manage the time you have?* To hold your pace, you must study your workflow habits and find ways to work smarter and more effectively with the time you have. You must think about when you work, how you work, and what you need to be as efficient as possible.
2. *How do you use tools and technology to help you get things done?* You need to understand the tools of productivity that are available to you. By learning something about productivity technology, the processes you follow, and the organizational tools you can use, you may find you're saving time, getting more done faster, and working at a more easily sustainable pace than you have in the past.
3. *When do you relax and rejuvenate, to reset the pace?* Resting and resetting doesn't just happen. And scheduling a vacation or sleeping in one morning a weekend may not be enough rest and relaxation for you to completely reengage in what you're doing.

To survive and thrive, you need to be productive with consistency, professionalism, and excellence. The old time management tricks no longer give you the help you need. Rewriting your to-do list takes up precious minutes each morning. Getting less sleep each night isn't healthy. And, certainly, watching the clock won't help you get things done.

When I was young, I remember hearing repeatedly that "practice makes perfect." Parents, teachers, and coaches said it about many of my activities; I tried to learn to play the guitar, practiced baseball, and took art classes. Though I never quite reached a level of perfection in any of those efforts, I did achieve a feeling of comfort with them. I could go through the motions, even though I knew I wasn't going to make a career out of any of these endeavors.

What I know: Practice doesn't always make perfect, but repeating something over and over again will eventually make it seem normal and feel comfortable.

Take Inventory

What *is* comfortable for you? What have you practiced so much that you do it easily, without even thinking about it? Once you know what that is, ask yourself if there is anything you can change, if there's more you might be able to do by implementing new concepts of productivity and pacing to your workday.

Let me share three inventories you can take to identify what you're already doing, and offer some tips on how to maximize the effort you put in to get those things done each day.

Inventory 1: What Do You Do By 10:00 AM?

Have you ever looked back on a day just ended and thought, "I just didn't have enough time?" or "Where did my time go?" No matter how much time you have, how many meetings get cancelled, or how you "time-block" your calendar to make space for the work you have to do, there always seems to be more work than time left at the end of the day. The busyness of business (and life) fills the day, dawn to dusk (or, for many, dark to dark!).

To complete this inventory, take out a piece of paper, or use the lines provided here, and write down *everything* you typically do by 10:00 AM each day that takes your *time*, *energy*, and *focus*. Start with the little activities, the easy ones that are small and seemingly insignificant. Carry this list around with you and add to it over the next week. Write. It. All. Down.

_____

_____

_____

_____

Here's the question to ask yourself: "What do I do from the time I wake up in the morning until about 10:00 AM?" Here's just some of what one of my clients wrote one day a while ago (notice, it was all in the present tense):

1. Wake up with alarm; press snooze—twice.
2. Check e-mail on BlackBerry (in bed).
3. Check calendar on BlackBerry (still in bed).
4. Let dog outside.
5. Turn on bathroom television to news channel.
6. Shower.
7. Get dressed; listen to news/sports on bedroom television.
8. Drive to the park-n-ride.
9. Listen to news while driving to the park-n-ride.
10. Take train to work.
11. Read news on tablet computer.
12. Check e-mail on BlackBerry.
13. Walk from train station to office.
14. Stop at coffee shop for breakfast—coffee and a bagel.
15. Get to office; walk toward desk.
16. Check in with two key staff; ask them for any updates.
17. Review e-mail inbox; clean up, delete, file e-mails reviewed that morning.
18. Dial in for morning conference call.
    His list went on and on.

The first few items you write down will be easy. As you carry this list with you (or track it on a sticky note on your desk where you can see it throughout the morning) for the next five days, you'll add more, and more, and more. Don't be surprised if you come up with 20 or even 30 different things you do by 10:00 AM. None of these items is inherently wrong or bad; it is what it is. These are, simply, the things that take your time during the day, the reason you don't have all the time you need, and why you generally have more tasks undone than done at the end of each day.

The good news is, once you get this inventory close to complete, you have an opportunity to "create time." Change what you do, and you'll change what you get! You have three choices to make regarding each item you've put on the list: keep doing it, delete it, or delegate it to something or someone else.

Keep Doing It You've had years, perhaps even decades, of practice honing these morning rituals. By applying the concept of pacing to this exercise, you'll most likely realize you're already working at an efficient and effective rate. Therefore, you're probably going to keep many of these daily habits in place. Nevertheless, review your long list of routines again, this time inserting a checkmark next to only those you're certain you need to keep doing, those you absolutely cannot change. Ideally, you'll identify some you *can* stop doing.

Delete Some Things Efficiency reduces waste. One of the first weeks I tracked my own morning routines, I recognized there was a deep chasm between the things that, early in the morning, I thought about doing, and the things I actually got done by the end of the day. I used to spend time each day re-creating an oversized to-do list, writing down more than I could possibly have gotten done. Worse, I usually knew it! One of the improvements to my system, as a result of studying my morning routine, was to stop breaking agreements with myself. My advice is to eliminate overcommitting and stop the self-sabotaging behaviors. You'll be amazed at the amount of energy it frees up.

Now when I sit down at my desk to work in the morning, I focus on my MITs and the to-do list for the day. I am very careful to choose consciously how much I take on. Don't get me wrong, I'm always open to overachieving, but I don't want to let myself down. I choose no more than four items as my MITs for each day (though on some days, when high performance and productivity are critical, I choose even fewer).

A teacher of mine once gave me this very simple advice: "Don't set your alarm knowing you will press snooze the next morning. Set your alarm for the time you're actually going to get up, then get up! Make and keep this first agreement of the day with yourself." I've always remembered this piece of advice, and to this day I set the alarm for the time I intend to get up.

Another cause of time-wasting that I've heard a lot lately from clients is "information consumption." By creating an inventory of habits and routines, you'll be able to realize just how much information you are attracting each day (via print, video, audio, web, daily meetings, status updates, etc.). With this knowledge, you may see that spreading your attention that thin gets in the way of achieving your MITs.

Three Ways to Minimize Interruptions

1. Schedule a meeting with yourself—start with just 45 minutes—and get away from your desk/office. Find a conference room or coffee shop where you can work without being interrupted by coworkers for that block of time.

2. If you can't get away from your desk, set a digital timer to count down 15 minutes at a time. Put it where you can see it, and commit to working on one piece of work or project for that entire period. (Consider asking your colleagues to respect this focus time; they may be able to wait a few more minutes to interrupt you, while you finish that report you're writing or research you're reading!)

3. Think about the one or two coworkers or clients you antici-pate will interrupt you during the day. Then, interrupt them first! By this I mean, find a way to reach out to them when you're in an in-between time. When I do this, I first mention that I'm about to go into a one-hour-focused work session, and ask them if there's anything they might need from me in the next 60 minutes or so. Many times, by giving them the chance to "interrupt" me right now, we act on things earlier in the day, even staving off possible crises that could have come up later.

Recall the client whose list I shared with you earlier, in particular the fact that he used his BlackBerry to check e-mail while he was still in bed. Note that he didn't *do* anything about those e-mails while still in bed; he waited until he was commuting to work (he had a 40-minute train ride to the office each day). Then, he said, he "rushed and stressed through his morning routine, continuing to think about the e-mails [he] had seen that morning."

Together, he and I designed a five-day experiment (I've mentioned the five-day experiment before, and I will explain it in detail in Chapter 10), during which period he would leave his mobile device in another room and use an alarm clock to wake up instead of his phone. He would shower, dress, eat breakfast, and *then* check e-mail on his train ride to work.

Initially, he expressed concern that he might miss the "thinking about what I have to think about" time he had built in to the early part of the day, but he was willing to give the experiment a try. When I called him the following week, he had good news: "It worked, Jason," he said. "I'm getting up; and I'm not as stressed and scattered when I go through my morning routines. And I'm using my commute time much more productively, as I'm clear-headed and ready for those e-mails." This change in his routine gave him a higher quality of life (less stress, increased productivity), one he didn't know was possible without putting him behind.

What habits do you have that drain your energy or prevent you from taking your performance to the next level? Remember, pacing is all about sustaining improvement. You're not throwing *everything* out; you're not changing it all, all at once. You're simply slowing down, looking around, and then picking up the pace!

Delegate Other Things Is this what you're thinking now?: "But, Jason, I *need* to know what's going on every morning! I *have* to check my e-mail from bed. *Everything* I wrote down on my 'by 10:00 AM' list is *absolutely* necessary!"

I understand, believe me. It seems there's *always* a digital screen vying for my attention. Instant messages, e-mails, and "do-you-have-a-minute" phone calls can easily fill the day. I also read two newspapers every morning when I can: the *Wall Street Journal* and the *Financial Times*. Whether I'm traveling domestically or abroad, and while I'm at home in Ojai, California, I count on these publications to give me the business news for the markets I advise: finance and technology.

That said, now I spend much less time reading those papers than before. While conducting one of my own inventories (what I was doing by 10:00 every morning), I realized I was scanning these papers daily looking for articles by specific authors, and I followed topical stories (for weeks or months at a time) that I or my clients were interested in. Even just scanning the papers looking for those articles would sometimes take 10 or 15 minutes. Instead now, I delegate some of that to research.

I also use a search aggregator/clipping service (such as Google Alerts) that automatically searches the Internet for important events, clients, and keywords or terms I am interested in following. It's what I use to find out whether my favorite authors have recently written a new article. I also get alerts about companies or projects I'm following. Each morning, I receive one e-mail that provides me with links to videos, newspaper or magazine articles, online news feeds, and more, containing specific information about these topics. And if I want to read one of the articles in the print version, I know exactly where to look. Using Google Alerts, I now spend only a few minutes each day reviewing the news that would ordinarily take up significant time. Thus, I have more time to focus on getting other, more pressing work done.

Throughout the year, I work with local colleges to create short-term internship programs with students interested in learning about business development, entrepreneurship, and strategic advising. These interns are responsible for sharing a weekly review with our whole team. They choose something to track each week—a company, an industry, a conference—anything that is potentially related to our company's growth. Throughout the week, they look for information that relates to what we do, and then we meet to talk about their research via conference or videoconference call. Over time, the formats change as to how they present their reviews, using written documentation, a photographic slide show, a PowerPoint presentation, and so on. Once, we even got the weekly update presented within Tweet restrictions—each comment limited to 140 characters!

You may not be in a position that affords you access to an internship program and students to help you get your work done; but, I believe, chances are good that if you look around for some kind of assistance with the work you do, you will be able to delegate some aspect of it. My question when I am delegating is, "Will this give me back 15 to 30 minutes a day?" If the answer is yes, I'll do what I can to set it up.

Spend a little bit of time each morning over the next week to identify what it is you actually spend time *doing*. If you intend to keep going at your current pace, you'll have to decide just how much you're planning to do on your own, what you'll stop doing, and what you'll ask for help to get done. You will surely be ready to make some changes.

Inventory 2: What Tools or Assistance Do You Use to Get Things Done?

This second inventory will take you on a very important journey. To prepare for it, write down all the tools, systems, technologies, and gear that you use to get your work done—in both your personal and work life—every day. (Note that I define "work" here in the more general sense of "getting something done." Whether for my job or in my personal life, if something takes effort, I consider it work!) You can start with the obvious items; then, over the next week, you'll identify exactly how much you count on each of them to get your work done.

To get started on this inventory, ask yourself this question: "What do I never leave the house *without?*" Similarly, ask this question when you're about to leave your desk: "What do I always want with me during meetings?" And when you're packing your suitcase for another quick trip, answer this question: "What do I want with me for this trip?" Include all of these items on your tools list. As before, use a blank sheet of paper or the lines provided here.

_____

_____

_____

_____

Sample List of Tools

Phone/mobile calling device

Laptop computer

Desktop computer

Digital camera

Pen and paper/notebook

Corporate intranet sites

Whiteboard in your office

E-mail (Outlook, Gmail, Lotus Notes, other)

Microsoft Office Suite (Word, PowerPoint, Excel, etc.)

After you've assembled your list of items, it's time to make some decisions: What do you keep? What do you combine? What do you stop using altogether? Do you need an extra phone charger at home and at the office? If, say, you learned a few shortcuts on your phone, would you use it as a business tool more, or more effectively? The important point of this inventory is to find out how your pace is being slowed, or speeded up, as a result of the tools and gear you use.

In 1997, I was meeting regularly with a master teacher I had asked to mentor me during my second year of teaching. We met once a month for 10 months, and at each meeting we'd discuss the progress I was making, the challenges I was facing, and what I would do next to develop as a teacher. I recall distinctly during one meeting, as we were talking, he reached across the table and took my notebook away from me *while I was writing*!

You see, for a few moments prior to doing that, he had been watching me flip back and forth looking for something I had written earlier in the month to ask him about during our current meeting. In those days, I took notes, wrote ideas, made to-do lists, even doodled, in one particular notebook I carried with me everywhere. Everything I needed was in it. He took that notebook, opened it to the beginning, and said, "Jason, from front to back, write your ideas." Then he flipped to the very last page and on the top of it wrote: "My Actions." He said, "From the back to the front, make a list of what you have to do."

That conversation, over a decade ago, changed how I think and work. Today, I capture ideas freely in my notebook, and make a single list, starting with the last page of the notebook, where I write my action reminders. It has worked all this time!

Do You Really Need It All? I was working with a client some time ago when we discovered that she had three different labeling devices on her desk. She labeled files, folders, and notebooks, and found during this exercise that she always had to think about which labeling system to use. Something that was meant to save her time was actually taking up more of it. After she made her tools list and studied her productivity over just a few days, she was able to identify the label maker she used the most often (in this case, the easiest one to use), and so returned the other two to the office supply cabinet.

I also worked with someone who had set up hundreds (there were more than 300!) of reference folders down the left-hand column of Microsoft Outlook, her e-mail management system. While I watched, she showed me how she organized her e-mail (which at the time had over 7,500 e-mails stored in the inbox alone) by moving messages one by one. After I watched her file 50 of them, I gave her my feedback. On average, it was taking her 32 seconds to open, review, close, click, drag, and file each item. That's right: organizing those 50 e-mails took over 25 minutes. And because she was receiving over 100 e-mails a day, many of which needed to be filed, she calculated she was easily spending over 3 hours a week just organizing her messages. And that didn't include the time she knew she'd have to spend catching up—putting most of those 7,000 e-mails in those folders!

I have been working with clients who use Microsoft Outlook since 1999. I've watched hundreds of people use, get frustrated by, and master that program. Over time, I have picked up some tips and tricks to save others using it minutes a day. So I shared with this client a few of the specific features (rules and search folders) of Microsoft Outlook that would enable her to cut down considerably the time she spent organizing her e-mails. As a result, she now spends less than an hour a week filing her messages.

Every e-mail system has its own tools and organizational features. It would be well worth your time and money to sit down with an expert and have him or her observe you working with your e-mail program. Just one insight or recommendation could save you hours a year! You too may need to learn more about the software you're using, so that you can be more effective. I will always remember the CoffeeChat that wound up saving me dozens of hours one year. It happened one morning during a conversation I was having over latte in New York City.

[An aside: I host local CoffeeChat meetings in the cities I travel to worldwide and let the community know where I'll be and what time to show up. You can follow along at www.Twitter.com/JasonWomack. The goal is to get together for an hour or so, meet new people, share some conversation, and then go on to work. They're great!]

During this particular CoffeeChat in New York, I told a colleague about the segment of my workshops when I show clips from short videos. (I am a huge fan of www.TED.com, and the organization has made those videos available to download straight to my laptop.) I often find a 20-minute video and edit it so that I show only the 2 to 4 minutes that demonstrate a point I am making. Then I share the actual link with the audience so they can view the entire clip on the Internet.

As I was sharing with my colleague how I did this, he said he could give me some tips—show me an easier way to do it. Whereas it used to take me from 45 to 60 minutes to edit and save one of the video clips to my PowerPoint presentation, I can now do it all in less than 30, thanks to this short tutorial he gave me on a couple of digital tools. That one conversation immediately saved me time, the first week I learned it. All I had to do was share what I was working on and be open to learning something new. My point is, the more fully you understand the tools you use the easier it will be to learn even more about their features and how to use them to your advantage.

I encourage all of my clients to sit down with others and watch them work. Do you know someone who is a tech wizard? Watch them use their favorite technology gear and tools. Do you have a colleague who is a spreadsheet genius? Invite that person to lunch to discuss tips that could make your spreadsheet experience easier. By seeing what other people do and use, you can decide which new tools and systems to add to your work process.

Think specifically about routine tasks such as printing multiple attachments, filing e-mails into folders, and moving information to and from your e-mail, calendar, and address book. Also, learn the speed keys and shortcuts of the software you use. By maximizing your tools, you have the potential to open up large windows of time throughout your workday.

Inventory 3: What Could You Do to Relax, Rejuvenate, and Reinvent Yourself?

For this last exercise, begin by writing down at least 12 things you could do to incorporate relaxation, rejuvenation, and reinvention into your life. What have you done in the past three to six weeks that was relaxing, fun, and/or exciting?

Remember, this chapter is all about pacing. If you're going to keep going at the speed you want to work at, it's important to back off, reflect, and recalibrate, regularly. If you're going to work smarter, think bigger, and make more, you're going to need the inspiration, motivation, and energy to maintain that pace over the long term!

Take out a pen and notepad now, and begin to create your list.

_____

_____

_____

_____

Relaxation Ideas

Go for a walk.

Call a friend.

Ride your bike.

Go for a run.

Play a videogame.

Play golf (or the sport of your choice).

Take a hike.

Get involved in a craft (e.g., knit, crochet, sew).

Cook a delicious meal.

Take a bath.

Go to the farmer's market.

Get a massage or manicure.

Spend time with family.

I sincerely hope you will sit up and pay attention during this exercise. I've witnessed two common reactions to this activity:

"Wow, there are things on this list that I have not done in a really long time, and I just don't see how I can get to them. I know they would be good for me to do, but . . ."

"Okay, I want more of what's on that list in my life, more often. This has made me realize the importance of making my best better. It's time for me to study my routines and habits, and utilize all of the tools and systems at my disposal to give myself more time, energy, and focus to engage in those things."

What was *your* reaction?

This final inventory was designed to increase your awareness and challenge you to think again about what it means to work smarter. It is intended to prompt you to recognize the reasons you should want to change. It's no longer just a good idea to learn a new technology or manage meetings more effectively. If you want to be able to do something from your third inventory, you *have* to manage your time better.

Remember, your willingness to change isn't an indication that something is wrong with you or the way you work. In fact, it's likely that many of your habitual and comfortable workflow habits have served you well in getting you where you are. It may be, however, that to get to where you're going, or want to go, you'll have to do something different; you'll have to change the pace.

Now that you are well prepared with a firm commitment to make your best even better, let's move on to improving your use of time, the subject of Chapter 3.

3

Improvement and Time

Get the Most from 1 Percent of Your Day!

WHEN DO YOU start feeling the need to manage time?

Let's assume for a moment that you begin working the moment you wake up in the morning. Whether you awaken to the jolt of an alarm clock, or naturally as the first rays of light fill your bedroom, when do you start planning another day of getting things done? Most people tell me that almost immediately in the morning they start thinking about what they need to do that day; many clients tell me that they check e-mail on their phones while they are still in bed, and mentally plan out the day throughout their morning routine before they even leave the house.

In Chapter 1, you read about the limitation of time. Remember, you have only 1,440 minutes between now and tomorrow at this time. That equates to just 96 15-minute blocks of time to do everything you think needs to be done. I focus on these blocks of time for three reasons:

1. I can imagine what 15 minutes is like. For me, it's about the equivalent of a 2-mile run or a 4-mile bike ride. I can write two thank you cards in about 15 minutes; and that's about how long it takes to make an airline reservation for one of my multicity trips. It's also approximately how many minutes *late* most meetings begin.

2. Fifteen minutes is enough to make a difference. If I focus on just one topic for a full 15 minutes, I can go deep into thinking about it. It's possible, in just 15 minutes, using some of the ideas you'll learn about in Chapter 9 of this book, to focus in on a project or event and develop a strategy and plan for action to move that project forward.

3. Fifteen minutes is not too long a stretch to work at one time. Instead of thinking "I'll work on this one project for 2 hours," think about making progress over 7 or 8 sessions of 15 minutes each. You will still work for about 2 hours, but by giving yourself interval-designed tasks, you can continually move forward while holding yourself to a predetermined schedule, which may keep you on course to finish on time.

Whether it is a weekday during which you're going to the office to make things happen, or a weekend or vacation day and you're on your way to experience something out of the ordinary, you have a limited time to do it all. To see for yourself just how valuable your time is, I suggest you do a time-budgeting exercise. At the top of a blank piece of paper, write "My Time Each Day." Then, starting with 96 blocks of 15 minutes each, subtract those blocks that are already accounted for each day. For example:

Sleep (e.g., 7 hours = 28 blocks): Now, you're down to 68.
Meals (e.g., 1 hour = 4 blocks): Now, you're down to 64.

Finish the exercise as it applies to you, listing other entries that are applicable, such as:

Commute to/from work =
Work (meetings, deskwork, interruptions) =
Exercise =
Downtime with family/friends =
Media (television, radio,
    reading, video games, Internet) =

_____

_____

_____

_____

If you're like most people I work with, the first time you do this exercise you may be surprised. Many find they are overcommitted, that they try to spend more of their time budget than they have. For example, the first time I did this, I realized that to do everything I intended, I would actually need more than a hundred 15-minute blocks of time.

Obviously, you can't get any more time in a day, and the only way to manage your time is to maximize what you *do* in time, so that you do what needs to get done *and* you have the time you need to do what you want to do!

How Valuable Is 1 Percent of Your Day?

I recently flew to New York City for a preliminary meeting with Annya (not her real name), a managing partner of a large financial firm interested in the *Your Best Just Got Better* coaching program. To find out whether we would work together over the next 10 months, Annya's company had flown me out to meet with her, with a twofold goal: to discuss the issue of time management and identify some solutions to her biggest problems.

The clear, spring morning of the meeting, I put on a new suit and my favorite blue tie and walked the 18 blocks from my hotel to her office in midtown. On the way, I stopped at a favorite coffee shop, ordered a balanced breakfast of oatmeal, juice, and scrambled eggs, and wrote my ideas for the meeting in my journal as I ate.

With about 15 minutes to spare, I walked to the building where Annya works. This gave me ample time to check in with the security desk downstairs and arrive at her office my "normal" three minutes early. While I walked, I thought about how the meeting would go, what I would say to begin the discussion, and the kinds of questions I could anticipate coming my way. This kind of preplanning gets my mind ready and focuses me on the job at hand. (Have you ever done this sort of thing? Maybe before you fall asleep at night, or on your way to work in the morning, do you ever make a mental list of things that need your attention? Most people I work with can relate to thinking about their work before they can actually do anything about it.)

A quick aside here about my arrival time to meetings: I no longer arrive at them as early as I used to (anywhere from 10 to 30 minutes ahead). I learned from a senior director in the U.S. Navy whom I worked with long ago about the importance of timeliness and arrival times for meetings. "Jason," he told me, "I book my meetings in 45-minute increments. I start them on the 00:15, and I end on the hour. If you arrive to a meeting with me early, you interrupt the only 'think' time I have in a day."

That idea has stuck with me for about a decade. Today, you can expect me to arrive right about three minutes early to my meetings. Yes, that's all. This way I am ready to go, but I don't show up so early that I impose on someone else's schedule. I have found this to be a very effective time management technique, and more than once clients have commented on my timeliness. I always show up when I say I will.

After I checked in at the security desk in Annya's building, I stepped through the elevator doors and pressed the button to go upstairs to her office. As it made its way up, stopping at a couple of other floors, I looked at my watch and thought, "Right on time." When I got to the thirty-seventh floor, I met with her assistant, who was waiting in the lobby. He led me to a small conference room and said, "Annya will be with you shortly; she's just finishing another meeting that is going a little longer than expected."

Sitting alone in that room, I realized I had just two minutes until our scheduled start time of 10:00 AM. So I did what I always do: I took out my small black notebook, opened to the back pocket where I keep ready-to-mail thank you cards. (I have traveled with stamped, return-addressed envelopes and thank you cards for years. Every week, I write at least one.) Since I had a couple of minutes to wait, on the envelope I wrote out the address of the hotel I was staying at, as I planned to send a thank you card to the hotel manager for the assistance the front-desk late-night manager had given me while I was checking in the night before. That took only about a minute, so at the appointed time, I cleared the table in front of me and waited patiently for a few minutes.

I looked down at my watch and the time was 10:03. I waited some more. At 10:05, the assistant returned, apologized, and told me that his manager was going to need at least *15 more minutes* before we could start. "Are you okay waiting here?" he asked. I said yes, and decided to use the time to run an experiment. Here was my hypothesis: I knew I could get a lot done with this 1 percent of my day, so I set a timer on my mobile phone, and consciously and deliberately worked for the next 15 minutes—with amazing results.

Here is what I accomplished during that time:

1. I handwrote the thank you card I had addressed just a few minutes earlier.
2. I reviewed my calendar for the next three weeks.
3. I called a hotel chain to make reservations for upcoming trips.
4. I called a car rental agency to make a reservation for a car.
5. I listened to my voicemail messages.
6. I used my smartphone to send e-mails to my office and clients.
7. I drafted a quick mind-map into my journal about an article I was working on for *Training Magazine*, even though it wasn't due for another few weeks.

When, at about 10:20, Annya appeared for our meeting, I had a big smile on my face. I had gotten some really important things done; even better, it meant I was going to have a bit more free time later that night to read the novel I had started on the plane from Los Angeles the day before.

"I have a question," I said to Annya after she sat down at the conference table: "How often do the people you work with arrive about 15 minutes late to meetings?"

Keep in mind she and I had communicated only via e-mail for the previous week; this was our first face-to-face meeting. I knew I was taking a big risk in moving immediately to the point, but I wanted to explore the very issue she had wanted to cover: time management. I wasn't going to waste any of *her* time.

"Oh Jason, all the time!" she exclaimed. "It seems that all I do each day is go from meeting to meeting, each one starting and ending a little later than the one before it. I print my daily calendar each morning, and it looks like someone is playing the video game Tetris!"

Then she raised the most common question I'm asked by clients: "So, really, can you help me get more time?"

I slowly nodded my head to indicate that I understood her situation, and then waited a long moment before starting to talk. I knew I was going to discuss with her the same content contained in the first two chapters of this book: how she managed herself, her ideas, her actions, her responsibilities. I also planned to eventually talk about the importance of pacing, and the danger of taking on too much, too soon, and trying to do a little bit of everything all the time.

I wanted her to understand that I knew what she was talking about, and that I took it very seriously. Only then did I begin to describe to her the issue of managing time, explaining why this process is so difficult for so many people. I showed her the list of things I had done in the 15 minutes of extra time she had inadvertently given me by being late to our first meeting.

When we are managing time, we're managing much more than the tick-tock of the clock. We're managing our areas of focus and responsibility; we're fielding interruptions from others; we're listening to our own self-talk; and we're generating all kinds of other ideas. All the while, we're inhibited by very specific influencers to our productivity.

Initially, Annya was completely taken aback by this idea (though later she told me she was immensely impressed by it). Years ago I realized that people give me extra time all the time. Meetings start late, people fail to arrive on time, flights get cancelled. These things happen. Depending on the week, I can count on anywhere from 10 to 20 extra 15-minute blocks. So I'm ready for them when they come.

Many years ago I came up with this saying: "If you're waiting until you have time to figure out what you'll do when you have the time, you'll always be behind." Isn't *that* the truth?

I shared with Annya my time management approach, which I just described to you:

I plan to arrive to meetings about three minutes early; never more than that. Showing up too early for an appointment can be just as disruptive as showing up late. I also believe in ABR, which stands for Always Be Ready.

With that presented to Annya, I continued summarizing my approach to her:

This morning, I was in this conference room by 10:00 AM. I have a system for making good use of waiting time. When you came in at 10:20, I had been as productive in my work as if I had been at my own office.

Now Annya was looking at me with eyes wide open and the beginning of a smile on her face. "You did all that in about 15 minutes?" she asked.

"Yes," I assured her. "Think about it this way: That was just about 1 percent of my day! What *else* could I get done today? You see, every day we have 1,440 minutes to get things done, and I figure I've got to be ready in case someone gives me an extra 1 percent of my day."

The next step in setting yourself up for success is to make sure you have the tools available for success. The reason I was able to (1) write the card, (2) make the hotel reservations, (3) send the e-mails, and (4) start on my article while waiting for my client to appear for our meeting was that I was *already ready*. Remember the concept I just mentioned—ABR, Always Be Ready. I coach all clients with it. I can promise you that sometime during the next month, *someone* is going to arrive late for a meeting with you, cancel a meeting, or otherwise keep you waiting. When that inevitably happens, you can look over your to-do list and pick something—anything—to work on.

A word of warning here: When a window of time opens up like that, most people tend to only check e-mail on their phones. Although that may seem productive in the moment, it doesn't have the long-term effect of moving your MITs forward. Of course, you might have to check your e-mail, but also prepare yourself with other work you could do in that "gift of time." A good exercise is to make a list of 20 to 30 things you could do in less than 15 minutes. Then set yourself up with the supplies or information you would need in order to accomplish those tasks, and make sure they are with you when you go to meetings, leave the office, or otherwise think you may have a bit of extra time.

Sometimes clients ask why we create such inventories of work in 15-, 30-, and 45-minute time blocks. The answer to this is the following: I have found that I very rarely have extremely long blocks of unscheduled, open time. That's why I need to be ready to take advantage of smaller chunks of it. If there is something you're planning to work on for which you know you will need a couple of hours or more, then do yourself a favor and schedule it on your calendar. (And, of course, see if there is a way to break that work in to smaller chunks of focus time.)

Why Do You Manage Time the Way You Do?

Why was I able to get seven tasks, at various levels of priorities, done in the little bit of extra time I had while waiting for Annya? Because of what I call my Time Management Profile. Have you ever stopped to consider *why* you manage time the way you do? To become a better time manager, I recommend you start by clarifying *your* personal Time Management Profile. You are who you are, you do what you do, and you think what you think based on all your life and work experiences.

To help you create your profile, I will first share mine with you.

My Personal Time Management Profile

At the venue for a conference I spoke at some time ago, there was an exposition hall divided into dozens of corporate booths. In each of them, a person behind a table attempted to capture my attention and time in order to offer me something in exchange for my business card and, more specifically, my e-mail address. I walked by one booth after another, barely making eye contact with most of the vendors until I saw one that caught my attention. Not only did I stay and listen to the sales pitch, I willingly gave up my e-mail address. In exchange, I got more than a prize; I had an epiphany.

To explain, I want you to picture a booth in which two cameras are set up: one on a tripod, to take my picture, the second on a table, to take a picture of staged items on the table. I stood in line and posed for the camera, then moved to the next line where, on a tabletop, were arranged several circular pieces of paper, about the size of a dinner plate. I was instructed to place an item that I had with me on top of each circle. The items were supposed to describe "who I am." This was to give visitors to this booth the chance to look at themselves through the lens of the answer to this question: "What are the things you have with you that best describe you?"

After I placed the sixth and final item, I realized there was more to this activity than met my eye. Looking down at the tabletop, I realized that those items did much more than just describe me. Together, they created something that I now call my Time Management Profile. Each item represented a part of who I am, what is important to me, why I want to make my best even better, and why I want to get the absolute most out of each day.

Following is the list of the items I had with me on that spring day. After you read these descriptions, I urge you to create your own Time Management Profile.

Item 1: Things to Write with and On I write every day. That's right, every day. I put my ideas on paper, whiteboards, flip charts, even business cards. I find that if I have a place to write something down, I'm more prone to ideate wherever I am. For the past several years I have used a medium-sized, hardback notebook that I carry almost everywhere with me. (As I was writing this chapter, I had it open and off to the right of my computer. When I thought of something I wanted or needed to do later, I simply paused, wrote it down, and returned to the keyboard. In three hours, I had added five items.)

At the end of each day, I write a full page of thoughts in a journal that stays on my nightstand. The last line of that page is reserved for my word of the day, a single word that describes what I thought about, what I saw, and what I learned that day. An interesting aspect of this practice is that I see themes begin to appear over a period of weeks or months. I get an interesting snapshot, one day at a time, of how and what I'm doing, and what the most important things to me really are.

And in order to always be prepared, I also designed a foldable note card that fits in my wallet, which I can write on at any time, wherever I am. On the front it says "I.D.E.A.," which, as I explained in Chapter 1, stands for:

> **Identify:** There are times when the most I can do is to see or hear something that I want to see or hear again later. I love the freedom of writing an idea down on a piece of paper, combined with the habit I've formed over the years of reviewing those ideas to find out which ones I need to *develop*.

> **Develop:** These are the ideas that I bring back to the office. They deserve a bit of my attention or maybe even a conversation with a colleague, client, or mentor. I filter through all the good ideas, looking for the great ones so that I can design an *experiment*.

> **Experiment:** It usually takes only a little experimentation to determine whether or not the idea has any value. Let's say someone recommends a book to me (identify), and later that day I download

an electronic version to my reader (develop). Within a couple of reading sessions of 10 to 20 minutes apiece, I can usually decide whether it's worthwhile to go on reading so that I can *assess*.

Assess: Now I look back and assign some kind of value to the effort I expended in phases one through three. Was it worth it? This is a *fantastic* question to ask at the end of your experiments.

So far, what have you thought about doing while you've been reading this book? My challenge to you is: *Just get started.* Try something for five days then stop. Look back and determine the *effort versus payoff* of engaging in that habit, trying that new product, or doing that new thing.

(By the way, if you e-mail me, I'll gladly send you a couple of my I.D.E.A. note cards: Jason@WomackCompany.com)

Item 2: Bottle of Water I always have water handy. For the past 10 years I've been racing in triathlons and traveling almost weekly to cities around the world. I know how much I need to hydrate. When I fly, I set a goal: eight ounces of water for every hour in the air. Even when I'm at my desk writing, I have a glass of water right next to me.

The water represents my commitment to my health, fitness, and physical well-being. It's kind of a trademark. Often, while I'm facilitating a workplace performance and productivity workshop, I'll walk around with bottles of water and offer them to participants. I find that the days I drink a bottle or two of water, I am more aware of my time, and I even use it differently. I think about my health and well-being with every sip I take.

Item 3: Thank You Card I mentioned earlier in the chapter that I write thank you cards. What I didn't say is that I send one to someone at least every week (and, frequently, more often than that). I really love to let people know how appreciative I am. I travel quite a bit, I have friends I talk with almost every day, and I consume a lot of media (books, articles, videos, movies). With all of these contacts, I can always find *someone* to send a card to. Several years ago, I started writing thank you cards to authors, to let them know how their work impacted me and how appreciative I was.

When I tell people that I write more than 52 thank you cards a year, many will look at me in surprise, and ask, "How do you have the time to do that? Aren't you busy?" Yes, I am, but I've created systems and processes that make it easy for me to send at least one card a week. Here's how:

1. I'm always on the lookout for someone to thank.
2. I travel with thank you cards in a file folder in my briefcase.
3. I have with me various denominations of stamps ready to use.

The very act of stopping long enough to write a thank you card demonstrates three very specific things to me: (1) I remain aware all the time. I'm constantly on the lookout for good times, good things, and good people who are doing work that matters. For these things I am thankful. (2) I acknowledge that I *have* time. I have a few minutes to stop and let someone know how thankful I am. (3) At the end of this activity, I always feel a little bit better, a little more energized, and a little more ready to get something else done.

Item 4: Membership Cards During each of the past 10 years I have traveled more than 200 days. To continue working smart, I have memberships for several airline frequent-flyer programs, hotel chains, and health clubs. When it comes to recognizing the value of time and the need to travel effectively and efficiently, I highly recommend this strategy.

During one trip in particular, in a single day, one flight was delayed, my connecting flight was cancelled, and I wound up having to drive several hundred miles (overnight from Chicago to Cleveland!) to be at work at the client site early the next morning. I fully utilized the airline, car rental, and hotel membership programs I'm enrolled in to ensure a safe and successful trip for myself.

Joining a membership group gives you something else: access to a network. While waiting for flights or eating appetizers in hotel lounges, I have met authors, actors, fellow road warriors, business executives, and professional athletes. In Chapter 5, I will cover the importance of and methods for building your social and professional networks. The motto Always Be Ready applies to networking as well!

Item 5: Coffee Shop Loyalty Cards I'm naturally a morning guy, so I don't need coffee to get me going. Over the years, however, I've noticed that many others *do* need their morning cup of joe! And because more local coffee houses are now serving as community hubs, where conversations happen and updates are shared, I like to be a part of all that, so I became a café latte and tea drinker.

Just now, I looked in my wallet and counted loyalty cards for six different coffee shops in the United States and United Kingdom. I visit the same ones where I travel, and about once a week I set up meetings at them before the workday starts. There's something about meeting first thing in the morning over a cup of tea or a latte that gets the day started in an engaging way.

Several years ago, I started organizing CoffeeChat Meetups (hashtag: #CoffeeChat). Whenever I travel to a city, I plan at least one morning CoffeeChat and let my online communities (Facebook, Twitter, LinkedIn, and Plancast) know about it—and, yes, people do show up.

Sometimes, it is just a few of us; other days, in other cities, the meetings are much more heavily attended. A typical CoffeeChat is a small, informal networking meeting of 10 or so people. I usually schedule them for 45 minutes in the morning, before we all go our separate ways to work. When people tell me they don't have time to network (or any other activity like working out, writing, reading, etc.), I encourage them to incorporate their new desired behavior into one of their existing activities. Creating the CoffeeChat Meetups has transformed a morning routine of drinking coffee into a resourceful networking opportunity.

Item 6: Digital Camera I carry a digital camera everywhere I go, and have been doing so for more than a decade. I stop to take pictures of landscape and cityscape views, events, client buildings, relevant advertisements, and more. Recently, I started taking photos of meeting notes. That's right, after a meeting, I take a picture of the notes I've written in my notebook, a whiteboard, any flip chart pages; even during a meeting I'll photograph a PowerPoint slide that is being projected on a screen.

Taking a photo is faster than writing everything down—and certainly more effective than hoping I'll remember it later! I can also more conveniently share it with coworkers, directly via e-mail, and add it to my notes in an online database.

■ ■ ■

These six items I carry with me almost everywhere make up my Time Management Profile. They represent who I am; more than that, they describe *why* I want to manage time, and *how*. Because I've studied this topic for so long, I know that time management isn't just about the clock anymore; it's about how we use our environment, our tools, our energy, and our focus to drive our ideas and actions toward completion.

Your Time Management Profile

To create your own Time Management Profile, start by going through your pockets, bag, purse, and/or briefcase. What items do you always carry with you? Also, think about items you wish you carried with you more often. How do they help you be productive? The reason to do this is twofold:

1. *The items you have with you might help identify what takes up your time.* For example, if you bring a notepad and pen with you to every meeting you attend, you may find that later, either the same day or week, it takes you a lot of time to go back through those notes and find what you need when you need it.
2. *The items you carry with you serve as physical reminders of why it's so important to manage time, work smarter, think bigger, and make more.* For example, you might have a picture of your family in your wallet. You want to look at that picture from time to time to remind yourself how important it is to pursue effectiveness and efficiency, since these are the people with whom you get to spend more time when you do.

Take the time to make a list of these items now, on the lines provided here.

Your Time Management Profile

Item 1: _____

Item 2: _____

Item 3: _____

Item 4: _____

Item 5: _____

Item 6: _____

Managing Your Time Better

When I start my on-site workplace performance seminars, I ask participants to reflect really deeply on this question: "When was the last time you took two days of your time, energy, and focus to study *how* you work?" As you can probably guess, many people say never.

Developing and learning time management strategies and methods does indeed take time. If you look at the way you currently manage your time, you will likely see that you do what you've always done because it has worked—until now. But to make your best better, it is probably time to change *how* you use your time.

During the next few days, I encourage you to be especially conscious (and curious) about how you spend your time. Recognize how often other people interrupt you, how frequently you have to stop and look for things, or how long it takes to complete certain job functions. As you continue studying your methods, look for new practices that you can implement immediately that will help you manage your time better.

The following are some of my favorite strategies for making immediate improvements to your time management process:

1. *Start meetings on the 00:15 of each hour.* Invite your colleagues to a meeting that starts at 9:15 AM and ends at 10:00 AM, or starts at 2:15 PM and ends at 3:00 PM. In my experience, most one-hour meetings can be handled in 45 minutes. In fact, they usually are as, often, especially later in the day, people are generally running 5 to 15 minutes late for meetings anyway. If it's part of your corporate culture to run late, start your meetings at 9:15; because people usually get ready to leave their desks *on the hour*, you may be pleased to find that your colleagues actually show up "on time."

2. ABR: *Always Be Ready*. I'm repeating this because it's *that* important. Bring small chunks of work with you wherever you go. Then, while waiting for a meeting to start or for a delayed flight to depart, you'll be able to reply to an e-mail or phone call; in other instances, you might have enough time to review materials for another meeting or project you are working on. If you're prepared, you can also confirm appointments, draft responses, or map out a project outline.

3. *Gain some ground early in the day.* When you get to the office or sit down at your desk each morning, begin by working on something that you can finish. After a few weeks, you'll find that you've completed a lot of little things that needed to be done, and may just have a bit more time, mental space, and inspiration to tackle some bigger issues. Completion increases your energy level and sets the standard for consistent forward motion on projects at all levels of importance.

4. *Interrupt people less.* Consider keeping a piece of paper off to the side on your desk. This way, when you think of something nonurgent that you need to tell or ask someone, write it down instead of e-mailing, calling, or talking to the person right away. Experiment with this approach; instead of interrupting someone three times per hour with one thing each time, you'll only be contacting him or her once an hour with three items.

Of course, you'll only really know that you are managing time more effectively by implementing the next two areas of improvement: *decide to focus* and *debrief success*.

Decide to Focus

Are you managing your meeting time well? Before you leave the office tonight, review your calendar and reprioritize your meetings, appointments, and planned work for the next day. Look to see if you can reschedule a meeting with anyone for the *following* day instead. Review the next week on your calendar and ask yourself if two people can meet with you at the same time. Find and schedule 30 to 60 minutes at a time (perhaps even multiple times per day) during which you can close the door or go to a conference room by yourself and focus on a single project or priority without being interrupted.

Clients have found this evening review to be the ideal time to become aware of what changes they might be able to make to have a more productive, engaging day. Decide what you want to focus on and how you're going to do that. Understand and take advantage of everything that influences your productivity, and you'll find you can manage time more effectively.

Debrief Success

Next, open your calendar to Thursday, at least one week from today. There, write this question: "How have I been managing my time lately?"

The next time you see this reminder, you'll have had a week or so to study how you use time and how you take advantage of small blocks of time. This is when you can assess the work you've done and the progress you've made. I coach my clients to do this kind of weekly debriefing on Thursdays (not Fridays) as a way to acknowledge that week's work, as well as organize anything that must be done before they leave the office the next day.

When people ask me why I do my debriefing on Thursday (early to midmorning), I give them the following reasons:

1. Friday afternoon, I generally want to: (a) go for a bike ride, (b) do aimless online research along my lines of interest, or (c) meet up with friends for happy hour.
2. Friday afternoon, I do *not* want to have to think!
3. Thursday, midmorning, is the time I start to think about bringing the week to a close.
4. Thursday, midmorning, I can remind people of (a) what I am doing *for* them, and (b) what I need *from* them. This gives all of us the rest of that day and all day Friday to get those things done.
5. By seeing the progress I've made over the previous three days (Monday, Tuesday, Wednesday), I get an extra shot of energy to move on to the next two days with gusto.

Between now and next Thursday, practice some of the time management ideas I've presented in this chapter. Here are three specific topics to think about, as you move toward working smarter and improving your efficiency and productivity:

- Is ABR working for you?
- Are you making progress on some of the more important areas and goals you've identified?
- What could you change that would move you forward on the path of productivity, so that you get done more of the important things during the day and increase the amount of time, energy, and focus you have when you get home?

Three Influences on Our Productivity

You're now ready to work smart, be productive, and get more of the great work you're doing done. That said, even if you have a plan for what you're going to do today or over the next week, sometimes a shift occurs and you're just not able to complete everything you thought you could. In this section I describe three influences that positively and negatively impact your daily productivity. As you read, consider how they impact what you focus on and what gets done during your 96 15-minute blocks of time each day.

Influence 1: Homeostasis

We tend to do what we've always done, how we've always done it, and in the same order we've done it. We seek "normal," and we love routines!

Here's a simple way to experience homeostasis: Put this book down and cross your arms over your chest. Notice which wrist ends up on top; we'll call that the outside arm. Now, for you, that's normal, right? I mean, if you find yourself waiting for someone, or you sit back in your chair and start thinking and fold your arms over your chest, that is how you'd do it.

Okay, now that you know what normal is for you, let's do a quick experiment: Stretch your hands out and again fold your arms over your chest, but this time do it so that the other wrist is on top. It feels weird to do it the opposite way, doesn't it? Most of my seminar participants say, "It's not normal."

Another word for normal is *homeostasis,* defined as, "the tendency toward a relatively stable equilibrium between interdependent elements." As I've said before, during the workday we tend to do what we've always done.

Let's say, for example, you've just taken a new job in a different part of the country and you now have a much longer commute to work. At first, this may weigh heavily on you; you may really feel the loss of the time it now takes to get to work; but as you adapt to your new routine, the longer commute will begin to seem like the "new normal" for you.

Similarly, if you've been working with your colleagues a long time, you probably feel you know what to expect from them (well, usually!). Likewise, when you have an open block of time (e.g., when a meeting gets cancelled), you tend to fill it up with another meeting, or by organizing your space, or getting a quick meal (all of which are important). And when you're especially overwhelmed, you tend to do what you've always done to impose some balance: cancel a meeting, get out of the office for a walk, delegate work, come in early in the morning or stay late.

Think back to the work you did while you were reading Chapter 2. Review your daily routines. When you get into the office, what are the first few things you do? Do you boot up a computer program? Do you check in with someone on your staff? Do you review or seek out important information you'll need that day?

My friend and mentor, Marshall Goldsmith, wrote a book called *What Got You Here, Won't Get You There*. The title says it all. If you stay in a comfortable state of homeostasis, you'll never take the risks and introduce the improvements you need to make your best better.

Influence 2: Context

Where you work changes what you do.

Read that sentence again, and then think about yesterday or another recent workday: Where were you? What did you get done? What made it easier/harder to accomplish the items on your to-do list?

When I consider context, I think about my surrounding environment and what I need to be able to work and manage my time most effectively. Say, for example, I have devoted a day to coaching. On such a day, I generally get up at 4:30 in the morning, drink a glass of water, and head to the gym in whatever hotel I'm staying at. During my workout, I watch a TED.com presentation, drink a little more water, and visualize an upcoming race I will compete in (a motivating factor, to be sure). By 6:30, I am done with my workout, have showered and dressed, and make my way to breakfast.

Breakfast is when I usually "put my head in the work-game." I write several notes in my journal; I draft questions, draw diagrams, and organize thoughts that are rolling around in my mind. This gives me a chance to "see what I'm thinking," and is a very powerful productivity technique.

During the coaching day (and any two coaching days are rarely alike), I support my clients by identifying their Time Management Profiles and discuss their priorities, projects, and workflow methods—how they get things done.

Over the course of the coaching session, I focus on studying exactly how each individual works in his or her current context, using the systems and tools he or she has available. Here are a few important questions to ask when you're addressing the context in which you work.

1. *Where* is *that thing?* If you waste time looking for items—printed forms, electronic files, e-mails, or other information—then it is time to update or upgrade your context. As rudimentary as it sounds, you waste more than just time when you search for misplaced items. You also squander your energy and focus when you invest them in such low-value activities.

   Think about it this way: If you invest only 30 minutes a week, perhaps in two 15-minute sessions, organizing, returning, recycling, and trashing items in your workspace, you will enjoy a return on that time two- or threefold next week. Reduce the amount of time you spend looking for things you "know are here—somewhere" by formalizing the time you spend organizing.

2. *Does "it" work the way it should?* Does the printer, the scanner, the new app on your mobile device, or that rule/filter you set up for incoming e-mail work the way it should? One of my clients bought a new tablet computer to take with him on business trips, only to find after two trips that the tablet was not the replacement he had hoped it would be. After discussing his situation for several minutes, he admitted that he knew this device wasn't doing what he wanted it to. He confessed, "I have to accept that, for now." Just acknowledging this fact forced him to identify the functions he needed from a travel computer. Once he spent time mapping out the productivity function of the device, he was able to identify a new solution (a new tool), one that provided exactly the results he wanted.

Think about your workspace: Is there some tool, system, or resource that you think should work a certain way, yet intuitively you know it's just not there yet?

3. *What are other people using to . . .?* Watch the way other people work. Ask them if they have a few moments available to give you a tour of their desk space, their office, or their briefcase/travel carry-on. Afterward, when you're back at your own desk, experiment with different models of productivity and organization. Use your research to figure out which systems and aesthetics will make it easier for you to get things done during the day. When you're traveling, watch what other people do to maintain a level of focus, productivity, and relaxation. What can they teach you?

4. *Do I like the way "it" looks, sounds, feels, works?* It's amazing, but over years of coaching I see repeatedly one simple cause for clients failing to get things done: They just don't like the way something *is*. For example, I worked with one executive who didn't like the appearance of her computer screen. So I showed her how to increase the font size on her e-mail/task management/calendaring application on both her computer and her smartphone. That one simple change made it easier for her to see information, which in turn enabled her to make decisions faster and get more done in less time. Again, take some time to study how you use the tools and space around you; you may find an instant upgrade or improvement, which turns out to be not just a good idea, but a *necessary* one.

5. *Does this space inspire me to do great work?* Look around where you are working right now. My belief is that you either garner or lose energy from what you surround yourself with; there is no middle ground. In one New York City office I visited, I saw an entire shelf of awards and plaques for "deals done," however, they were on the *other side* of the room from my client's desk. What *was* on his desk? All his unfinished business—printouts of deals gone bad, letters, articles, notepads (multiples)—in short, all things representing what he had *not* done.

We spent a good portion of our time together creating a physical space on his desk and in his office that helped him to realize when he was working on important deals, reminded him he had "won" in the past, and made him aware when he was ready to engage, when the time was right.

Influence 3: Network

It's not what you know, it's who you know. You've heard that one, right? My life has changed for the better time and again as a result of my willingness to take a risk, introduce myself, and meet someone new. Building and maintaining a social network are very important to everyday productivity—so important, in fact, that I dedicate all of Chapter 5 to the topic. For now, I want to introduce a couple of thoughts about influence and networking.

Years ago, I made a list of the five people I spent the most time with. I realized something pretty interesting: The more time I spent with these people, the more they influenced my behavior and mind-set, in both positive and negative ways.

I started tracking the number of vacation days they took. I kept track of how many books they'd read, the concerts they'd gone to, the movies they'd seen. I even guesstimated their annual salaries. Do you know what? I realized I was living about the average of the five people I spent the most time with!

Let me explain what I mean by that: Let's say those five people took a combined 35 days of vacation over the past 12 months. I divided 35 by five and came up with seven. As it turned out, I, too, had taken about seven days off during that same year. That synchronicity held true for all the other things: number of books read, amount of money earned, and more!

Here's another example: When, in 2007, I added one new person to my social network, who I learned had taken 40 *days of vacation* (his annual goal) the previous year, I noticed that the number of vacation days *I* took jumped as well. (In 2008, I enjoyed an 11-day vacation to Costa Rica, plus several long weekends.) Next year, my goal is to take 35 days off—by which I mean, not checking e-mail or voicemail or doing any other work-related activities.

If you are going to *make more* (the third purpose of this book, and my promise to you when you implement the ideas I present in it), you will have to add new people to your network. And by "your network," I mean beyond your online networks such as LinkedIn.com and Facebook.com.

Here is what I know: Who I am, where I have traveled, and what I think about are direct results of the people with whom I have spent most of my time. I realized years ago that if I alter who I surround myself with, I'll change more of how my life works. In fact, the bigger the changes I want to make, the more important it is that I immediately change who I spend my time with. As I learn new things and identify new goals, I'm always looking to meet new people.

In Chapter 5, I'll explain that your social network goes beyond online profiles. Just keep in mind for now that any network, whether online or face-to-face, is responsible for, and ready to help with, getting you from where you are to where you want to be. To do that, you have to start thinking big! Over the next four chapters I will show you how to do just that.

PART

2

Think Bigger

SOME TIME AGO, management expert and world-renowned author Marshall Goldsmith told me, "There's a fine line between taking on a lot of work and [taking on] *too* much." As you start using the ideas from the first three chapters of this book to work smarter, it's going to be tempting (and even easy) to take on more, you'll automatically start thinking bigger! You'll be getting things done more effectively and efficiently, and you'll undoubtedly begin to work in a completely different way.

When you direct your attention toward new possibilities, you'll immediately begin to notice new opportunities. There are several specific factors that will affect, and enable, you to make your best even better. Here are a few:

■ **You've got to believe.** Ask anyone who works at the highest levels of professionalism—from business to athletics to government institutions—about the secrets to their success, and they are bound to talk about their mind-set. Mental rehearsal—that is, visualizing something *before* it actually happens—is a great way to set yourself up for success. It establishes the foundation for the results to come.

- This isn't just positive thinking; it goes much deeper than that. As one of my clients, competitive swimmer B.J. Bedford, told me about competing in the Olympics: "I earned the right to be in Sydney. Twenty-two years of training, competing, making good choices, and working hard was culminating in one swim meet, a handful of one-minute races. If everything went according to my plan, I knew my team and I could break the world record and come home with a gold medal that day."

- Give *this* thought experiment a try: Ask yourself, "Who do I spend time with that limits my thinking?" If you want to think bigger, spend an hour (each week, once per month; whatever works best for you) with someone you know who thinks big. Chapter 5 will provide you with specific ways to tap in to your existing network of family, friends, coworkers, and community members to expand the way you think, as well as the topics you think about.

- Do you ever stop to ask yourself, "What is getting in my way?" In other words, what are you doing that's *preventing* you from reaching those targets? Think about the tasks and projects around you that limit your time, attention, and energy. Sure, you could make another to-do list and write down more than you know you can do in a day. Consider instead writing a "stop-doing" list. I'll show you how to study your habits, your workflow, and your comfort zone so you can figure out how to do a little less of the low-impact stuff, and more of the bigger-picture projects.

- **What's your why?** Ever notice that as you get busier and busier, your Most Important Things get a little (or, sometimes, a lot) less attention? Now is the time to review, reconfirm, and/or rewrite your purpose. Knowing what you're thinking bigger *for* makes it easier to Think Bigger!

4

Improvement and Self-Efficacy
If You Think You Can, You Probably Can

WHY DO YOU think the *way* you think?

How you answer that question sets the tone for this chapter and Part 2 of this book: *Think Bigger*. Your mental response—what you're telling yourself right now—forms your outlook on productivity and performance, all the way to the goals you set for yourself. Over a long period of time, your work, your experiences, and your expectations all blend together in your life, to create your belief in what is possible, what to expect, and what to dream for.

Let's begin with a definition. According to the online Merriam-Webster's Dictionary, efficacy is "the power to produce an effect." So when I use the term "self-efficacy," I'm referring to your ability to think about what you are going to do, and to do that which you are thinking about.

You think many thousands of thoughts in a typical day; of those, which take most of your energy, time, and focus? Which do you ignore? Which do you think about again and again—and again?

If you believe you will succeed, you're inclined to engage, learn from experiences—both positive and negative—take on newer, bigger goals, and continually go for the win. Think back to some point in your life when you identified, worked on, and achieved a dream.

73

Perhaps it was acceptance at a college; one of your first jobs; the day you decided to get married. Whatever it was, when you look back on that experience now, what thoughts come to mind?

I have spent the past 15 years around some very successful people, listening very carefully when they talk about what got them from "where they were" to "where they are." When I listen to someone with an efficacious mind-set, I know it's worthwhile to spend as much time as possible in conversation with him or her. People who have made a habit of achieving their goals will often make such declarative remarks as: "I did it once, I can do it again." I like to hear those stories.

I believe effective and directed thinking lays the foundation for taking any effort to the next level. If you want to improve your performance and build your productivity, start by studying your thinking. Look around at the life you have, the work you do, and the organizations you're involved in.

Here is a bold statement: "Things are the way they are *because of* the way you think."

Let's reflect back to the beginning of the book. In Chapter 1, you thought and wrote about you "at your best." Now is the time to bring that inventory to mind; review the kinds of things you can do to improve the chances that you will be able to focus on your priorities and do what you think about getting done.

By now I hope you have posted at least a rough draft of your "I'm At My Best When" statements where you can review them every morning. (For more ideas, go to www.AtMyBestWhen.com.) To get maximum value, be sure to review this list each morning. I hope you've been doing that for the past few days. If not, start tomorrow morning! Once you have experienced practicing this routine at the start of your day, you're ready to take it even further; it is time to think big. Then bigger. And then *biggify* that!

This chapter isn't about positive thinking or affirming what you hope one day will come true. It's about having what I refer to here as an "efficacious mind-set." I learned the concept of self-efficacy when I met Lou Tice, cofounder of The Pacific Institute. I had long believed in this concept of placing my focus where I wanted it; I just didn't know it had a name. The way Lou taught me about efficacy prepared me to rethink my entire outlook on productivity, development, and even my relationships and personal health!

Now is the time to take full accountability, by completely embracing this philosophy. Accept the single most important asset you control to make your best better. I call it *deep thinking* (which I write more about later, in Chapter 9 on the importance of focus). Thinking bigger is the natural by-product of working smarter. In addition, in my experience, professionally and personally, as an athlete and an advisor, I have seen that *how* I think is often more important than *that* I think, or even *what* I think.

What do you do when it's time to get your "head in the game"? The characteristic that separates the good from the great, the highly successful from the folks who are just getting along is their ability to think about themselves *as successful*. The way I learned it, they are efficacious; they have *and* trust in their ability to produce results.

There is more on your mind than you think. And each independent thought has the potential to take you off track, cause stress, or redefine your priorities. An important skill, now more than ever, is the ability to think without acting. Let me explain how this manifests for busy professionals.

It All Starts Where You Are

One Saturday morning, I met a client in her Philadelphia office. It was her choice to work with me over a weekend. "Because," she said, "there are just too many distractions during a workday." Our coaching session started in the same way I begin all of my client meetings: We discussed her roles, needs, and goals for the time we'd be spending together (two back-to-back, 10-hour days). After a while, she asked me the same question most clients do at the beginning of a one-on-one executive coaching program: "So, Jason, where do we start?"

I placed a ream of paper (500 pages) on her desk and asked her to get her favorite pen. I then asked her to write down one thing that she was thinking about on the first page. Next I instructed her to move that page off to the side of the desk and then to write something else on the next page, and then to move *that* sheet of paper to the side of her desk.

At first, she was hesitant and only recorded "big" items. Then she began to add a few large, multimonth projects she was managing. We made eye contact; I smiled my encouragement. She wrote more.

Occasionally she paused, then wrote another and another. After 10 minutes, she had written about a dozen items. When she looked up at me, I asked, "Is there anything else?" She wrote a few more. I sat and watched her add all kinds of thoughts to those pieces of paper, from big items to small "reminders." She wrote things like the stores she had to go to and the meetings she had to draft agendas for. Every time she looked up, I asked her to write just two more.

Over the next few minutes she went on to specify more and more items, among them office supplies that needed to be changed and the vacation she was planning later that spring. She kept on writing. Soon she had gone through 30 pieces of paper. Then 40! She wrote down ideas to discuss with different staff members, and topics to discuss with her husband that weekend. This went on for more than 4 hours! That's how long it took her to write something on each page of an entire ream of paper. That's right; she ended up identifying *500 items* that required her attention.

Afterward, we spent some time debriefing the activity. I shared with her that all those things she'd written down could have a significant impact on her productivity. We reviewed the kinds of items she wrote, looking at both size and scope. We uncovered big things and little things, personal projects and professional tasks, long-term goals and short-term priorities. She wrote such things as "hire a new staff person" and "coordinate summer camp for my daughter." She also had to organize her past travel receipts and set up an end-of-year off-site retreat. And there was much, much more. Yes, she had a lot on her mind.

I will always remember what she said to me at the end of that long, quiet, deep-thinking morning: "Jason, looking at that pile of what's on my mind, I think I know now why I feel so stressed!"

One of the biggest stressors we experience is the concept of incompletion. *I* didn't have to think about it; I *knew* why she was stressed out! The fact that we have so many things going on, competing intentions and multiple priorities, means we're not able to fully focus on what we are doing at any one time. Why? Because we're constantly bringing to mind things we're *not* doing! Don't take my word for it. Prove it to yourself by answering this question: Have you ever been reading a book, realized you'd finished an entire page and had no idea what you just read?

Imagine that you did this same mental exercise, writing each thought, to-do, reminder, idea, and so on, on its own sheet of paper. What do you think your response would be if you saw everything you're thinking about? Really, what would happen if you gave yourself the opportunity *and* time to write down every single thought that passed through your mind for four hours (or a day, or a week)? How long would it be before you started repeating thoughts? What might show up on the list that is new? Old? That you thought was done? Would you be excited by this inventory, or would just reviewing it bring you stress? More important, consider this: The things you write might actually stop you from "thinking you can."

What you write can both positively and negatively affect your ability to think efficaciously. There are two primary reasons for this:

1. *It's hard to take on more when you already have more to do than you can manage.* When you take out a blank piece of paper and challenge yourself to write down a goal, an intention, or a project, you're compromising something very near and dear to your heart: your comfort zone. Immediately, your mind and your body start reacting to those things you're writing down. The inventory might even remind you of an outdated goals list or a to-do list, neither of which you've ever kept up consistently.
2. *You're probably used to writing those things down.* Simultaneously, you're probably thinking, "Yeah, this is familiar." How do you begin to even think about, much less record, things that are more daunting than what you're already facing? Your to-do list—or e-mail inbox, or saved voicemail messages, or stacks of papers on your desk—are unconscious descriptions of what you believe is possible.

Here is something that gets in the way of making your best better: your ability, or lack thereof, to *think* you can. PR expert and fellow triathlete Peter Shankman's first book *Can We Do That?* walks readers through the process of creating outrageous PR stunts that work. Want to know the big secret of why they work? Because the really good ones answer the questions: "What do you want to be known for? What do you want to do? What is possible?"

By now, you probably have spent years (or even decades) honing your efforts and endeavors to your current level of comfort, clarifying your beliefs about what is possible, and creating a work and life style that matches your current professional and personal requirements. But I'm here to tell you that more, and better, is possible. What is your current thinking saying to you?

How Is Your Thinking "Talking"?

After reading this chapter, spend the next few hours just listening to what people say—really *listening*. We tend to give ourselves and our positions away in conversations; it's a lot like poker, when someone has a "tell" that lets the other players know how good (or bad) the cards are that he or she is holding. We use words and phrases to let others know what we think about creativity, possibility, goals, even our own performance preferences and methods. Consider even a casual conversation like this one:

Friend 1: "Hey, how are ya?"
Friend 2: "Not bad. How are you?"
Friend 1: "Busy. Seems like I'm always behind. Too much to do, you know?"
Friend 2: "Oh, wow, I know. I'm completely stressed, too. In fact, just last week I had to . . ."

Maybe you've overheard or participated in a conversation like this recently. Think about it for a moment: This kind of discussion is predisposed to go one way: spiraling downward. If someone begins a conversation claiming to be "not bad," "busy," and "always behind," how likely is he or she to spend the next few sentences talking about taking on more opportunities, thinking bigger, making his or her best better, or setting new goals? Not very.

Change begins with your vocabulary and your self-talk about what is possible. When I first began learning about efficacy and the very real conflict between the unconscious and conscious minds, I immediately recognized the impact this has on my own productivity. Years ago, I started looking for ways to manage the two thought-streams that are always flowing through my mind:

Stream A: What I consciously *think* about doing.

Stream B: What I subconsciously believe is *possible*.

It is critical that you study your ability, propensity, and comfort *to think you can* en route to making your best better.

I once told a client I was coaching who worked in a large investment firm, "You've got to study *you*." During our conversation, he told me that he had spent years trying to figure out the market, understand his client base, effectively work with his team, and even how to better understand his wife; but in all that time, he had not studied himself with that same rigor. This aha! moment set him on a path to develop his own level of efficacy and realize the significance of understanding his comfort zone and the impact of self-talk.

How Do You Build Self-Efficacy?

Do you think you can? What comes to mind when you review the goals and milestones you considered in Chapter 2? What does a review of your current to-do list tell you? And what would you think, really, if you actually spent a couple of hours and wrote down 500 things you could think of that need your attention?

The thoughts you choose to focus (or *not* focus) on are absolutely critical to this stage of improvement. I've heard people say, "If you change your thoughts, you can change your life." Well, what's the fastest way to change your thoughts? The answer: Start by changing your words. Tell yourself these four statements to help develop efficacious thinking:

1. "I *did it before*." Bring to mind a time in your recent past when you marked one in the "win" column. From start to finish, focus on what you did, how you were, who you talked to, what you did to complete that goal.
2. "They *were able to do it*." Look around at other people doing it (whatever "it" is). This is the main reason I continue to read biographies (and the prefaces and introductions to books). Simply knowing that other people are achieving their dreams gives me a line to hold onto, and something to work toward.
3. "They *think I can do it*." In Chapter 5, where I delve into the power of your social network, I discuss the importance of surrounding yourself with your fans and supporters—friends, mentors, family— anyone who cares about your success and is willing to push you

toward your goal. Knowing there are people who think I can do "it" (write a book, start a company, advise a board), makes it easier for me to think so too.

4. *"I know I can do it."* This is a powerful statement. Knowing you've worked, prepared, rehearsed, and anticipated success gives you confidence as you move toward your goals.

What Pulls You Off-Course?

Take a moment to look around. You may see some things nearby that instigate a "thought trail," *away* from efficacy. Recall that one of our most limited resources is focus (the topic of Chapter 9).

Since you started reading this chapter, what have you thought about, and what in your current environment is competing for your attention? If you completed the written exercises I encouraged you to do earlier, you're no doubt aware of just how many thoughts are circling in your mind and taking you in opposite directions.

Anything around you that is not started, about halfway finished, or simply "not the way you wish it was" will significantly, and often severely, impact your ability to concentrate and complete important tasks. It's easy for most people to stay busy. What is challenging for many of us is to ignore that which needs our attention *later*, and focus instead on what we're doing right now.

During a seminar at the University of California–Berkeley many years ago, I led an audience of over 100 through this exercise. I asked everyone to take 10 minutes, in silence, to write down what they were thinking about. Less than 5 minutes into the activity, I saw a woman in the back of the room waving her hand at me. I was about to walk over to her when she broke the silence of the room by saying, quite loudly, "What if there's nothing else on my mind? I already wrote it all down?"

Immediately, every head was up and 200 eyes were *on me!* "What should I do?" I thought to myself. Quickly, I recalibrated. I looked toward the woman who disrupted the exercise, past the dozens of people who were listening to what I was about to say. I smiled softly, and replied, "If your manager or director were sitting next to you in this seminar, looked at that page, and read what you wrote, what would he or she remind you that you forgot to write down?"

Then I turned toward the rest of the room and said, "If the person who cares the most about your success—a friend, a mentor, a spouse, a coach—were sitting next to you right now and looking at what you'd written, what would he or she encourage you to add to your list?"

Do you know what happened? The entire room went silent again, and every single person wrote faster and more than during the previous five minutes! And at the end, we had a very rich discussion. This is why it is so important to think deeply about what you do have to think about. In order to make this choice—"I'm not working on *that*, because I choose to work on *this*"—it is critical that you know what you're *not* working on. The way to do that is to write it all down, look at it, and make choices about your priorities.

How I Learned the Importance of Self-Efficacy and Vocabulary

In 2002, I drove toward Santa Barbara one early, dark August morning with a colleague, mentor, and racing buddy, Quanah Ridenour. It was on this Sunday morning so many years ago that I realized firsthand the power of efficacious thoughts; that the reality I experience is limited, and can be expanded by the thoughts I have leading up to any engagement. In other words, when I start to think about something, those are the thoughts that tend to manifest.

It was the morning of the third triathlon of my life, a sprint race in our neighbor coastal town. When we were about 15 miles from the site of the event, Quanah turned to me and asked: "So, you think you're going to place today?"

My mental voice immediately kicked in. How could he ask me that question, about an objective that, to me, was obviously impossible at that time? This was only my third race, and there would be over 400 other people competing, more than a dozen in my age group alone. How could he possibly ask me if I were going to finish in the top 3 percent of the competing field? Here's how I remember responding: "Nah. I think I'm just planning to go for finishing with a good time today," I said, and left it at that.

The start of the race was exciting for me. As a relative rookie, I was a bit stressed during the entire event. At the end of the short swim, I ran up the sand into a bit of headwind. I remember looking up at the

Los Padres Mountains, wondering exactly how far ahead Quanah was. When I reached the bike transition, his bike (and those of many others) was gone. That meant he had finished the swim and was already charging away on the bike course. As quickly as I could, I changed out of my wetsuit, put on my cycling shoes, and started the bicycle portion of the race.

The bike course was what's called an "out-and-back." About 600 yards before reaching the turnaround, I saw Quanah riding back toward me. That meant he was a couple of minutes ahead of me and on his way to rerack his bike, and head out on the run. "Okay," I thought, "I know where he is; let me put the chase on." I rode as hard as I could for the next 15 minutes. I didn't think I'd catch him, but I figured if I could keep the distance the same, I might make up some time on the run.

I reached the next transition point, hooked my bike to the rack, changed into my running shoes, strapped my race number belt around my waist, and bolted out along the beach running path. The sun was above us by now, and people were milling around everywhere. Though most were yelling for other participants, I felt the roar pushing me faster and faster. The run was flat and fast. To my surprise, I saw Quanah again; he had increased the distance between us! Not only had he outbiked me on the entire bike portion, he was running faster as well!

I gave all I had—or at least all I thought I had; I was running as fast as I could. When I did finally reach the finish line, I was exhausted, but excited as well. I had finished my third triathlon.

I walked over to the results posting area to see how I'd done, thinking, "I bet I didn't place today." When I finally did see the results, my mouth dropped, my shoulders sagged, and I swore out loud. Quanah must have seen the disappointment on my face, because when I walked up to join him and the group from Ojai, he asked me what was wrong. It was all I could do to say, "Forty-five seconds, man. I can't believe it; 45 seconds." I had missed placing in my age group—and going home with a trophy—by less than a minute!

As I mentioned, earlier that morning Quanah had asked me, "Do you think you're going to place today?" My thoughts, as well as my response and subsequent mental planning and organizing, had launched a chain of events that would take place over the rest of that morning. Because I couldn't imagine myself placing—most of my thoughts simply involved just "making it through the course"—I didn't place.

Simply put, I didn't see myself placing as a possibility toward which to work.

What Are You Thinking?

You will know what you are thinking when you see what you're saying.

Read that sentence again. This time, slowly; and let yourself think it through. That statement is a significant part of the process of iterative improvement, that is, how it is possible to get better over time. Because you are so familiar with what you think, do, and say, it is crucial to get another person's perspective on these matters, an outsider's view. One way to do this is to ask the people with whom you spend the most time to give you honest feedback. Just be aware that they, too, probably are comfortable in *their* thinking of what's possible, and so may have a hard time giving you ideas on what you could do to improve and grow.

For example, think back to Chapter 1 and the exercise asking you to write down some of your MITs, your Most Important Things. Was yours a long list? Did you write down only things that you know you need to do? Did you leave any room for dreaming, identifying fresh goals, or acknowledging new opportunities? Now that you've read the discussion about the power of thought, focus, and productivity, I challenge you to go through that process again.

Take out another few pieces of paper or a brand new notebook, set a timer for 15 or 20 minutes, sit down, and *write*. Write one item per line, and undertake this thinking process again, but this time, write *more*. If possible, try to imagine and record at least 100 things—big, little, personal, professional, and everything in between. Why so many? So you can discover what you're really thinking, of course!

What You Believe: That Is What Is Getting in the Way

While studying the psychology of improvement and professional development, I have had the opportunity to speak with Olympic athletes, business owners, politicians, as well as many others of diverse professional and cultural backgrounds. It seems that the more successful people become, the more willing they are to turn to outside resources for assistance. For example, many of the successful professional athletes I know work with a variety of coaches, and not necessarily in their sport.

A commonly shared trait of people with a high sense of self-efficacy is an awareness of the "thought-trails" along which they move through the journey of life. Much like a trail that is cut through a meadow or along a hillside after years and years of use, these tracks can actually *force* you to continue thinking the way you've always thought. That can prove to be especially challenging when your goal is to experience something new and to "change your mind."

The following is an exercise you can complete in just 15 minutes to clarify ways to operate from a mind-set that's ready for action and making things happen. I give you several prompts below to get you started and help you become aware of your own thought-trails. Later on, we'll look at how you can begin shifting your thinking in a more efficacious and positive direction. For each prompt, write down at least two statements, or "truths," that come to mind.

- Life is . . .
- Money is . . .
- Coaches are for people who . . .
- Goals are . . .
- Work is . . .
- Organized people are . . .
- People who get better are . . .

In the table here, I list a number of responses I have read from people doing this activity over the years:

Life is *good*	Life is *hard*
Money is *what I use to create opportunity.*	Money is the *root of all evil.*
Coaches are for people who *are moving forward, faster.*	Coaches are for people who *have money to burn.*
Goals are *necessary to achieve more.*	Goals are *nice, but I'm always busy managing a new crisis.*
Work is *what I do to express myself.*	Work is *never over.*
Organized people are *productive.*	Organized people are *type-A workaholics.*
People who get better are *leading the way and setting an example for the rest of us.*	People who get better are *obviously lacking in some area of their life.*

Writing your own truths gives you a chance to examine your work, your world, and your life as you think about and see it now. Giving yourself this opportunity to see what you think can go a long way toward shifting your willingness to initiate action, seek out information, and engage in the change process.

Remember, improvement does not mean something is *wrong*; it simply indicates a movement toward something new—and, possibly, better.

The Truth Is What You Think It Is

Think back to my Ideal Day I described in the prologue to this book. If you skipped it, go back and read it now. (And, if you haven't already done so, write one of your own!) I had no idea how I was going to achieve that ideal scenario when I wrote it over a decade ago, or even whether it was possible to do so. I wrote it out of trust in a mentor who suggested I "just write what I want." He reminded me, "You don't have to show anyone." So, I wrote out my dream, and I didn't show anyone.

What I did do, however, was continue thinking about those few paragraphs. Over months, and then years, I continued to reflect on what an ideal day would look, sound, and feel like. And then one day, I experienced it to almost the smallest detail, in the Sierra Nevada, in California.

For the past several years, my wife Jodi and I schedule a month during the summer when we move to the mountains or a coastal town. We do this to "get out of what's normal," practice different routines, and search for new ideas. Some of our favorite places to travel are Tamarindo, Costa Rica, Homer, Alaska, and Lake Tahoe, California. At the end of one summer day during our month-long sojourn in a cabin in Tahoe City, we were sitting on the porch overlooking the lake, when I smiled and said, "I did it."

I went on to describe my day to my wife, letting her know what had happened since I woke up (always a bit before she does) and all I had experienced during the next several hours. I could finally say I had achieved a dream of having an Ideal Day! I told her I had written about this day years before, and that I had now experienced it all, coming together in one day.

Now it was time to up the ante. Since I realized that it was possible to have *those* things come together for a great day, I'm ready to write the next level of what's possible.

The truth is that the work you're doing and the life you're living right now is the sum of all the parts of your thinking, your beliefs, and your explanations of what it is, why it is, and how it came to be. Therefore, the process of making your best better begins when you start *believing* it is possible to do so. By identifying what you'd like to experience, personally and professionally, you then can begin to develop habits and actions that move you closer to those goals. Over time, you will make seemingly trivial decisions, decide to meet certain people, collect specific information, and spend time planning to make great things happen.

So what are you waiting for? It's time to get started.

What Builds Your Self-Efficacy?

Spend a few moments considering the things that affect your ability to turn your beliefs into action. The short answer is, anything you let influence you, your focus, and your thinking. It is whatever you let into your sensory area, what you see, hear, and feel. If you want to increase the likelihood that you'll achieve what you want, and are setting significant and realistic goals, then you need to invite in new information. The following subsections describe sources I've recommended clients use for that purpose over the years.

Biographies

Start here. Pick a professional area—sports, commerce, politics, history, or whatever sparks your interest—and find a well-researched biography about a leader in that space. If you set a goal to read five biographies in a year, you'll give yourself a unique opportunity to study how other people "did it," succeeded. You'll identify patterns, pick up ideas, and read an occasional how-to secret of someone's success. This will help you develop your own ideas about how to build up your ability to achieve your goals, and figure out exactly what that means to you.

I remember reading a biography of Helen Keller long ago. Of course, I had heard about her, and as a child I was reminded of how lucky I was compared to her. What I didn't know, however, was the love for language she developed after she learned how to communicate. Not only did she learn how to "speak" in American Sign Language, she also learned to read Braille in other languages, including French and Latin. To this day, when I'm traveling abroad, I carry with me a sense of efficacy derived from her: "I can learn a few phrases and words while I'm here; it's what Ms. Keller would have done."

Stories of other people's lives are full of lessons for all of us to learn. You'll be amazed to discover what might motivate you when you're reading about the challenges another person faced—and overcame.

How-To Books

If there is a professional skill you're looking to hone or something you want to learn, diving into a book or series of books on the subject is a great way to build your knowledge base, confidence, and action list of what specifically you need to learn. Identify one or more authors who have written about the skill or information you are interested in. Consider buying a copy of the books they wrote; but don't stop there. Do a search for these authors on YouTube, Google, LinkedIn, Facebook, and any other forum where they might be sharing what they know and how they parlay their knowledge.

While preparing for a week of coaching several senior executives at a professional service firm in New York City, I bought a few books on leadership and motivation. I was so inspired while reading one of them—Daniel Pink's *Drive*—that I thought "There *has* to be more I could learn from this person." So I searched the Internet on Dan and found a series of videos; I started following Dan's Twitter feed, as well. Next, I wrote him a letter; and finally, I interviewed him by phone and shared it on my YouTube channel for others to listen to.

What kinds of skills are you looking to develop? What topics arouse your interest? Determine the subjects about which you'd like to gather more information, and then start gathering it.

Conferences/Seminars

Look ahead to the next 8 to 12 months and ask yourself: "What do I want to know more about?" Once you've answered that question, ask your peer group and your professional network if there are any upcoming conferences or seminars on that topic. Search the Internet using key terms related to the subjects you'd like to learn about, adding the words "conference" and "seminar."

For example, when I was seeking to learn more about workplace communication and effective teamwork among colleagues in different offices around the world, I decided to find, and attend, any conferences where I could learn about those issues. Over the past 10 years, doing this has enabled me to blend my travel with a day or two at a time of conferences. Not only do I have the opportunity to learn about those topics that have grabbed my interest at that time, I get to meet other people who are also interested in growing and developing in those areas.

Write about It

There's something invigorating about slowing down long enough to put words down in your own handwriting. You own everything you've done, both successes and failures. If along the way you give yourself time to write about how you see things going, you can look back over time and notice themes, issues, and areas on which you'll want to focus going forward. For the next five or so nights, I recommend that you stop at the end of the day and record everything you can remember about the day.

Each evening, I stop and write a 100- to 150-word entry in my daily journal. This is when I give myself the opportunity to slow down and see the words appear on the page. Sometimes I look back on a day with wonder: "Where did the time go?" Other times, I have the pleasure of acknowledging a win or two—something I did really, really well. Oh, and another thing I've been doing a while now is this: At the end of each entry, I write one word that I think best describes the day. Yes, just one word. Doing this goes an incredibly long way toward summarizing my thoughts and making everything seem crystal clear.

Mentors and Influential Friends

You are a reflection of the people with whom you spend the most time. If you're going to make your best better, you may have to reevaluate the group of people in your world. Needless to say, this will be very difficult in some situations—for example, you simply can't get away from a negative coworker, or your morning commute is full of ill-tempered people. Still, look around, no matter where you are, and see if there is someone with whom you can spend a little more time who can encourage, push, and challenge you.

At least once a quarter, I find someone to meet with at least five times for coffee, breakfast, or lunch. These conversations are designed so that I can share a situation or opportunity I am facing, and then listen as the other person shares stories about what he or she thinks I can do about it—how to approach the situation, and some ideas about possibly moving forward. (I'll discuss these meetings in more detail in Chapter 5, which is all about building your social network).

■ ■ ■

Keep in mind, you'll only get as far as you believe you can. This is not the time to disillusion yourself (or freak yourself out) by taking on a humongous, intimidating goal. Begin by practicing on smaller things so that you can perform successfully on bigger ones later; choose just one or two areas to study over the next couple of weeks. Consider implementing any one of the preceding suggestions, and watch how your own efficacious attitude toward what can be done begins to shift, ever so slightly, in a positive direction.

So, now that you think you can, what big things *would* you take on?

5

Improvement and the Social Network
If You Want to Go Far, Fast, Go Together

YOUR SOCIAL NETWORK is much more than just your "online presence," and it existed long before Facebook, Google Plus, LinkedIn, and Twitter came on the scene.

Where you work, where you live, where you go to dinner—these are all places that influence your network every single day. You've attended various schools, conferences, and events. You've met a lot of people, exchanged business cards with some of them, and followed up with a much smaller number over the years. While networking may happen naturally from time to time, by implementing just a few tips and practices I introduce here, you can meet more people "on purpose" and expand the influence of your own network.

A major factor influencing what you do and what you think about will be to surround yourself with people who encourage, support, and challenge you to think bigger. That is the theme of Chapters 4 through 7 of this book.

While it is true that millions of users worldwide check in daily via their digital networks to make connections and get status updates, this chapter is all about identifying the people who are around you now, and the people who need to be around you, to help you think bigger.

It's Not What You Know, It's Who You Know

Think first of the people who have had the greatest impact on your life—individuals who have coached, counseled, befriended, or mentored you. Now, bring just one of them to mind. Is there someone in your past from school, a job, your community, or a personal relationship who has changed the course of your life?

Often, when I ask people to do this, they remember someone they haven't talked to in years, raising the question, "Why do we let such relationships fade, when they were such important influences in our lives?"

The people around you can help greatly with the process of thinking bigger. You can turn to them for ideas, advice, and coaching; and you can learn a lot just by asking them questions. The point is to recognize just how important your social network is to your professional and personal development. It's not just *what* you know that counts, it's who.

Building Team You

Would you agree that the network you have built until now is (at least in part) responsible for your current life and work experience? If so, then to create new, bigger opportunities, it should make sense to study and build an expanded social network.

Now is the time to think about the people who care most about you and your development, who want to see you expand the most, and who are willing to meet you where you are and help you grow from there. Your team is made of the people you talk to most often, work with every day, and spend time with throughout the week. Here's a point to ponder: "Do you have the 'right' people on your team?"

In an article in the October 2001 issue of *Fast Company* magazine, management thinker Jim Collins wrote, "[L]eaders of companies that go from good to great start not with 'where' but with 'who.'" Think about your own performance, professional development, and the opportunities you anticipate coming your way in the next 18 to 36 months.

When I meet with executives who manage companies, and managers who lead teams, we talk about their networks; not just people promoted to positions of leadership, but the informal groups of people they spend time with throughout the day, at work, at home after work, on the weekends, and on vacations. As you continue the process of thinking bigger and making your best better, focus on the following prompts:

Who you are

What you do

How much money you make

What possibilities you envision

All of these develop in direct proportion to the collective and expansive mind-set of the people you spend the most time with in life and at work.

Spend time with people who think bigger and you will think bigger too!

You have probably heard the saying "garbage in, garbage out." If only bad data goes into the processor, it makes sense that only bad data will come back out.

Though this concept originally was applied to programming computer software, it works in a similar fashion when it comes to the human mind—with one important difference. Sometimes, when we think about our plans and our social network, it may be "garbage in, garbage *stays*." The purpose of building up your social network is to make sure you have better, and bigger, information going in!

The fact remains that the groups of people with whom we interact contribute the most to our mental outlook—the way we see the world. It is undeniably clear how important it is to engage with the kind of people who can influence you positively on practical and subtle levels. So, surround yourself with other leaders: people who inspire you, design new realities, and do the seemingly impossible.

They may be entrepreneurs, educators, or artists; they may be individuals both inside and outside your profession. You may have someone in mind already, someone who inspires awe each time he or she responds to the simple question, "What's new with you?"

Start Where You Are

To begin this exercise, start where you are. Instead of identifying the next meeting invitation to send out or deciding which conference to attend, simply acknowledge some of the more significant people in your current network.

Get out a sheet of paper and write down the names of the first people who come to mind in each the following categories:

- A list of 10 people you *look up to and admire*
- A list of 10 people you would like to *spend an extra hour* with this month
- A list of 10 people you would like to spend *less time* with

You don't have to do anything about these 30 people right now; the purpose in making these lists is to help you begin to discern who is already on your team, determine if there are others to add, and decide whether there is anyone you might need to spend less time with.

Build Your Leadership Support Network

Some people see their list of 30 people and immediately realize they are well on their way to expansion. Others find this exercise makes them feel isolated, because they realize they don't currently have a group of colleagues to meet their needs. If that's your situation, then it's time to start thinking about *and* building your own leadership support network, your *real* social network.

Establishing both an in-person and virtual community can play a significant role in expanding your horizons. You can keep feeding the hunger you've developed for wanting to discover what's possible by seeking out who's doing the impossible. You want to identify individuals who are taking on the serious issues, the ones that are especially important if, say, you're the person directing the vision and focus for your organization. Odds are that if you aren't getting rejected enough or pushing up against boundaries, then you aren't playing in a challenging enough game.

A great resource for finding influential leaders you can learn from and "spend time with" are podcasts, audio and video presentations you can download for free from Apple's iTunes platform. Two other places where you can surround yourself with "good information" are Pop!Tech and TEDTalks, annual conferences that host some of the world's most fascinating people, who have been invited to contribute based on their innovative research, products, or studies. The presentations range in length from 5 to 20 minutes and are selected for their valuable contributions to the global dialog. The presenters share "inspired talks by the world's greatest thinkers and doers."

Ever since I was a high school teacher, I have coached my students and clients to "watch their associations." You must be mindful of more than the membership cards you hold in your purse and wallet; you must pay close attention to the one-on-one interactions and small groups of people with whom you spend time. In order to make your best better, you must challenge the strength and value of the people in your personal and professional networks. One simple test is to ask yourself the following question when you end a conversation with someone in your network: "How do I feel right now, having just finished a conversation with _____ (the person's name)?"

I have been asking myself that question for years now. Whether it is in response to time I spent with a friend, a client, a coach, or a family member, I check in to see if I'm feeling better or worse than when I started that conversation. My colleague Susan Scott, author of the book *Fierce Conversations*, reminds us that relationships in life and at work are not made up of individual conversations; they are one, long, continuing, ever-deepening conversation. Do you surround yourself with people who build you up, support you, and encourage you through those conversations? You have to create your team with an eye toward building this kind of rapport.

Students and clients I have met with on four continents have seen the "Team You" Mindmap exercise you will read about here. It is an easy way to visualize your connections with the people in your circle, and strategize how to spend more time with those who really add to your endeavors, and conversely, less time with those who don't. By directing your focus now on the following activity, you'll find that it's designed to—and will—provide you with specific and actionable information.

Identify Team You

It is best to sketch your "Team You" Mindmap on a large piece of paper or whiteboard, but a page in your notebook will do if that's all you have at hand. Write "Team [Your Name]" in the middle at the top of the page. Then ask yourself: "From the original list of 30, who are the 5 to 10 people who care the *most* about my personal and professional success?"

It is important to think about both your personal and work life. My suggestion is to write down the names that come immediately to mind. Certainly, you can always come back later and add or replace a person's name, but I find it's best to kick off this exercise simply by writing the names of people who come to mind immediately. These represent the group of individuals to whom you turn for ideas, with whom you share your problems, and who would want to help put you on a path to personal and professional improvement.

Occasionally, some of my clients will record peoples' names then look back over the list and realize they have not heard from or contacted someone on their "team" in a long, long time. If that's the case for you, the message is clear: It's time to reach out!

Your team is the group of people who are willing to support you, and want to see you improve. Yet they must also be individuals who are willing to challenge you, question you, and encourage you to achieve greatness. One of the fastest ways to engage in that development is to assure the people around you that you're doing just that!

In Figure 5.1, you'll see a diagram of a TeamMap I drew while I was writing this chapter; on it are the names of people I know I can go to for ideas, advice, or counsel. Some are family members; others are friends; and a couple are clients. Your team can be made up of like-minded people, or be as diverse as you need it to be. Often, I'll make new TeamMaps based on individual projects I'm working on. And note that I don't list the names in any particular order; my goal is to simply transfer the list I have in my head to paper, and then move to a developmental, explorative process to determine how I can move even further, and potentially faster, by reaching out to my team members.

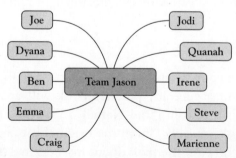

Figure 5.1   My Team

Who Is on Your Team?

I came up with the idea of TeamMapping at the same time I started working as an executive coach, in the year 2000. I had spent that year surrounding myself with information, education, and practices that led me to understand and experience a successful work/life balance, as well as to develop my brand as a thought leader in the personal productivity space of coaching and advising. I trust the importance of coming back to my team to help me continue to expand my own objectives, reach my goals, and enjoy the life that I do.

Here's how it sounds in my head: "We're smarter together."

I have a few people on my team to whom I turn constantly for advice and ideas. They each have different strengths. In Figure 5.2 you can see what Team Jason looks like, and some of the areas of focus I direct to each person. How has your team evolved over the years? Who have you added (and perhaps removed)? How has each member helped you get to where you are now?

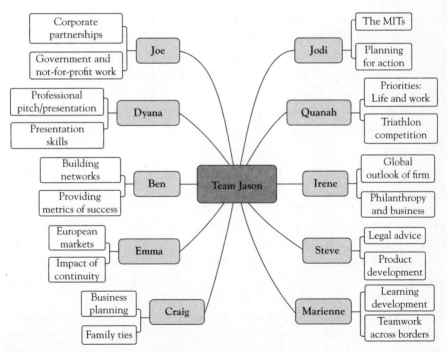

Figure 5.2   Expansion of Team Jason

You Are Your Network

You may be wondering how to add the task of identifying your social network and building these relationships to your already busy schedule. For this purpose I refer you back to Part 1, "Work Smarter," which gives you tactical solutions to managing your current level of work more effectively, so that you can now build Team You and step up to the next level, a higher level, in your life and your work.

Think about what you have done lately. Consider the places you have gone, the books you have read, the movies you have seen, the technology you use; simply bring to mind anything you have done over the past three to six weeks. It's likely that the people with whom you spend time influenced at least some of those activities.

Here's a simple example: I'll bet that someone recently said something to you along the lines of, "Hey, you should try this restaurant. I went there with [name] and it was terrific!" Remember, *you* are your network, so make your network work for you.

Now let's move on from restaurant recommendations to consider more important issues, like how much money you make, how many vacation days you take, and how many and what kind of books you read. With those categories in mind, again think of the people with whom you regularly associate. As you read further, keep a running list (either on a piece of paper or in your digital system) of who comes to mind as you think about where you *are*, where you *were*, and where you *are going*. As you undertake this exercise, consider the questions in the following sections.

Whom Do You Talk To?

For example, on your way to work, do you ever think about the conversations you plan to have that day? Are there specific people you look for or listen to, individuals you hope to hear from when you check your e-mail or voicemail? One way to get the most out of your social network is to expand its size and continue meeting people who can help you get from where you are to where you want to be.

"Change who you spend your life with, and your life will change." Les Brown, author and motivational speaker, said this to me backstage when we were both speaking at the same conference. I had approached him later in the day, after I heard him speak, to ask "just one more question." (That's my style: I always have another question!) I wanted to know what he had done to change his life so dramatically over the years, and find out exactly how he had moved on from where he had been to become the person he is today. His answer to me was the quote above, which he said with a smile. I immediately understood what he meant.

How Do You Meet People?

Where do you go to meet new people? How do you find interesting men and women "on the edge" of your normal routines and interests? Of course you're busy; we all are. That is precisely why it's so critical to choose where, how, and with whom you're going to spend your limited time and efforts. Clarifying your goals and homing in on the specific areas you'd like to improve makes it easier to prioritize your time and make yourself available to spend time with these people each week.

As I noted earlier, during my travels around the world, I host a weekly CoffeeChat in local coffee shops before work each morning. I send an invitation to this very informal get-together to my network in each city I visit. On any given weekday, in cities such as Zurich, London, New York, San Francisco, and my hometown of Ojai, California, 2 to 12 people show up to meet, talk, and build their networks. Over the years, new friendships have been forged and new jobs created, just by bringing people together to talk about new things.

What Do You Talk about When You Meet Someone New?

What do you talk about with people you already know? The topic of discussion is just as important as the people with whom you're discussing it. Build your capacity to make connections and talk about things that are related to, as well as that go beyond, the topic of conversations you're currently having.

Experiment by subscribing to new magazines, reading a different genre of book, even taking a class or attending a seminar. In short, expose yourself to fresh ideas and experiences.

Where Do You Go and How Much Time Do You Spend There?

For better or for worse, most people spend the bulk of their waking hours during the week (and sometimes on the weekends) in some kind of office or professional environment working or thinking about work. You should immediately recognize the impact this has on growing and nurturing your social network. Simply put, it makes it hard!

By spending most of our time with the same people, we tend to talk about the same things. Breaking free from your normal, day-to-day routines, even for one day every two weeks, will give you a chance to meet someone new and discover whether you share any interests that you might like to discuss and explore.

I always have my next conference planned. Over the years, I have taken art classes, gone to triathlon camp, attended professional skills improvement seminars, and sat in on local community development workshops. Each one of these events has given me a few new things to talk about and a few new people with whom I can discuss my growing range of interests.

This kind of networking also gives me the opportunity to learn about places I've not been to, organizations I've not heard of, and events I haven't yet participated in. And when I return to many of these cities, it also makes it easier to reach out and catch up with someone I met on a previous visit. (Since I travel almost 200 days a year, this kind of global network really helps.)

Why Are You Meeting the Kinds of People You're Meeting?

Hint: It has to do with the questions in this series asking you to describe your network and how you participate in it.

The people around you and the situations in which you find yourself will usually connect to the types of questions you ask yourself and the kinds of topics you're interested in. I will talk later in the book about the importance of identifying, developing, and living your own "so that . . . ." This requires you to identify your own "why?" and work to create opportunities to spend more time *working toward* an answer to it.

At the end of each day, I pause to reflect on the people with whom I spent time that day. I find it easier to capture these thoughts in the small notebook I keep on my nightstand, so I compose a daily assessment where I write about the individuals with whom I spent the most time and energy over the previous 24 hours. I then begin to see patterns emerge over the course of a few days. I also become very aware of who is getting most of my attention, and how that is affecting my own engagement and productivity.

When Are You at Your Best?

When might it be a good time to get out and meet people in your line of business, your community, or anywhere else where others might share your interests? Just as there are cycles throughout the day (some of us are morning people, while others work best after the sun goes down), there are also cycles inherent to building, maintaining, and cultivating a social network. Fortunately, there are a variety of events you can tap into throughout the day, from early-morning Toastmasters meetings to weekly lunch networking events to after-work Meetups. Likewise, there are conferences, seminars, and workshops offered in your area(s) of focus and interest throughout the year. Take some time over the next three months to identify a few new events you might be able to attend. Sign up, show up, and see what happens when you get there and begin meeting and interacting with new people.

I already mentioned the CoffeeChat meetings (hashtag: #Coffee-Chat) I coordinate on an almost weekly basis. In addition to these, my wife and I have made it a point to get away every year for several weeks at a time. One year we moved to Homer, Alaska, for a month; another, we traveled to Costa Rica for two weeks. While we're away from home, we make it a habit to reach out to the local community to learn about its people, understand the culture, and look for ways to contribute what we can while we're living among them.

While in Homer, for example, I raced in the local Breast Cancer Awareness 5-mile run and finished in first place. The local paper ran the story and my finish-line photo on the front page, whose link I shared with my virtual networks via Facebook, Twitter, and LinkedIn. Overnight I became a recognizable face in this small town, and "big-city" clients were intrigued by the quaint Alaskan fishing town and wanted me to send them info about visiting. I learned two memorable lessons that day: (1) when we share a bit about ourselves we learn how much we have in common; and, (2) that people prefer to do business with people they like.

The Next Questions

I teach an idea I call the "Next Questions." Think back to the last meeting or networking event you attended. Did you meet anyone new? Or, did you introduce two people you knew but who had not yet met each other? Now think about the first questions you typically are called upon to answer during a conversation with someone you've just met. Surely, you introduce yourself and ask the other person his or her name. Then, there are usually three questions you ask, usually in this order:

"Where are you from?"

"Where do you work?"

"What do you do?"

These are followed by still more questions. What are yours? Do you have different questions for different venues you attend? I do! Some of the questions I have asked over the years include:

"What's a great book you've read lately?"

"Have you heard any good speakers or been to any conferences lately?"

"Where have you traveled lately that really made you think differently?

I have others; and I'm sure you've asked some I never have. The important point is, if you're going to develop a new relationship, and use that first conversation to think bigger, you need to set up to do just that—where it can be done!

Let me raise a couple more questions relevant here. Whenever I attend these events or conferences, or meet someone while flying around the world, I anticipate that those first three questions are going to come my way. Of course, we need those kinds of questions, as they get the conversation going. After you've asked and answered them, however, I recommend asking two more questions (these are the Next

Questions I mentioned at the beginning of this section) to take the conversation to a whole new level. They are:

1. "What is interesting to you these days?"
2. "How can I help you?"

What Is Interesting to You These Days?

Over years of asking people these questions while at dinner parties, networking events, and conferences, I still am pleased by the first look I get when I pose this one—usually one of surprise! Admittedly, it doesn't always go over as I'd like. I have met some people who aren't interested in going into further detail (I call them the "business card collectors"); however, I've met many others along the way who are happy to elaborate. They tell me about a project they are working on, a situation they are managing, a trip they are taking, or something else important and interesting to them.

How Can I Help You?

This question, too, might not be the most typical one to ask at an after-work, evening networking event, but I find it is a good way to gauge the enthusiasm and seriousness regarding the projects someone is working on, or other matters of interest.

Later in the book, I'll go into more detail about asking for, receiving, and using feedback and peer-to-peer mentoring. But for now, realize that simply offering to help will occasionally open a door to a deeper connection and continued conversation with someone. Over the years, I have seen it lead to friendships and business relationships that continue to grow far beyond the event where they began.

Who Got You Here May Not Take You There

Recall I mentioned in Chapter 3, the book titled *What Got You Here Won't Get You There: How Successful People Become Even More Successful* by Marshall Goldsmith and Mark Reiter. (I highly recommend you get a copy as soon as possible.) While you think of that title, please recognize *this* as well when you're considering your social network: *Who* got you here, may not *take* you there.

That is, your current friends, coworkers, and managers, those who have been around you for a long time, have greatly influenced what you are currently doing (or not doing!). If, now, you look around and realize that you need to start doing something different, think deeply about how, or if, those same people should be a part of your new plan: Who among them is going to understand, support, and encourage you in your new ventures? While some will enthusiastically encourage and support you in making these proactive changes, in your life, you may discover that you will ultimately be spending less time with others. Now is the time to add new members to your TeamMap.

Who Do You Know Who . . .?

This is one of my favorite paradigm-shift questions to ask during a conversation. It changes the way we look at a situation and produces the kind of connective thinking that involves everyone to tap more fully into social networks, peer groups, and address books. When you take the opportunity during a conversation to identify a topic that is interesting to you, describe the help you are looking for, or identify who else may be able to contribute, you're changing your perspective and opening the door to making your best even better.

For over a decade I have served as a facilitator, workshop leader, community volunteer, and executive coach, and I have used this very question to build my practice, continue learning, and develop new ideas and processes that help people improve their productivity and workplace performance. Several times per week, I ask this question to learn about the people around me, and the people around them, as well.

That's right: The more you develop Team You, the better prepared you'll be to tap into the networks of other people's teams. Now *that's* a way to make your best better.

Three Kinds of Conversations

It's important to identify the kinds of conversations you regularly have throughout the course of a typical day. As you continue reading, ask yourself the following questions: "Who did I talk to earlier today? What about yesterday? What kinds of things did we discuss?" As you remember the people you talked to and the tenor of those conversations, it's important to focus on the topics that were discussed. Going forward, you may want to expand your social network by including people who are knowledgeable about specific areas you need or want to learn more about.

Remember, your social network weaves the fabric that creates opportunity, so make each conversation count. Of course, there is much to talk about when you do meet with someone, so it may help to focus on the kinds of conversations you have with the people you regularly talk to. In your conversations, are you:

1. Managing transactions?
2. Developing a relationship?
3. Addressing challenges?

Managing Transactions

Often, you're looking to manage a transaction when you call someone on the phone and ask if he or she "has a minute." When it's just information you're looking for, and someone else has it, you can save a lot of time by simply "going to the source." You're getting in touch because you want to ask or tell this person something. This kind of conversation tends to be content-specific and action-rich.

On the plus side, a transaction-based conversation is a quick way to get the information you need, but be careful. I've seen teams (and even entire organizations) that have "practiced" interrupting each other so much that some individuals have habituated coming in early in the morning or staying later in the evening to get their work done when there are fewer people in the office.

Developing a Relationship

If you are talking with someone about a problem he or she is having, or the way he or she is responding to various specific and important aspects of life and work, then you may have the opportunity to develop or strengthen your relationship with this individual. When you talk about the "real stuff," you often get the chance to meet that person in a new place, or discover something about him or her that you didn't know before. The requirements for this kind of a conversation are basic: two people who are interested in learning about each other, coupled with the time and mental bandwidth to engage in that interchange.

Addressing Challenges

Finally, we involve ourselves in conversations that require us to see our way through a challenge or crisis. Though this exchange is sometimes called "problem solving," I find that, more often than not, determining a solution to a sudden or long-term problem actually comes down to identifying and then changing our perspective. Once you've handled the transaction-type conversation (i.e., "Did you . . .," "Why didn't you . . .," "When are you going to . . ."), you can begin to develop a deeper level of rapport with the other person. The more trust and understanding that exists between the two of you, the easier it will be to manage the crises and problems as they arise.

■ ■ ■

Always remain aware of the kinds of conversations you're having, and be careful not to engage in too many of them simultaneously. Many people make the mistake of attempting to develop a relationship with someone by asking very transaction-based questions. Consider how valuable it is to deal with serious issues and challenges once you've established relationships, understandings, and partnerships with those around you.

For several years now, I have attended the South By Southwest (SXSW) Interactive conference in Austin, Texas. Each year I participate in this huge event and meet about a dozen people with whom I stay in touch throughout the year. By expanding my social network, I create new opportunities for both my life and my work.

One year, I noticed that Pam Slim, author of *Escape from Cubicle Nation*, was chairing a panel discussion called "From Blog to Book." The panel featured three leaders in the print media space: one from a company to which I had submitted a book proposal months before (and had never gotten a response); the second I had known as the editor at a large publisher; and the third I would meet for the first time that day.

During the discussion and subsequent audience-led Q&A session, I realized that I wanted to meet one of the panelists: Matt Holt from John Wiley & Sons, Inc. When the presentations were over, I walked up to him, introduced myself, and said, "There were some things you said that really resonated with me. I'd like to get your card; I come to New York every month and will reach out to you soon. I'd like to talk about a project."

I saw Matt again later that afternoon at a crosswalk, waiting for the light to change, as we were both on our way back to the Austin Convention Center. I told him a little more about the book proposal I had been working on, and asked if I could send it his way. He said yes, and we parted ways again. Later that day, I sent the proposal. Over the next couple of weeks we e-mailed a few times, and ultimately I signed a contract to become a Wiley author. You're now holding in your hands the book I proposed that day!

There's a saying that you have to play to win. I say you have to *show up to play*! I truly believe that it isn't just what you know, it's who you know.

More, it's who you follow up with and stay in touch with over time. If you don't know the right people yet, what are you waiting for? Get out there, use the ideas from this chapter and the rest of this book to think bigger and make real the opportunities you once only imagined.

6

Improvement and Tracking

What Is in the Way,
What Is Along the Way?

I RECEIVED THIS message via voicemail: "Jason, I can't believe it: One person on my team interrupted me 27 times during the past two days here in the office. I knew I was getting distracted at work, but I had no idea how much!"

I had spoken to this client, an architect, by phone 10 days prior to our scheduled coaching session. During the conversation I asked him to tell me about his work area, how it was set up to support his focus while he was addressing his priorities. He designs office spaces in the San Francisco Bay Area, so naturally I was curious how he had designed his own. We talked about his office layout and how he schedules and delegates daily and weekly projects. We also discussed what his staff did both to support *and* inhibit his productivity. Toward the end of the conversation, he asked, "Is there anything I should do to prepare for our meeting?"

Since we had discussed both his physical work environment and the type of high-level development and deep-thinking work he was doing, the answer was obvious to me. I asked him to think about how he could use significant blocks of time to focus on his MITs, his Most Important Things.

I gave him the task of tracking interruptions, specifically the number of times people on his team asked him for "just a minute" of his time. I suggested that he keep a note card on his desk to tally the number of times each person in his office interrupted him with nonurgent matters.

If You Can Track It, You Can Change It

One thing I know about workplace interruptions is that people rarely want "just a minute" of your time. More realistically, they expect you to stop what you're doing and focus on (or at least pretend to) whatever is so important to them. Then, as *they* talk, ask questions, complain, or just suck up your time, *you* begin thinking about what else you could be doing if you weren't listening to them. Your mind wanders, you begin to feel anxious, and, as a result, you aren't really all that attentive or effective during the conversation. Sound familiar?

Think about the last day you were at work. If you've been implementing the ideas from the first three chapters of this book to work smarter, you're now in a position to think bigger. In order to accomplish that, however, you may need to do some things a little bit differently—that is, alter your habitual behavior. The best way I know to change habits is to first identify those that are already in place. The way to do that? Study what you're already doing. There are all kinds of factors you could track to help you in this effort, and any one of them is bound to give you significant information.

- How many times were you interrupted?
- What time did you arrive?
- When did you take a morning break?
- How many minutes (or hours) did you spend away from your desk in meetings?
- What time did you leave for home?
- What time did you go to bed?

If you can't answer those prompts with 100 percent accuracy, don't worry (most people can't). All the more reason to start tracking. The first, and perhaps most important, step in making your best better is to gain awareness of what you're currently doing. This is the secret ingredient to making positive, iterative, and sustainable change.

One week several years ago, I worked with a client group in Colorado Springs, Colorado. I had planned to spend an extra day in town, to visit the USA Olympic Training Center (USOTC). Since I was a kid, I've been a huge fan of both the Summer and Winter Olympics. The opportunity to meet a real Olympic athlete was too good to pass up! I don't remember exactly what I was expecting, but I can say that the five-hour visit I enjoyed that spring day changed me forever.

The USOTC is designed for visitors. Everything about it, from the beautiful grounds to the tour guides showing people around the campus, made me feel comfortable and supportive of our nation's athletes. And while I was there, I met two Olympians, a skeet shooter and a gymnast. I remember asking the marksman, "What is the most interesting thing about your training day?" He talked about the mental workouts he did—"visual rehearsal," he called it. He described sitting in a chair and imagining shooting a clay pigeon for several minutes at a time. Then he said, with a smile, "You know, the best thing about it is the fact that, in my mind, I *never* miss!"

He explained that the purpose of this kind of workout was to train his psyche to *expect* to win, to anticipate success, and to create visual-motor memory of what it looks and feels like to succeed. From that brief encounter, I took away the importance of "seeing before I see." If you think back over the first few chapters of this book, it's probably obvious to you the powerful impact this conversation had on me. Activities such as "I am at my best when . . ." and "Creating Team You" were derived from it.

Unfortunately, our tour group didn't get to talk to the second athlete we met, the gymnast. There in the state-of-the-art gymnasium, he was practicing a floor routine in front of us and his three coaches. Even after 30 minutes of watching him, I didn't want to leave!

I took in as much of the scene as I could. I observed as he jogged to one corner of the mat and balanced on his toes. I took note of the chalk on his hands, the shoelaces perfectly tied, and the electronic sensors strapped to his biceps, quadriceps, and calves. "How can he do it with all those extra wires strung along his arms and legs?" I heard myself say aloud.

Next, in a burst of speed, he sprinted toward the center of the mat and seemed to fly in an explosion of powerful moves that included a hand-plant, a flip, a turn, a spin, a roll, and more running. Then, just as fast as the routine started, it was over. The energy he had expended seemed minimal; the memory of human flight the only thing left for me to think about.

He jogged back to his coaches, who where standing in front of two video monitors. On one, they watched a video playback of the gymnast's routine. On the other, a series of calculations appeared, measurements of the power and force generated from his arms and legs.

The expression on my face must have given away my feelings of awe and surprise to the tour guide. She moved a little closer to me and whispered an explanation of how the technology strapped to his body was measuring the feedback in real time. Everyone on the team could see exactly what was going on there on the mat. She went on to say that the focus of training now was on what to take away, what to minimize, and what to stop doing completely. With only so many square feet to work on, the entire routine was studied through the lens of limitation. The more the team could observe and track, the more they could fine-tune the routine, decide what to eliminate and what to keep (obviously, keeping only the best of the best).

There may be days when you're so pressed for time and stressed by the demand to perform that you feel like a "corporate athlete," running from one meeting to the next, measuring your productivity with spreadsheets and reports, managing the strategy and vision of your team, while dealing with day-to-day issues of customers, the market, and/or office politics.

You might sense intuitively that you don't have all the time you need during the day; and chances are you've identified some of the things you can do to manage your ideas, actions, and results more effectively thanks to reading this book. This chapter gives you a double opportunity: (1) to identify exactly what *does* take up your time and pulls you away from the object(s) of your focus, and (2) to set you up to establish new habits and routines. Measuring in the way I describe here is the only way I know to gain a clear picture of what is really happening at work.

I'm going to show you how to apply tracking and measuring exercises to your workflow, with one purpose in mind: to help you free up time, energy, and focus, so that you can think bigger, plan more effectively, and achieve more every day. I have read dozens of comments from clients who have decided to incorporate multiday tracking exercises over the past decade and they are surprised by the results, every time.

Before you continue, I have a question for you: How can you make *anything* better unless you know what you are currently doing?

Until You Notice What You Do, You Don't Notice What You Do

I spent years complaining about and trying to improve my own methods of time management. Looking back, I now recognize that I had incorrectly identified the actual problem: I had confused the effect with the cause. I kept blaming my lack of productivity on the fact that 24 hours were simply not enough to do "it all." I can remember saying, like so many of you, "I just wish I had an extra hour in the day." And this was when I had already implemented a plan to sleep just four to five hours a night, because I was working well past midnight most nights during the week. And I was still teaching high school. You can imagine how well that worked out!

Believing that my time management was the reason I didn't have enough time in the day, I kept on trying different methods of, well, time management!

Fortunately for me, I accidentally came across the solution to my time management problems: I had to pick the things I was *not* going to do, that I was *not* even going to focus on!

After three years of teaching high school in Ojai, California, I was confident my methods and pedagogy were sound. My students were performing well; in both the history and Spanish departments, test scores were up. This was critical because, in California, as in many other states, there is a lot of pressure on teachers, schools, and districts to improve scores at all costs.

Meanwhile, over those three years of teaching, I recognized an undercurrent to the success I was experiencing: There were other teachers, those I considered the "good" ones, who seemed to be working *all* the time. It wasn't just me! When I left school at the end of the day, often around 5:00 or 6:00 PM, other teachers were still there, working in their classrooms. Likewise, in the main office, the lights were on and administrators were still at their desks. And there were students sitting at tables, at the bus stop, on the curb in the parking lot, reading, writing, and doing homework. I heard from parents of the students in my classroom that their children were regularly doing their schoolwork until 9:00, 10:00, or even 11:00 most nights.

In the fall of 1999, I designed and taught an elective course called "Pathfinders: Action and Ambition Management for Teens." We met for eight weeks, three times a week, from 6:00 to 7:00 AM, before the school day started. In these sessions I focused on what the students were actually *doing* with their time, not just on what they *should have been doing* with their time. Since then, with over a decade of experience behind me, I've updated those themes and programs and applied them to the contemporary corporate market.

During this period, I came to recognize a crucial fact: In order to effectively use those 96 15-minute blocks of time throughout the day, we have to manage (a) *where* we direct our attention, and (b) *what* we can actually ignore for the next 24 to 96 hours. In other words, we need to notice what we are *currently* doing so that we can identify what we could do differently, and better. To achieve our highest-level performance, we must identify what we can *stop* doing, with little or no negative impact on overall results.

Current Reality

What is real? For the sake of the exercises in this chapter, try to avoid describing how you *feel* about your workspace and routines, and stop looking for external reasons (i.e., excuses) for your lack of focus during the workday. Likewise, don't think about or try to explain what it *seems* like. Instead, attempt to make observations as objectively as possible about what truly *is*. Much like an Olympic coach would track the finest details of an athlete's effort and progress over time, your goal here is to do that with regard to your work, your life, your actions, and your results. The subject of this study is not the workplace, your boss, a direct report, or a coworker; throughout this chapter, you're studying only you!

I worked with a client in New York City in the financial services industry. His job consisted of: (1) managing 10 staff members, (2) actively trading on positions for current clients, and (3) building a book of business by reaching out to new clients. I asked him, "What's the activity that generates the most potential for increased revenue?" He answered matter-of-factly, "Jason, I've got to be on the phone, talking to current clients, reaching out to other traders, and calling on potential clients."

I asked him approximately how many outbound calls he thought he had made the day before. "Oh, about 10," he said. "Bull," I said out loud, before I had time to think and censor my comment. ("Uh-oh," I thought. "I may have just offended him.")

It was a gamble, but I had a feeling and decided to go with it. I waited for what seemed long, silent moments as he looked me straight in the eye. Then he cracked a smile and said, "Okay, you're right; I probably made about five. It was a busy day."

This is why clarity is key. You've got to *know*, not just think you know. The whole purpose of tracking is to clearly identify what you *are* doing, compare that to your current results, identify tasks or activities you *could* do differently, and after a period of implementation, compare the new results against the old.

In the case of this client, I wanted to meet him where he was and help him grow from there. I knew that he moves money for a living. So, to make it a money-moving game, I gave him a stack of 10 quarters. "Each morning," I said, "Stack these quarters on *this* side of the desk," and I put them next to his phone. "Whenever you make one outbound call, move one quarter to the other side of your desk." It wasn't rocket science, but it worked. When we talked a week later, he assured me he was making more calls—all because we made it a game.

As you read along here, keep a notebook close by, open to a blank page, ready to write things down. As I've said before, in my coaching program this is where we always begin. It's absolutely crucial that you start writing more notes, more thoughts, down. By getting these concepts, ideas, questions, and reminders out of your head, you can study them in a new way.

As I shared at the start of this chapter, before I ever arrive at my clients' workplaces, I ask them to track something, an activity or project that they perceive takes their time, energy, and focus during the day. Additionally, I ask them to become aware of how they're using their systems, tools, and technologies to manage (or fail to manage, in some cases) their workdays, workflow, and priorities. I know it's a lot—often, too much—for people to do on their own. Nevertheless, when I arrive, we use it at a starting point for the discussion.

Developing an understanding of "current reality" is critical to change management and success. As I say in all of my seminars, "Start where you are and grow from there."

What's Your Normal?

Depending on the time of the year you're reading this, the room, house, or office building you're in may be using some kind of climate control system—air conditioning or heating—and that, essentially, acts as a barrier between inside and outside. Have you ever shared that space with someone who has a different temperature "temperament" than yours? For example, let's say it's summertime and that you like air conditioning on to take the ambient temperature down; but your colleague prefers the windows open to allow a warm, airy breeze to come through the room. As soon as this person adds his or her preference to the mix, your "normal" is compromised. The same concept holds true when it comes to your productivity, your ability to do more of what you want to do.

Remember the activity in Chapter 3 when I asked you to cross your arms over your chest one way, and then the other way, to experience how different *different* feels? What you found was that you have a normal, comfortable way of doing that, and that the other way just didn't feel right. When it comes to having a productive day—and, thinking longer term, developing a career of making your best continually better—it is important to question your normal. You see, what you've normally done until now has produced the results you've achieved. By studying the effort you're expending, and tracking your habits, actions, and results, you can quickly and effectively identify what you need to, or could, change.

In Chapter 2, I asked you to create several inventories by thinking about what you do and how you do it. By examining what you do by 10:00 AM, identifying the tools and systems you rely on to get your work done, and how you build time for relaxation and rejuvenation into your monthly routines, you identify the information you need to question your patterns, routines, and procedures. This chapter will teach you how to take your productivity and performance to a whole new level.

Maximize Your Four Limited Resources

You hear many people say, "I didn't have enough time to get it all done." But remember, time is just one of your four limited resources. You have *three other* resources, albeit also limited: energy, focus, and tools.

- Your ability to make the most out of your *time* is a function of the *energy* you have available to apply to your work.
- The *energy* you can apply to your work is determined by your ability to *focus* on your work. This helps you manage your priorities more effectively.
- Your ability to *focus* on your work is determined by the *systems* and *tools* you use to manage your responsibilities. You will get more done each day when you develop a "focus-to-finish" mind-set.
- When you use your *systems* and *tools* efficiently, you work in a more focused manner, and habits of *completion* will begin to affect you and your team. With completion and accomplishment comes the knowledge that you are using your time wisely.

Time

As you are well aware by now, there are only 1,440 minutes in a day. Keep that in mind as you ponder these questions:

- How do you use yours?
- Are you getting the most from your time?
- Are you wasting time?

To begin getting more from the time you do have during the day, regularly stop while you're working, or before you take on new work, and ask yourself and your team "time-aware" questions like:

- How long will this *really* take?
- Who can we ask for ideas or advice, to get an answer sooner?
- Instead of an hour, can we schedule that meeting for just 45 minutes?

I encourage everyone I work with to be very careful of the promises they make, as it is easy to *under*estimate the amount of time it will take to do tasks and, conversely, *over*estimate what they can do with the time they have. Mastering workplace performance requires that you develop habits and systems to identify, track, and deliver the work you have made a commitment to complete. Clarifying your objectives and constraints will allow you to identify which of those constraints you can change.

Be mindful, too, of time-wasters like meetings that start late, cancelled appointments, and other people's tendency to procrastinate; all of these limit your effectiveness if you don't plan for them. Make the most of the time you have by anticipating these scenarios.

- Bring materials to review while you're waiting for meetings to start.
- Call to confirm your appointments a day in advance, so you will not have unexpected cancellations.
- Be very aware of what other people say yes to. Make sure they have a system in place to organize and track their work.
- Have a system in place to track your commitments so that you're able to focus on and prioritize your MITs when you get back to your desk.

Energy

As I explained in Chapter 3, our minds and bodies seek homeostasis, a return to normal. We therefore need to make an effort to take part in activities that help us engage both mentally and physically, since full participation, in both our personal and professional endeavors, requires mental and physical energy.

To help you discern how you can best do this, try the following experiment: For the next week, identify which projects and activities increase, and decrease, your energy. For example, you may find that you're tired after meetings, or that taking a walk during your lunch hour gives you the extra boost you need to finish out the day productively. When you have identified exactly what these are, you can implement procedures that will help you add to your energy increasers and subtract from your energy decreasers.

Focus

I believe most people task-switch several hundred times a day. For example, consider the number of times you reach for the computer mouse and click on a different application each day. You don't need a research report or survey to prove that people get interrupted by their coworkers dozens of times daily, and that they think about other work and other meetings during current meetings on a regular basis. Think about this: When people are checking their BlackBerrys and holding side conversations during meetings, they distract everyone else in the group, as well as themselves. It's even worse when someone is on a conference call, presses the mute button, and looks over his or her e-mail. What happens when people who do this miss a significant point during the meeting, and later are asked about it?

These kinds of interruptions have a more powerful impact on your productivity than you might realize. Reestablishing your train of thought and attention after such disruptions requires you to expend energy and resources that you could have used for something more critical. Having to constantly refocus on what you were just doing compromises your workflow, prevents you from completing your most important tasks, and essentially forces you to spend more time than necessary getting things done.

This is precisely why you must be sure to bring awareness and focus to each task *as* you work on it. If you adopt a focus-to-finish mind-set, you'll get things done accurately and appropriately from the moment you begin concentrating on them.

Systems and Tools

Whether paper-based or electronic, you can use your systems and tools—in other words, your *gear*—more to your advantage. Learning just one new aspect today about the tools you use the most often will go a long way toward saving you time and energy throughout the course of each workday.

Think about how you can manage your time and improve your productivity over the next few work sessions, and be very aware of how you use your energy. Your mental energy is what gives you the opportunity to tap in to your knowledge, experience, and business acumen, while your physical energy allows you to stay alert and engaged.

Finally, bear in mind that these very same systems and tools can easily act as distractions or detractors if you don't invest the time to figure out how to use them wisely and effectively. Make sure you learn everything you can about them in order to minimize the number of times each day you need to change your focus.

I make a conscious effort to use my systems and tools to direct my focus to completion. My energy increases when I finish something; I'm able to focus more clearly, and I feel like I've managed my time successfully that day. When I am able to use my systems and tools to compel myself to concentrate on my most important endeavors, I am more likely to finish them; and when I finish these crucial tasks, my energy intensifies. Doing so helps me focus even more clearly, and shows me that I am making effective use of my time.

Track Your Limited Resources

Consider this section your personal Self-Coaching Guide. In it, I will share with you the actual coaching steps through which I lead my clients, as well as step-by-step instructions to track your way to success. The next few pages might seem overwhelming, since I give you more ideas than you can possibly implement this week, but the reason I do this is to make you aware that you have options.

As you read through them, you can choose those that make the most sense to you, and begin your tracking process. I encourage you to choose one limited resource, track it for a week or two. Then come back to this chapter every month or so.

Time

Chances are you've tried the time-blocking approach before. I have worked with people in offices around the world who set aside time on their calendars by "making up" meetings, to guard against doing anything else during those periods of time. Unfortunately, they don't always adhere to that blocked time, which is why this approach is not the right way to start.

To effectively track your time over a two- to three-day period, you're going to need a couple of low-tech tools—namely, a countdown timer, a pen or pencil, and a notebook or note card on which to write.

I prefer a wearable timer, either a digital watch or a timer I can clip to my belt or briefcase. By having this simple time management tool available, I'm much more likely to use it.

Two things happen when I set a timer:

1. *I remain conscious of the time I have.* I set the clock after I consider two factors: (a) What time of the day is it? and (b), How much time until the next thing? I'm a morning person; I know this about myself. So if I look at the clock and it says 2:34 PM and my calendar shows I have another meeting at 3:30, I will choose to do something relative to the energy and time I have available. If it's only 5:30 in the morning and I don't need to be on the phone with a client until 9:00, I choose something very different.
2. *I get more done.* It's true: When I'm working with a countdown timer nearby, I use it to help me refocus. You see, if I'm sitting at my desk working for 30, 45, or 60 minutes and I feel like getting up to take a quick break (or check e-mail or talk to a colleague), I simply glance over at the clock. I'll see that I have 17:37 to go, and I tell myself, "Focus, Jason, focus. Stay here for another 17 minutes."

You should begin by deciding which days you're going to track. I recommend to my clients that they start with two continuous workdays. So, if you're reading this on a Sunday afternoon, let's say you'll track your time next Tuesday and Wednesday. At some point in the future, you may want to do this over two weekends, picking a day to study how you're using time then as well.

It's usually best, and easiest, to track in 30-minute blocks, as this is something most people can feasibly do. That said, you'll get twice the information if you track in 15-minute blocks. The 30-minute tracking is a great way to start for the first day you do this. If you think you can move up to every 15 minutes for day two, then give that a go.

Begin your tracking process the day before your official start date; thus, using the example above, you'd begin on Monday. (This is why I suggest you start two days from now, as you're reading.) You will need to collect your supplies and put some kind of basic tracking sheet together in order to succeed with this process. Following is a sample tracking sheet you can use. It matches the one I use when I do my own two-day tracking process, which I conduct about once every 12 to 18 months.

Blank Time Tracking Sheet

7:00–7:30
7:30–8:00
8:00–8:30
8:30–9:00
9:00–9:30
9:30–10:00
10:00–10:30

I think you can see and appreciate the simplicity of this matrix. The left-hand side has designated blocks of time, while the right-hand side provides room to write short notes. The purpose of having just a little bit of room is clear: You don't have to spend minutes a day writing paragraphs of observations. For the most part, you'll stop for 10 to 30 seconds every half-hour to write things down. Here's a sample.

Sample Time Tracking Sheet

7:00–7:30	Commuted to work, read on ereader, checked mobile e-mail.
7:30–8:00	Stopped at coffee shop for breakfast, reviewed newspaper headlines.
8:00–8:30	Arrived at office, handled surprise call from client.
8:30–9:00	Reviewed, filed, and responded to e-mail.
9:00–9:30	Arrived five minutes late to morning meeting; shared research.
9:30–10:00	Delegated two tasks during meeting; ate nutrition bar.
10:00–10:30	Worked on presentation deck at desk, handled interruptions.

Energy

Are you a morning person? An afternoon person? An evening person? Yes, we all need to be productive throughout the day, but I have found that each of us prefers to work on bigger or important projects at certain times of the day. I know that I'm a more effective writer, a better presenter, and a stronger athlete between 6:00 and 11:00 AM. (Of course, I *can* write, present, and train in the afternoons.)

When you're tracking your energy level over a few days, it helps to anticipate the qualities and state of mind you're seeking to be in. My clients are interested in such things as engagement, productivity, and focus.

The next tracking exercise is similar to the previous one, tracking time, but as you'll see, you're looking for something a bit more subjective. Here's a blank chart.

Blank Energy Tracking Sheet

Morning

Late morning

Afternoon

Late afternoon

Here again, you will choose what to write in each row of the right-hand column. Starting with the morning session at work, you can briefly note where your energy level was, what happened to enhance or diminish it, and how you responded to the various inputs you received throughout the day. By tracking your energy use and level for about two to three days, you will gather critical information you can use to change how, when, and what you do at certain times of the day. Remember, you won't notice what you do until you notice what you do!

Here's an energy tracking sheet filled in.

Sample Energy Tracking Sheet

Morning	Checked e-mail, read client feedback, felt excited.
Late morning	Started next quarter's budget; felt unfocused, a bit stuck.
Afternoon	Went to lunch with Joe, talked about next project.
Late afternoon	Felt effect of that extra cookie at lunch; energy low.

Focus

Take a look around the area where you are reading this book. Are you at the office? On a train? In your living room? Now look around again and ask, "What around me do I think could or should be different?" Whether these items are under your control (e.g., the decorations on the wall, the placement of the television in the family room) or not (e.g., the advertising on the train and subway stations), you'll find your focus moves from one thing to another very quickly once you start paying attention in this way.

One of the culprits of a mis-time-managed day is not, in fact, the clock, the ticking of seconds going by; rather, it's the number of things to which we need to shift focus throughout the course of the day. Imagine, for example, that you're sitting in a meeting and you hear someone's cellphone ring. Everyone's focus immediately goes, if only for an instant, to their own phones. I've even seen people check their own phones when they see someone else take a phone call.

There are two points to carefully note while you're tracking your focus during the day: what you accomplished while you were multitasking, and what you accomplished when you turned off all the other inputs and worked solely on one project. Notice that I'm not suggesting that one or the other is a superior approach; I'm simply asking you to pay attention to the specific nuances of working one way or the other.

Next you'll see a sample of the kinds of things you may do while you're busy getting things done during the day.

Blank Focus Tracking Sheet

Multitask	
Single Task	

Sample Focus Tracking Sheet

Multitask	While on conference call, pressed mute and organized a few e-mails.
	Attended meeting, brought mobile to respond to e-mails.
Single Focus	Took project notes and calendar to work in conference room.
	Worked offline: organizing and deleting e-mails.

Systems and Tools

Today, tools, apps, and gear are almost synonymous with time management. I can remember the very first electronic device I purchased to manage my information, actions, and time: It was a Sharp Wizard, back in 1992. With 32K of memory, it had a memo pad, an address book, a calendar, and scheduling capability with alarms and repeating events. I spent hours inputting people's names and addresses. Then, while visiting friends in Palo Alto just days before moving to Mexico City, I accidentally left the device at a restaurant, only to return hours later to find it had disappeared. Since then, I make sure I back up my organizing systems to at least one other digital device.

Blank Tools Tracking Sheet

Paper-based tools
Digital tools

You'll notice here that I assume you're working in a dual tools environment (i.e., using both paper- and digital-based equipment). As paperless as your office and personal organization might be, you're going to turn to a pen/paper system at some point during most days, even if it's just to sign a receipt at the restaurant where you eat dinner tonight.

For a couple of days, make notes, either on a note card, on a page in your notebook, or in some kind of online matrix organizer, of the tools you use, and for what purpose, during the day, as in the sample here.

Sample Tools Tracking Sheet

Paper-based	Took all notes today in a Moleskine journal; typed up tasks and to-do's into digital system, to sync to mobile device.
Digital	Set up Out of Office for the next two days of off-site meetings with senior management.

The Symptom versus the Cause

Not having enough time at the end of the day is, in fact, a symptom of a much bigger issue; it is *not*, as I have said before, the issue itself. In order to find ways to more effectively manage your time, it's absolutely critical that you identify what you're doing currently and what you're using to manage your time. That way, you can begin to experiment with various other ways of working, thereby freeing up a bit of time each day. Even if it's just one or two 15-minute blocks, you'll notice a positive difference.

Pattern Recognition

I have written in a notebook every day for over 20 years. Over those years I have experimented with different formats, changing contextual prompts and specific times of the day to write things down. It seems that I fall into routines that generally last anywhere from six months to two years, although I have been doing some things the same way for longer periods of time. For example, in the pages in the back of every notebook I own, I write down the actions I think of during the day, whereas I use front pages to take notes, jot down what I think about topics, and draw diagrams.

For example, I spent over six months one year following a specific ritual: At the end of every day, I wrote in a diary-type journal. The pages were about the size of my hand, so it didn't take long to fill in a page each day with the things I had seen, done, and remembered. Essentially, I just wrote freely whatever came to my mind.

At the bottom of each page, however, I did something a little different. I used this space to record a single word (always just one) that came to my mind after I asked myself this question: "What one word stands out from all the others today?"

What was very interesting to me was that, after 180 days, I could look back and notice themes, trends, and unique words. When I was on the road (which was quite often, since I coach and speak 100 to 120 times per year), the words generally concerned learning, travel, and outside influences. When I was home, in contrast, I tended to choose words about family, friends, and community. Over those months of tracking, my set of priorities became (by default) very clear to me.

Once I recognized my daily areas of focus, it forced me to address questions I hadn't been asking before, questions about purpose and significance.

Tracking Failures

What will you discover by becoming much more aware of what you're doing and how you're using your time? You're bound to discover somewhere along this journey of making your best even better that some of the habits and routines you had put in to place over the years no longer work for you. Yes, what you used to do with your time, how you used it, and the tools and systems you used to manage it, have gotten you to this point; but it may now be time to move on.

I read that Richard Branson, chairman of Virgin Group, said, "[J]ust remember that most businesses fail, and the best lessons are usually learned from failure. You must not get too dispirited. Just get back up and try again."

I can make a very strong case for tracking attempt. Something I say to my clients who are implementing new habits and routines is, "Hurry up and fail, to find out what *doesn't* work." Such a mind-set emphasizes the fact that we must examine the lesson(s) we learn both prior to and after failure. The most important part of this is developing the attitude and ability to move on after a failure.

I do not, however, encourage my clients to set out to track failure; I don't think it's healthy to start the day waiting for something to go wrong. What I do suggest is that they be ready to capture when something does *not* go according to plan!

What Will You Track?

What will you gain by observing your actions, routines, and behaviors? Over time, you will gain a heightened awareness of progress and detraction. Believe me, if you were to capture 16 to 24 "data points" of activity throughout a typical workday, you would find something to enhance. Will it be what you do, how you do it, or what you use to get it done? Only time will tell.

Before moving on to the next chapter, I recommend you review this one and make note of any section that you think is important to improving your workflow and style. Consider, too, reviewing how you are currently using your four limited resources—time, energy, focus, and systems and tools—and then pick just one to watch closely over a couple of days. It's important to point out that you don't need to track it all to benefit from this process. I have seen over and over that some clients automatically experience a carryover effect into other areas of their life and work by focusing on just one.

Decide how and where you're going to expend this effort today, and supersize the process of making your best better. Once you know what depletes your time, energy, and focus, you can begin to plan for it, set up processes and systems to support you, and continue to think even bigger!

7

Improvement and Purpose

Clarify and Promote Your Own "So That . . ."

WHILE ATTENDING THE South By Southwest Conference (SXSW), in Austin, Texas, I met Tony Deifell, creator of the popular Internet meme "Why Do You Do What You Do?" Over breakfast on the morning Jodi and I were scheduled to fly back to Los Angeles, he asked me a simple, though not-so-easy-to-answer, question: "Jason, why do you do what you do?"

I remember putting my glass of orange juice down on the table, looking at him, and in my best corporate-speak voice beginning to respond, "Tony, I do what I do . . . ," but he interrupted me and said, "Oh no. You have to think about it for a while." Then he smiled and sat back in his chair. The conversation had taken a new turn.

Over the next hour, as our discussion went deeper, I thought bigger. There were four of us at the table that morning; the other three continued posing questions to me, repeating back what they heard me say, then encouraging me to explain things in other words. At one point, finally, I said something that made them all go silent. I looked up, and they were staring at me. Jodi said, "Jason, that's it! *That* is why you do what you do!" Before we left the restaurant,

I wrote down what I had said on a piece of paper in big, block letters, and Tony took my picture to publish it to the world via his website, www.wdydwyd.com.

What did I write on that piece of paper? That I do what I do "because I am joyful when I feel the sense of completion." That's it. That is my purpose—so that when I work with people, I can help them to see, touch, experience, and *know* how important it is to finish things; *and* I want to show them how they can make it easier to get bigger things done! One thing I know for sure is that I will continue working toward my "So that . . ." in the years to come.

When I wrote my "why I do what I do" statement in my Moleskine brand journal at the breakfast table that morning, I felt something shift. I felt both enlightened and weighed down by a deeper responsibility. Whether I am working toward completion on a goal I've set or partnering with clients on multimonth projects as they plan, progress, and complete, I do what I do to experience completion.

What does "your best just got better" mean to you? When you picked up this book, no doubt you were looking for ways to achieve more—in your personal life and at work. Now it's time to press the pause button. Why? Because the more you focus on improvement, the greater the risk of adding more to your list of to-do items and bigger projects to manage. This is why the discussion on purpose comes here (and not in Chapter 1 of this book). I invite you to take a moment now and stop; and maybe even take a step or two backward.

Now let me ask you another question: "What got you into *this* in the first place?" By "this" I mean: Your career. Your community. Your responsibilities. Your goals and dreams for the future. To answer, compare what you *originally* wanted to accomplish in your work and in your personal life against what, currently, is *actually* taking your time, energy, and focus. How closely are those two realities tied together? If you are on course, can you sustain that momentum? If you're on a path of distraction, can you get off it and head back in the direction you want to be going in?

Distractions pull us off point and out of the game. Problem is, there is usually a way to justify the urgency of a distraction. Say for example you're about to sit down and focus on one of your work goals. Suddenly, the phone rings and you think, "Oh, surely it's just a quick question; I'll answer it really fast and then get back to my work." Or: "If I don't attend to this now . . ." Or (the famous one that keeps so many of us busy): "Here, let *me* do it; it won't take as long."

To truly make your best better, you need to reduce the number of distractions, the amount of "stuff" that pulls you out of focus. The way to do that is to know your "why"—why you are doing what you do.

If you recognize that in order to live more on point you may have to do things differently, this chapter is for you. Doing things differently often goes against what is most natural and comfortable to us. I remind you that everything you've done up to now has gotten you here. Knowing your own "So that . . .," and reflecting on it regularly, will go a long way toward keeping you on point and in the game.

What about you? Why *do* you do what you do? Set this goal, right now:

By the end of this chapter, you will think about and draft your own "So that . . ." statement.

This will be the most up-to-date-version of your personal mission, vision, and purpose statement—*why* you're doing *what* you're doing.

Have you ever noticed that when things are unclear, when you're stressed out, bored, or stuck, you don't perform at your best? Conversely, when you're contributing at the highest level possible for you, what is true? Chances are, you're working at your best. You're engaged, you're inspired, you're involved, and you can easily see that what you're doing has an effect on a larger cause. Take a moment now and go back to Chapter 1 to review your "I'm at my best when . . ." statements. Use what you wrote there to design a "So that . . ." statement that makes you think bigger and want to work smarter!

Distractions, whether work-related or personal, pull you away from your goals and out of the game of work and life. Have you ever been working on something important at your desk when someone walks up and interrupts you? Is your office designed as an open floor plan, where anyone who walks by "chips away" at your attention through the day? The problem is, when you say yes to the interruption, you're saying no to everything else.

To truly make your best better, to work smarter, and to think bigger, you need to slow down and focus with all your senses. Then answer this question: "Why are you doing what you do?" Really think about it.

Write a few different versions; perhaps even get together with a good friend or a mentor. Consider reviewing Chapter 5 and reaching out to a few of the people on Team You. Getting a solid answer—whether a sentence, a phrase, or even a word that gets to the core of you—will change everything, I promise.

Living from a purpose statement like this promotes change. You'll want to do things differently, to form new habits and take on new goals. Simultaneously, however, doing so may also go against what is natural and comfortable to you. That's precisely why it's important to be able to complete the statement, "I'm doing X, *so that* Y . . ." This is your "So that . . ."

I believe this with all of my heart: Knowing your purpose, and reflecting on it regularly, will *make all the difference* between keeping you on point and in the game and being taken off-course. Clients, family members, and friends who have identified their purpose, and then use it as a compass in decision making and before taking action, have told me that it just makes things easier. I've stopped counting the times I've heard something like this from a person I spend time with: "Now that I know when I'm at my best, and *why* I'm doing what I'm doing, it's easier to say yes to [the right] and no to [the wrong] things than ever before."

What Is the Point of All This Busyness?

I started studying time management in earnest more than a decade ago. I thoroughly enjoyed my teaching job; it was great to work with the students, and I fully accepted the challenge of making the world a better place. I felt like I was working in and on purpose.

Over time, however, I ran into a problem. I was ending each day with more unfinished tasks, more often, than I started with. Every weekend I spent grading papers and writing lesson plans. When I did have a week or more off, I used that time to sleep, catch up on rest. Jodi reminds me that over the five years I taught, I caught a cold at the beginning of every vacation and then had to spend the first part of my time off resting and recovering.

The truth was apparent: There was simply too much to do! In response to the ever-growing pressure not just to succeed but to continually improve, I began to arrive at my classroom earlier and earlier every morning. Then I started bringing work home on the weekends. "If I only had another hour in the day," was a favorite remark of mine until . . .

I attended a course sponsored by a local university. I had found a flyer in my mailbox one morning advertising a seminar titled "Time Management for Teachers." Exactly what I needed! I signed up for the two-hour evening course immediately. Upon arrival at the site, I was impressed. There were signs directing us to the room we'd be in, *and* the presenter started on time—something of a rarity, I had found, among teachers and in the educational world in general. (I have come to learn that the corporate environment has a similar problem, as most meetings start anywhere from 5 to 15 minutes late.)

Our first assignment at the seminar was to summarize our teaching philosophy in one sentence. Not a paragraph, not a white paper; a simple, single sentence. Throughout the evening, I wrote and rewrote what I was thinking at that time, way back in 1997. That sentence was a powerful one. I'll always remember it: "I teach *so that* students see beyond Ojai."

I didn't need any more words to describe what I wanted to accomplish. (Later, I affixed that piece of paper to the wall in my classroom, right next to my desk, and it stayed there for the next three years!)

I believe your own "So that . . ." is more than a mission statement; it is more than a resolution, or a raison d'être. Watch someone involved deeply in his or her own "So that . . ."—a musician, a farmer, an athlete, a parent, an actor, anyone who takes their profession professionally—and you'll see something amazing: full engagement, complete presence, a sense of contribution and joy, and, often, a feeling of completion.

People describe this experience as being "in the zone," "in a flow," or simply as "being there." Only a very fortunate few know their "So that . . ." from an early age and have been able to act on it, achieve it, and experience it over the years. Most of the rest of us need a little prodding. For this reason, let's start with a subjective evaluation.

Of the past 100 hours you spent working, commuting, sleeping, eating—all of it—how many were you deeply engaged in your own "So that..."? Review your calendar, notes in your notebook or on your desk, to-do lists, and the stacks of papers, files, magazines, and books on your desk(s). Seriously assess the past several days, hour by hour. Make a list of where you've spent the most time and, conversely, where you haven't spent enough time. Consider what you have done, whom you have talked to, and where you have gone over the past few days (that's enough time for you to cycle through several of your MITs, Most Important Things).

Realistically, you're currently managing some 10 to 20 of these. Based on my experience, thinking this way over the past several years, I know I can only be my absolute best dealing with about four of my own MITs on a daily basis. Whenever I've tried to perform well doing more than that, I've ended the day feeling behind and stressed out, because I didn't "get enough done." Because I know that, I also know I need to be very conscious and acutely aware of the specific areas upon which I am focusing.

For many years now, I stop at the end of each day and conduct a review/preview exercise. I *review* how I feel about what I did that day relative to my chosen MITs, then I *preview* my four MITs of focus for the next day. I complete this exercise at the end of every day; my goal is to cycle through as many of these in a week, month, and year as possible.

By working and living from this perspective it becomes obvious which areas of focus, MITs, and projects you're failing to address—or perhaps I should say, which are being "overcome by events," as a client of mine in the U.S. Armed Forces says. As this individual accurately explains, "I can have a plan for the day, and be ready to engage with all I've got, until there's a spill on base, or someone calls in sick, or we realize there is a threat we need to address."

Instead of ending a workday, leaving your office, and *hoping* something positive was accomplished, try this experiment: As you close out the day, review the areas you *think* were most important to you, and identify what you actually *did* relative to those objectives.

Additionally, before leaving the office today, and then every day for the next five days, identify your four (yes, just four) MITs for the *next day*; write them on a note card or sticky note, and leave that piece of paper where you will be sure to see it when you get back to work in the morning. It is important to note that these are not necessarily things to do, people to see, or projects to check in on. They are your MITs. You need virtually no preparation for this; you simply need to choose areas that are important to you, write them down, and plan to look at them from time to time throughout the next day.

You should always keep in mind the ratio between your *business* and your *busyness*. Doing so empowers you with the information you need to make significant decisions. Reviewing four of your MITs early each day and then assessing how you spent your time on them will, subsequently, give you a more objective and accurate look at how you spend your time, where you could improve, and who you need to talk with more.

You can facilitate the approach to your personal planning and prioritizing process by selecting your choices each day from a master list. First, consider how often things around you change. Is it weekly, monthly, seasonally, annually, or less frequently? I continue to update, change, add to, and delete from my own list of MITs. Change seems to occur for most people with some regularity about three times per year. For example, a new member joins your work team; new neighbors move in next door; you decide to go somewhere new on your next vacation; or you get a promotion.

The great news about defining your MITs is that once you build your inventory, you will be able to draw from it until something changes (a new job, move, opportunity, project, etc.).

Of course, you have more than four MITs; we all do, but I encourage you to choose only four each day for the reasons I just outlined. There are two very important reasons to pick only your top four (or fewer) at the end of today for tomorrow: (1) You can give everything you've got (to do your best) to this number of the important things every day; and (2) you need to see what you're actually choosing as your MITs. I firmly believe in choosing activities and projects at which I can excel—working toward my strengths, as Marcus Buckingham, author of *Now, Discover Your Strengths* says. My goal is to move through each day responding to as much as possible while holding that mental image of greatness, of engaging in my own "So that . . ."

By starting with your inventory of MITs, you equip yourself with powerful information you can use to create a tomorrow that is even better than yesterday. By identifying four (or fewer) areas to excel at 24 hours in advance of tackling them, you'll have all the information you need to plan, renegotiate, and engage. This practice allows you to set yourself up for maximum success in a very objective and iterative manner.

Since I began starting my days by focusing on my MITs, I find that I'm more closely aligned with my "So that"—which has, of course, changed since leaving high school teaching and moving into the profession of advising corporate organizations' leadership development initiatives and serving managers around the world as an executive performance and productivity coach.

Since that breakfast at South By Southwest I mentioned at the beginning of this chapter, I have updated my "Why I do what I do" statement. Here's what's on my office wall now, printed out on an 8½ × 11 piece of paper: "I share information and activities with leaders *so that* they have more time and energy for the things they want to do."

It's a bit longer and more inclusive than the one I wrote over a decade ago while I was still teaching history and Spanish. This "So that . . ." acts as my "North Star." I set the tone and direction for working with my clients by asking these two big questions: "Are you getting to the things that you *want* to do? Are you managing the things you *have* to do?"

Take some time right now to use what you've learned here to come up with your own inventory of MITs. Completing this activity will, in particular, help you to move away from focusing too often on the "latest and loudest," the most urgent—the crises, the problems, the situations that keep us busy but don't always move us in a positive, goal-oriented direction. Michael Bungay Stanier writes about this when he describes the difference between doing *good* work and doing *great* work. When you're working on your MITs, you're working on your *great* work.

A word of caution here: If you make your list right now, you might find that you're writing down items that you "know you know" are important. For this reason, it's essential to move beyond the top 10 mark on this list. Almost everyone I've met can come up with his or her own 10 important things. The real work comes when you get into the twenties or (gasp!) thirties. Give yourself an opportunity to think bigger. This activity might take 10 minutes, or it may take you 10 days.

Now ask yourself: "What am I committed to?"

While this may seem like a simple question, consider whether you're working with a current inventory these days. Schedule an appointment with the CEO of your life (that's you!) to identify the things that are most important to you. Begin by circling those that jump off at you from the following list. Then, add a few more that you know are a part of *your own* inventory.

Examples

- Family
- Health
- Career
- Recreation
- Community
- Spouse/Partner/Children
- Wealth
- Travel
- Volunteerism
- Friendships
- Continual learning
- _____
- _____
- _____
- _____
- _____
- _____
- _____
- _____
- _____
- _____
- _____

Keep in mind while you're creating your list of MITs that there is an element of subjectivity to this inventory. You're already well aware that your daily, monthly, and quarterly priorities will shift. You might, for example, get a promotion or volunteer at a new community program. Instantly, more MITs!

Now is the time to check your level of commitment and match it to objective actions and plans. Begin by clarifying the "So that . . ." of larger outcomes within your personal "ecosystem" at work and in your personal life. You can then examine your mission and vision statements to create a specific and measurable "So that . . ." statement for two to five areas of life and work that you've determined to be of greatest value to you.

The Night I Relied on My Own "So That . . ."

It was close to midnight and I had already been traveling for 10 hours that day, after earning a second-place finish in a 5K running race in Ventura, California, earlier that morning. I drove to Los Angeles International Airport, and then enjoyed an uneventful flight to Chicago. At O'Hare airport, I waited for an update on the new departure time of my next flight (it had already been delayed several times, due to weather). With less than nine hours until I was due to appear on stage in Cleveland, Ohio, I heard the announcement that no one wants to hear: My flight had been cancelled.

At that moment, I had a choice to make: Should I stay or should I go—by any other means possible? I called Jodi at home for advice. Within moments, we had enough information to make a decision. I would go. I had made a commitment to a client, and I believed it was still possible for me to get there on time by driving. The distance from the airport to the hotel where I'd be staying was about 330 miles, so I calculated I should be able to make it in 7 hours. Plus, the one-hour time change that would occur at the Illinois-Indiana border would give me a window of time to check it at the hotel, take a quick shower, and be at the client's site for the 9:00 AM event start time.

As I remember it today, the first couple of hours of that drive went just fine. I was still running on the adrenaline of my decision, and that kept me awake. From about 2:00 to 6:00 AM, however, I had to tap into a state of engagement, to really focus on my safety and a successful outcome. How did I do it? Around 3:00 in the morning, I stopped at a gas station and wrote on a page in my notebook while my tank was being filled. I used this time to clarify my "So that . . ." for the decision I had made that night. Here's what I wrote:

I am driving through the night in order to arrive to my presentation tomorrow morning on time *so that* I can demonstrate what it means to keep a promise to a client.

I have used the "So that . . ." technique for years now. Whenever someone offers me a new opportunity, or I think of a new project, I push it through a filter; I ask myself *why* I'm doing it. All my MITs have their own "So that . . ." next to them. It makes it easier and more engaging to focus on each, one at a time, on a regular basis.

Do You Really Want to Make Your Best Better?

In Chapter 2, I asked you to answer the following question: "Is the way you are working, working for you?" Read that question again, slowly. Consider writing down your answer. Capture both negative as well as positive aspects.

You go to work every day; you sit in meetings, make phone calls, and send e-mails. Additionally, when you work from home, you probably also clean your house, run errands, handle finances, and manage projects. When you think about all you're already doing, do you really believe you have the bandwidth (and inclination!) to make your best better?

Once you've identified your MITs and have done the work to clarify why they are important to you, it's time to take the entire exercise up one level; it's time to think bigger, by asking: *Why* are you concentrating on getting better?

Now is the time to decide and commit. It would be worth your while to reread the Ideal Day you drafted at the beginning of the book. If you didn't complete that exercise at the time, consider writing a draft of it now, now that you've come this far in this book. Then look carefully at what you've written; you will no doubt feel compelled to reengage and try to bring at least one part of that Ideal Day closer to tomorrow's reality.

Remember, my own Ideal Day exercise set me on a direction; over many years I have experienced individual elements of that Ideal Day—that is I've *headed* in the direction. But there have been only a handful of times I've actually achieved it, only a few times I've *arrived* at the predefined destination.

Even though you may not experience your Ideal Day in every detail, just by identifying the things you know are important to you will allow you to experience individual aspects of that day more and more often as you make your way through it.

What's Your "So That . . ."?

Now is the time to clarify your own "So that . . . ." You'll need some tools for this activity—something to write with and on—as it's a very active thought-experiment. In working with clients, I've used a notebook, a flip chart, the back of a restaurant napkin, and a whiteboard to explore the "So that . . ." of their different areas of focus.

To begin, choose something that has recently been taking up a lot of your time, energy, and focus. Whether it's an area of your professional or personal life, pick something you've been attending to, thinking about, and working on a great deal over the past several weeks.

Writing that one thing down—somewhere, anywhere. Again, just the act of getting it out of your head and onto a piece of paper or a whiteboard is a significant part of the "So that . . ." process. (By the way, I highly recommend doing this by hand initially, as opposed to on a computer. There's something about handwriting here . . .) Then spend 7 to 10 minutes writing whatever comes to mind when you ask the question "Why am I so interested in this particular area?" The first few answers will be obvious, so keep going. Once you get past the first few reasons, you might just be surprised at what comes up next.

The Layering Process

To make it easier to gain clarity about why you're doing what you're doing, consider moving each item through a layering process. One way to do this is to pick just a few things you're working on these days, identify several "So that . . ." responses for each one, and insert them into a chart, like the one shown here. (Note: It is easier to do this *after* you go through the clarification process, as then you'll have an entire page of ideas to choose from.)

In the sample chart here, you'll see that I wrote down a few areas of focus, some of my own MITs according to the various roles I have, and preceded each with "So that . . . ."

"So That . . ." Chart

	Triathlete	Author	Friend
"So that . . ."	Train toward a goal.	Research psychology of performance and productivity.	Connect with like-minded people.
"So that . . ."	Push my body and mind to mental and physical limits.	Share ideas with people, promoting individual contributions.	Hear the truth about how I'm perceived in the world.
"So that . . ."	Enjoy the outdoors in my local community.	Provide ideas and activities to groups in corporate, educational, and not-for-profit organizations.	Contribute to the professional and personal development plans of those closest to me.

Be prepared to discover something new about yourself when you go through this exercise. If possible, write down three, five, or seven "So that . . ." statements. On the surface, we all know why we do the things we do (e.g., "I work so I can pay my mortgage"), but there is much more to it than that.

There are several purposes for completing this exercise:

- It helps clarify your priorities.
- It provides direction and encouragement to work on your MITs.
- It gives you a reason to say no to projects and tasks that come along and distract you.
- It gives you something tangible to review at the end of the week, to check against your commitment and productivity levels.

What Purpose Is Not

This exercise is not designed to impose "should" on yourself. Your "So that . . ." statement should not discourage or bring you down in any way. That's one reason I encourage you to focus on just four MITs at a time. Again, at the end of each day, pick the four (or fewer) for tomorrow; do this for about a month. Instead of making you feel bad about the areas where you believe you're *not* performing or improving, consider this an exercise in positive *focus* (as opposed to positive thinking). I'll talk more about focus in Chapter 9; for now, realize that seeing, reading, and thinking about why you're doing things will prompt you to engage at a higher level of interest and development.

For example, after reviewing just one "So that . . . ," a client I had been working for over a month called me to say, "Jason, I don't need to feel bad about what I'm doing. [Rather], I can focus on it, know why I'm doing it, and continually get a little bit better at it. This helps me think that I don't have to be everything, to everyone, all the time." An important revelation, don't you think?

The Freedom of Boundaries

I used to think of boundaries as limitations. When I was young, I didn't want to be told what to do, how to do it, or when to do it. I spent several years of my life wishing, and sometimes acting as if, the rules just didn't apply to me.

What I failed to realize then was just how powerful it is to be aware of where the lines are drawn. Personal and professional productivity, how to work with other people, and where to gain the support I need to make things happen all exist within social, cultural, and economic boundaries. When I create, review, and make progress toward my own "So that . . ." statements, I do so within the constraints of modern society, but I don't feel constrained by those boundaries. And to make the kind of progress we're talking about here, we have to establish some boundaries.

So much of what we do and of which we are a part depends on "assumed affirmations" and agreed-to boundaries, which we all recognize. Take a simple example from the daily lives of most people, specifically in the realm of personal transportation. When cars stay on the "right" side of the roadway, when drivers stop at red lights, and when the taillights on the car ahead signal us to slow down, transportation works much more quickly, effectively, and safely. We all know where to go, we trust one another, and we avoid accidents.

Now consider another activity in which you are engaged and involved every day: your work—productivity and performance. Have you built in agreements and alerts to let you know when you're on- and/

or off-course? Do you have the sense that there is just too much to do and not enough time to do it? If so, you're a member of an overcrowded club. This is why it's absolutely critical to look at your "So that . . ." statements, as a way to gain freedom, to choose, to act, and to excel.

Even your workday is most likely set within the boundaries of (relative) start and end times, with a number of hours between them. Just how many hours *is* that these days? Many people I have met over the past few years have simply acquiesced to arriving at work increasingly earlier and, often, staying later and later, as their only option if they are to get everything done they need to. Now that you've read through most of this book, consider using some of the tools described in it—namely, "I'm at my best when . . ." and "So that . . ."—to determine the long-term sustainability of this approach. It may well be time to experiment with setting new boundaries.

Experiment with the following exercise for five contiguous weekdays: Decide when you're going to arrive at work and when you're going to leave. If you work for yourself or out of a home office, define when your workday will start and stop. It may be easier for the first couple of days to pad the times a bit on either side (7:30 AM to 6:30 PM, for example). Then you can ever so slightly begin to shorten the day by a few minutes. By the fifth day, see if you can manage to come in to work a few minutes later and leave a few minutes earlier. You'll find it absolutely amazing what happens when you put a boundary around what you call a workday.

Not only will you become a little more productive, but the people around you may notice the difference as well. When you come in on time (whatever time that is) and leave when you say you will, you send a very important message to others: that you value your time. This will help them do the same. When you fail to limit the time you spend working in a day, your work will continue filling up the day. This phenomenon is known as Parkinson's law, after British historian and author Cyril Northcote Parkinson, who said, in 1955, "Work expands to fill the time available for its completion."

You probably make some kind of to-do or daily priorities list (most people do so at the beginning of the day). There are ideas and tools in this book—including noun and verb working, and utilizing your systems and tools—that you can use to effectively manage your ideas, time, and activities throughout the day. By combining them with the ideas presented in this chapter, I am confident you will find a way to get more of your important work done, without having to put off other things or work late (or early!) to get it all done. If you end each day by identifying the MITs for the next one (remember, only four), you are building a boundary around what is (and, by default, what is *not*) important.

Keep in mind that your MITs are designed to rotate. Part of the reason for writing them down (again, I often do so on a whiteboard or sticky note that I put in an obvious place at my work station) is so that you can look back over the past week and observe how you are cycling through this list. I frequently receive compelling e-mails from clients who observe that they choose from a short list of only five MITs over several days (or weeks). "What does this mean?" they ask. The answer is fairly simple: Those "other" things that they thought were really important, the ones on their comprehensive MIT lists, just *aren't*, at least not right now. Don't make a big deal out of this; we all go through productivity and performance cycles. Keep in mind, however, that you do want to pick different MITs over a period of several months or quarters.

At the end of each day, you might look back and mentally review what you did and how you did it. As I told you at the beginning of the book, my long-standing definition of productivity is: "I am productive when I do what I said I would do in the time that I promised I would." That is important to me. Again, the reason I write down those MITs is *so that* I can look back and do an objective assessment at the end of a work cycle. How *did* I do after labeling *those* particular items as the important ones to work on? *What* did I do? And at how high a level of engagement, interest, and professionalism?

Promote Your Own "So That . . ."

Many years ago, I read a book that dramatically changed my life and career path. Keith Ferrazzi's *Never Eat Alone* gave me every reason I needed to meet new people. As I explained early on, from 2000 to 2006, I was a consultant with a fast-growing consulting firm, the David Allen Company. As part of my job I traveled a lot to speaking engagements and often ate out in restaurants by myself. For months, every time I went to a restaurant for dinner, I carried that book with me. And it helped! As soon as the host walked away from seating me at a table,

I took out that bright orange hardback book and placed it on the table where people around me could (if they bothered to look) see the title.

How many times did that book begin a conversation, get me invited to another table, or help me meet people while I traveled around the world? More than I can count. Even back then I was experimenting with my "So that . . . ." I wanted to meet more people *so that* I could increase my network, experience a more local view of the community where I was working, and really enjoy my time traveling. Some of the chance meetings I experienced over a decade ago have turned in to lifelong friendships with people I continue to see and talk to regularly.

How can you make your own "So that . . ." clear and present and easy to focus on daily? Here are five tips:

1. *Put it in writing.* This is the easy one, and it's something I hope you began doing while reading this chapter. If not, then consider writing a couple of your MITs on a note card or piece of paper now. Next to each one, write "So that. . . ." Then, put this piece of paper where you know you'll see it throughout the day (e.g., on your desk, in your wallet, near your computer, etc.). Make it a point to actively review it throughout the day over the next several days. At the end of each day, choose just four more for tomorrow!

2. *Take the mirror test.* Okay, let's move up a level: Get ahold of a dry-erase pen (the kind you use to write on a whiteboard) and bring it home with you. Before you go to bed tonight, write tomorrow's four MITs on your mirror, at about eye level. Consider adding the "So that . . ." for each one. By doing this, you'll have the opportunity to read through them again in the morning. But the most valuable part comes at the end of the day, when you return from work and can look yourself in the eyes while reviewing how you performed that day. (When I do this, I ask myself, "Did I do what I said I'd do?")

3. *Make a collage.* Find several magazines from your industry that interest you. Go through them and cut out words, phrases, pictures, and diagrams that relate to your MITs that have come to mind while reading this chapter. This activity may take an hour or more, but the result will be incredibly helpful. Tape or paste these cutouts on a large piece of poster board so that you're able to see

them all together. As you did for the mirror test, put this board where you can see it throughout the day. (Some of my clients have taken a picture of it and turned it into the background photo on their mobile phone or computer monitor.)

4. *Build personal brand awareness.* What do other people think of you, when they think of you? What do you talk about when you're engaged in a conversation? It's vital to continually build your personal brand through what you do, how you do it, where you go, and the people with whom you spend time. Many chapters of this book are designed with this in mind. Letting the people around you know what you believe in, stand for, and are engaged in makes it easier for them to help you when and where they can.

5. *Develop new habits.* How do you form a habit? Some people claim that time is the answer. It's often said that "You need to do something for 21 (or 35 or 60) days before it becomes a habit." In actual practice, there's a bit more to it than that. Sure, you need time to practice, but think about it this way: How many times can you practice what you want to think about or do, using 100 percent of your focus? If you do something repeatedly, with a high degree of focus (and, even better, knowing there is a high level of personal payoff!), the chances increase that it will become part of who you are and how you operate. Try this with each of your MITs and "So that . . ." statements.

What to Do Now That You Know Your "So That . . .": Three Steps To Success

Most likely, this chapter so far has been a lot of work for you—and that's a good thing! You've done a lot of heavy lifting so far; you've thought bigger and more deeply about what is most important to you, in your personal life, and at work. Now it's time to engage in what you know is important and act in ways that reflect that knowledge. (I will have more to say about practice in Chapter 10. For now, I ask you to consider the following: Practice does *not* make perfect; it does make comfortable.)

There are three keys to success when it comes to implementing the philosophy of working and performing "on purpose." To make your best better, you need to *show up*, *do good work*, and *stay in touch*.

Let's look at each of these in detail.

Show Up

When you think about purpose, consider the words "drive," "purpose," and "present" (as in "being in the present"). When I think about showing up in my life, I consider all three of these—they are big concepts. Showing up is about putting it all together. Whether I'm speaking at an event, meeting with someone, racing in a triathlon, or spending time with family or friends, I tap into the "drive." I ask myself the following question: "What is in me, at my core, that motivates me to spend my time doing this?"

Again it comes back to the *why* of it all. What is the purpose of my spending precious time, here, doing this? This is an excellent question to ask, especially as you consider the many places you're invited to show up.

Finally, be aware that showing up means more than just making it on time. When I am present, it means I am on time, prepared, equipped, and focused. I want everyone around me to know that what I'm about to do *is* the most important thing for me to be doing in that moment, and that they will get 100 percent of my contribution and attention while I'm there.

Do Good Work

I regard this particular tenet as becoming more and more important as workplaces continue to evolve, from blending multigenerational workforces together as never before to completely changing the basic concept of what it means to "go to work." First, consider the impact on coworkers, clients, and vendors, (oh, and friends and family, too) if you always do what you say you are going to do. Identify any place or way that you can take your work, your commitment, or your contribution to the next level. Doing good work often comes down to listening, and really paying attention to what the people around us say, care about, and ask of us during conversations.

When you show up at that next meeting or event, make a note of what you do, and observe the people around you who are doing good work. Really engage; make eye contact, ask questions, and contribute what you can throughout the interaction. When I think about doing good work, I often find myself wondering what or who I know as I'm listening to someone talk. I find ways to ask questions that are of genuine interest to us both, and I always make an effort to contribute to the conversation when possible. I also like to act as a "networking hub," introducing people to others who share interests and areas of focus. I believe that we are all just one introduction away from achieving that next level of our purpose.

Stay in Touch

This is one of the best personal and professional development practices you can follow. Try it for just the next five weeks: Simply stop once weekly and ask, "Is there anyone in my network I have not reached out to or connected with lately?" (Consider adding a reminder to do so on your calendar system for the next five Wednesdays.) If there are, contact the first two to five people who come to mind.

I do this daily. After meeting with someone, I add a note to my own organizational system to follow up with him or her. If it was at a seminar I presented, I may reach out to the coordinator and any participants who contacted me afterward. If I think about an executive coaching client I've worked with on different areas of leadership and organizational development, I may send along a book from Amazon. com that I've read recently and can recommend. If I meet like-minded people at a networking or community building event, I e-mail, write a card, or call them to share some of the things I'm working on, and to hear what they might be engaged in these days.

■ ■ ■

I attribute the substance of my success to following this three-step business model over the years. My purpose has always been to help people, as they take on more, stay focused on what's important to them, and complete the projects they commit to in different aspects of their work and personal lives. As you make your way through each of the three steps, consider where you might be able to improve and develop, and pick an action to complete today!

Significant Aspects Influencing Your "So That . . ."

Two factors will specifically and significantly influence what you choose as your "So that . . ." statements, as well as what you do about them once you've identified them. Here are two influences that will certainly encourage, change, and sustain you in achieving your own "So that . . .":

1. *External influence.* Your social network consists of people who live in your community, work for and with you, eat in the restaurants you frequent, and more. What you talk about with other people when you're standing in line for coffee, dropping your kids off at school, waiting for a meeting to start, or debriefing your day at work will impact what you believe is possible. Then there is the influence of the books and magazines you read, as well as the TV shows, movies, and video games you watch; they all impact your reasons for doing what you do and thinking what you think.

2. *Internal influence.* Consider your own moral compass, mind-set, and outlook, the natural gifts you have, and the areas both at work and in your personal life that interest you most. Naturally, external variables will have an effect on these internal influences, and the bulk of the decisions you make about what to "do next about that" will come down to the foundation that rests on a solid purpose statement.

Whether or not you identify with and focus on your "So that . . ." will also influence how big a part of your life you'll make this way of thinking. To begin with, simply write one of your "So that . . ." statements on a piece of paper. Write on a sticky note, a note card, or a page in a notebook. Then, for the next five days, look at it every day—better, if possible, a couple of times per day. I suggest to clients that they regularly review their purpose statements early in the morning. This gives them a reference point and a direction in which to head, which may gently (or perhaps a bit more forcefully) change what they decide to focus on as their day begins.

For those who naturally have energy to spare in the morning (the morning people), reviewing a purpose statement early in the day may serve as a launch pad for using their time, energy, and focus differently throughout the day. When you're ready to engage, and if you have more work to do than time to do it in, you need to be able to prioritize, focus, and produce.

For those who are *not* morning people, I suggest you review your "So that . . ." statements later in the day, to prepare for the next day by building momentum to do the things that will make a difference—personally and professionally.

It should be obvious to you by now that your social network influences your purpose. Here are four pertinent questions to ask about you and your social network and its influence on your ability to live and work "on purpose":

1. With whom do you spend time?
2. What do you do?
3. Where do you go?
4. What do you talk about?

What I have found about spending time with others is that there is a direct carryover effect between how much time I spend with them, what we talk about "there" (at work or away from work, on a weekday or a weekend), and what I focus on "here." Because of this, I continually search for ways to talk about my passion and mission with those individuals who show a genuine interest in them, and encourage me to go further along those paths.

With whom can you spend time over the next several weeks to fan the flames of your interest in professional and personal improvement? If, indeed, we are smarter together—and I believe we are—it makes sense to bring your "So that . . ." to someone who is willing to sit down over lunch or a latte and talk to you about it. Who knows? He or she may see or know something that you haven't noticed or thought about yet. It's an amazing way to build support for something that is so important to you.

What else influences whether or not you live "on purpose"? The support materials that surround you: the books and magazines you subscribe to and purchase, the websites you visit, the TV shows and movies you watch. All these come together to build your "portfolio of focus." You are currently reading a book that could potentially change the very topics that currently grab your attention and on which you spend time throughout the day. For example, think back to Chapter 6, on tracking. If, as I suggested, you studied some of your workflow habits, productivity tools, and ways to relax, reflect, and improve, you may have realized that you need to start doing some things (not everything!) a little bit differently.

If you combine these two critical areas of influence, your social network and the materials you've collected, you might then consider the value of engaging in some kind of formalized, structured program or class to take you farther along that path of engagement. Join a club, take a class, or enroll in a leadership program through a local organization or university, to clarify your thinking, catalyze your focus, and improve the chances you will live purposefully. This kind of commitment will, over a short period of time, pay you back in increased awareness of what is most important to you, as well as yield support to move you forward, faster.

Your Stop-Doing List

A lesson I learned long ago—and one that has been reinforced over time—is that it's just not possible to "do it all." Supply and demand, that very basic term I learned many years ago as a student in high school economics, dictates that there will not be as much of anything available as we'd like; and that goes for time, productivity, and the ability to do everything we want to do. I have also learned over the years that in order to do some things, I most likely need to *stop* doing others.

While listening to author and entrepreneur Nido Qubain some time ago, I quantified my commitment to studying those things I intend to stop doing as much, as I focus on how much I have decided to do. He taught me the importance of making a stop-doing list. Chapter 6, on tracking, is designed to encourage you to study and question what you're doing, and to identify as well what you can *stop doing*, without falling behind or losing momentum toward achieving your goals.

A purpose statement is a strategy. For it to serve you well, it must clearly describe the direction you're headed in and a plan of future action that distinctly and definitively sets you in motion. Developing this mission statement should be much more than a quick wordsmithing exercise. Devote as much time and energy to writing it as you would to creating a marketing plan, projecting a personal budget, or planning an upcoming vacation. If possible, include people from your social network (Chapter 5) in the process, to ensure that you heighten the importance and support of moving ever forward toward your purpose.

I trust you will find that by developing your "why," purpose, MITs, and "So that . . ." statements, you will move your mission forward faster, more effectively, and with better results than ever before!

PART

3

Make More

WHAT IS IT like when you have more—more time, more energy, more focus? These are all the things I want to make *more* of! The final three chapters of this book will show you what's necessary to take your work and your thinking to the next level: *completion and acknowledgment.*

Here's something you can do right now to begin implementing this philosophy: Make a list of some of the tasks and activities you've already done this week by answering these questions:

- Whom have you talked to?
- What have you read or seen or learned?
- Where have you gone?
- When did you have the opportunity to help someone make more of what he or she needed?

A critical component to making more is to use the information around us to our advantage. I call it feedback; you might prefer another word—perhaps *review*, *response*, *reaction*, or *criticism*. Whatever label we give it, we know it's incredibly valuable. When we seek out, accept, and test the information to which we have access, we can position ourselves to move even higher up. Whether you ask for a formal review at work or sit down with your friends and family to "talk about how things are going," listen very, very carefully; there will be information in these situations you can use.

One of the most limited resources I manage is not my time, and it's not my energy; it's my attention. Knowing how to direct focus on *more* is the first step to take in order to *make more*. You need to learn about the tools, mind-set, and practices that work to amplify your focus on what you want to do, while gradually eliminating the things that might pull you off-course and out of full engagement mode.

After you finish reading this book, I strongly encourage you to make a commitment to the practice of *practice*. When you were young, someone probably told you that "practice makes perfect." That's only a partial result of practice. Practice makes habit, and practice makes comfortable. It's that last one that is critical to understand. What we do—and do again and again—becomes our normal. You can use the ideas in Chapter 10 to create and maintain a "new normal" for making more—more time, more energy, and more attention—and, as you apply these methods to your business life, more professional success.

8

Improvement and Feedback

Knowing How to Ask for It and What to Do with It

Do you remember rock-and-roller Mick Jagger singing that he couldn't "get no satisfaction"? It seems that no matter what he did, whatever he had, it just wasn't enough. Do you wonder what filter he used to decide whether or not what he was getting was satisfying? I do!

I've been studying career and personal development for a while now, and what I've learned is that there are two factors that come together to make me feel that I've been successful in my endeavors: achieving what I set out to complete *and* staying aware of the experiences along the way. In this chapter, I'll show you that seeking and applying feedback is an excellent way to make more *and* enjoy what you do throughout the process. Let's start at the beginning.

This is the first of three chapters on *making more*. And, of course, there's more than just money to be made! In this section, I invite you to make a list of at least five *other* things that you make (and, ultimately, want to make more of), besides money. Look around while thinking deeply about the past month of your life and work, and ask yourself, "What have I created, built, and made lately?"

When I do this, I come up with categories like: Memories, Decisions, Connections, Relationships, Workspace, Big Ideas, Opportunities. Those are some of the other things I "make." By reviewing my "I am at my best when . . ." list (see Chapter 1), I can see the kinds of things I make right there in my own handwriting. On my best days, I'm doing things that take me toward achieving more of what I'm here for.

Go ahead and make your list. What do you make? What else would you like more of?

After you've identified at least five things you make besides money, continue reading this chapter. I'm going to show you how to *make more* of all of them, and then some!

Now ask yourself what you think of when you hear the word "feedback."

- Is it a positive or a negative thought?
- Are you attracted to it or do you run away from it?
- Do you work to receive and implement the feedback you get right away, or do you prefer to wait, putting it off as long as possible?

Write a definition here of what the word "feedback" means to you.

Let me share with you my view on the place and power of feedback from the recipient's perspective:

Proactively perceived, and appropriately applied, feedback offers one of the fastest ways to make your best better.

Is Your Approach to Work Working?

What are the symptoms you're experiencing that indicate it might be time to solicit some feedback?

On many levels, lots could happen to make it obvious that you need to make a change. Maybe you get a speeding ticket on your way to a meeting you were running late for. Maybe you lose a customer because you didn't return a bid soon enough. Perhaps you've gone up a pants size or two because you've been eating a little too much and exercising too little. Getting a ticket, losing a customer, and gaining weight are all symptoms of other root causes. These indicators pop up as course-corrective feedback. That said—and you may have found this—some of the symptoms that are feeding us information are not so obvious. Because of that we need to be especially tuned to receiving that information.

Here's a question to ask about your day *yesterday*: "Did what you accomplish move your mission forward?" Surely you were busy, whether it was a weekday spent in the office or a weekend day spent with your friends and family. What was it like? What happened?

My good days are those when I can look back and know that what I did made a difference. Then I seek out feedback to let me know if I'm on- or off-course. And feedback can come from the strangest places.

One day after school, in 1997, when I was still teaching Spanish at Nordhoff High, in Ojai, California, I met a local resident, speaker and author Martha Ringer. She had asked if she could sit in on my Spanish classes (she wanted to brush up on her language skills for a trip she was planning to South America). I said, "Of course." Well, after a couple of weeks of attending my classes (alongside high school freshmen and sophomores) she let me know that she was about to head south of the border and that she was extremely grateful for being allowed to sit in on my classes. But then she surprised me, by giving me some unsolicited feedback.

Actually, it was the *way* she gave it that surprised me. As we were ending our conversation, she looked me very directly in the eyes and said, "Can I offer you some feedback, based on my experience in your classroom?"

Think about that for a moment. When was the last time someone you knew, whether well or not, asked if he or she could "offer feedback?"

I know I was taken aback, and so said something like, "Yeah . . . uh . . . I mean, yes, I'd like your feedback." What she said next has stuck with me since that day in October 1997.

"Jason, you're an excellent teacher, but you're losing time, energy, and focus because you can't find what you need when you need it." This one sentence has proved to be a driving force behind my studies, my work, and my writing since then.

The next most memorable piece of feedback I ever received came from a former employer, David Allen, of *Getting Things Done* (GTD) fame. Four months before GTD was to be published, I joined the small David Allen Company (my wife was employee number 1, and I was number 6), training to be a seminar facilitator and workflow coach. Over those four months, for two days at a time, I individually coached a dozen leaders from local organizations in effective organization techniques. I also presented three seminars (each one lasting two days) to groups of 20 to 30 businesspeople from companies in Southern California. After my second two-day seminar, I sat down with David and some of the other facilitators to debrief our experiences.

The question David posed that day is one I've used since then, not only for myself after I complete a seminar or a coaching session, but also with the people I'm advising and mentoring. He asked, "Now that you've finished a successful two-day seminar, what would you do differently the next time?" On the one hand, I felt like he was saying "good job!" On the other, it seemed clear it was time to honestly assess my performance. One question, two distinct feedback experiences.

I remember talking for what seemed like hours, reflecting on those two days—step by step, activity by activity, and hour by hour of the seminar. I had ideas on how I would start the seminar differently, what I would change after participants returned from breaks, and what I could do different to end each day of the program.

These two feedback experiences—Martha asking me if I was open to receiving feedback, and David asking me to replay the last, and preplay the next, seminar—left me with an important thought: My best feedback comes when I'm ready, *and* it comes from the inside out.

Here are some questions for you to consider about your experiences receiving feedback:

- What is the best, most meaningful, and most significant feedback—professional or personal—you've ever received?
- Was it direct or indirect?
- Did you see it coming, or was it a surprise?
- Did you accept and use it, or did you deny and avoid it?
- Regardless of the feedback, what did you do with or about it?

Feedback Defined

Go back now and reread your definition of the word "feedback," the one you wrote at the beginning of the chapter. Keeping it in mind will go a long way to knowing when feedback is coming, and what you might do once you get it. According to Wikipedia:

> Feedback describes the situation when output from (or information about the result of) an event or phenomenon in the past will influence an occurrence or occurrences of the same.

Here's how I define it: "The information I collect about what I just did informs and directs me to make it better the next time I do something like this." Feedback to me isn't just about criticism; it's about a constant opportunity for improvement.

In an instant, one photo gave me feedback that changed my life. Have you ever seen a camera that can take pictures underwater? I remember the first time I used one. I thought it was *so* cool! I got one for the trip of a lifetime Jodi and I took to Maui, where I proposed to her on the beach one evening before dinner. Earlier in the day, we went snorkeling. Of course, I brought along the "cool camera" (that's what we called it). We were out in about 15 feet of water when I said, "I'm going to swim down toward the bottom, then I'll turn around and smile, and you take my picture. Okay?" And so I went.

Instant feedback.

Later that night, we were both excited to look at the photos we'd taken. After we scrolled through picture after picture of the ocean, palm trees, and the sunset, I saw a photo that immediately made the "coolness" of the camera melt away. There I was, underwater, a big smile on my face, arms outstretched, and in full view, the 40-plus pounds I had put on in the past couple of years.

I couldn't believe it. I did not recognize myself. I knew I'd been putting on weight; having to buy new clothes told me that. But that picture, taken underwater, really changed my focus. I had all the information I needed (you know the saying, a picture is worth a thousand words) to motivate me to make a change. The information I got from that photograph directed me to begin making healthy, sustainable, and positive choices and changes—which I have kept up to this day!

What kind of feedback have you received that had this degree of impact on you? And if indeed you have had such an experience, what can you do to set yourself up to experience it again, only this time direct it so that you set yourself up to take full advantage of the growth potential it offers?

Why This, Why Now?

Over dinner one night with one of my business development coaches in New York City, I brought up this chapter on feedback. I told him I wanted to focus on the recipient's experience *only*, as I felt most comfortable talking about receiving feedback; and I pointed out the many books written on how to give it.

"Jason, why is receiving feedback so important to you?" he asked between bites. "What does feedback do for you and your clients to make your best even better?"

I believe that when people collect feedback, they can use that information, apply it, to make the important stuff more important, the fun stuff more fun, and the easier stuff even easier. Here's a phrase you can use: "If I know, I can grow." (Kind of reminds you of the discussion in Chapter 6, doesn't it?)

Did you write a list of things you make at the start of this chapter? If not, please do that now, as I talk about it throughout the rest of this chapter. Once you've completed your list, I'd like you to stop and reflect deeply on this question: "Would you like to make *more* of those things on it?"

Whenever I have sought, received, and used solid and meaningful feedback, my goal has been to take advantage of it to its full potential, to work with it, and use it to make more of *some*thing. Over the past few years (true to my list of things I make), this has helped me earn a higher salary, take longer vacations, build more positive memories, and have more fun.

About midmorning on July 8, 2011, an interesting string of e-mails appeared in my inbox. Within minutes of the first one arriving, I received seven more with the exact same subject line: "Fw: Seth's Blog: Time for a workflow audit."

The senders were from all over—clients, friends, a vendor, even my wife! They had all received Seth Godin's e-mail newsletter that morning (remember reading in Chapter 5 about the power of the social network?) and they had all immediately forwarded a copy of it to me. The article Seth wrote that day and sent to his subscribers contained the following advice: "Have someone watch you work, and ask them for a 'workflow audit.'" Here was someone I have looked up to as an author and a speaker (I've been following his activities for over a decade now), describing part of the feedback process I conduct for my executive coaching clients.

Perhaps the most important—really, *only*—question to ask yourself as it relates to making your best better, in terms of the importance of feedback, is: "Am I achieving my intended results?" Before you even begin to answer this question, be sure you have read (and maybe even go back and reread) Chapter 7 on clarifying your purpose.

Once you have fine-tuned your "So that . . ." statement, it becomes much more important to ask for honest feedback, correct your course, and prioritize your MITs so that you pay attention to what you're doing and how you're doing it.

In the rest of this chapter I'll share with you the different kinds of feedback you may receive, as well as fundamental ways you can search for, discover, and use the information you take from it. Since the thrust of this book is about making your best better, as I mentioned above, I focus only on *receiving* feedback—the subjective and objective information you can use right away.

To begin, I point out there is a significant difference between the two: Subjective feedback will "feel" or "seem" like something. For example, you may say at the end of the day or after finishing a big project, "I feel as though the client is happy," or "It seems like that meeting went well." Objective feedback is arguably much more specific. "Today, I sent 67 e-mails to past clients to let them know about our recent award, which was promoted in a local trade journal."

From the Inside Out

Ever since that discussion I had on self-initiated feedback and ideas with David Allen after the seminar in 2000, I have continued to seek useful information that comes from the inside out. In other words, I ask questions and stir conversations that elicit discussion about the areas in people's work and personal lives where they need to question *their own* perspectives.

Obviously, feedback doesn't always have to come from *other people*. There are things you can do to change how *you* view what you just did, and positively change what you are currently doing to improve on it next time. In order to be valuable, however, the feedback you envision and receive must be based on something concrete; to know whether I'm moving in the right direction, I have to know where I plan to go!

Throughout this book, I've recommended ways to externalize and observe your goals, whether by setting an intention for the day, the week, or the year, or by planning a conversation, a project, or an event. It's only valuable to receive feedback if the person (even if that person is you) offering you feedback has some sense of what you were trying to accomplish in the first place. If a person offering feedback starts by providing you with an assessment that doesn't match your intention, it's perfectly acceptable to remind him or her of what you were trying to do in the first place. On the other hand, if the person *does* know what you were trying to do, and still is offering what to you seems like off-course feedback, it may be interesting to let it play out, see where it's going. You may, indeed, gain some information you can use to improve the situation next time.

Recall the three key influencers to your own performance and productivity I introduced in Chapter 3: *homeostasis*, *context*, and your *social network*. All put pressure on you to change what you do and how you do it. The first one, homeostasis, has to do with maintaining a balancing act between too much and too little, just right and not right, going for something big or new and staying comfortable. For better or worse, it's almost *always* easier to keep doing what we've always done, even if the feedback we're getting tells us we've gone off-course. To enact the changes you're thinking of making (to do something that's not "normal"), you're going to have to use every idea I've presented thus far in this book, plus implement the practices in this chapter and those to come! Feedback acts as the bridge between what you are doing and what you could be doing differently to experience different results.

Stepping outside normal routines is commonly referred to as "leaving your comfort zone." It is critical when you're seeking feedback from the inside out to have a reason and a place for that feedback to appear. Ask yourself: "Why this? Why now?" Feedback, after all, is meant to provide information and guidance as you continue experimenting with making things better. It is also meant to encourage you to continue moving forward, to the place you want to be.

A tool you can use to maximize this inside-out feedback process can be found in Chapter 1, the "I'm at my best when . . ." exercise. Take time to review it. As I said before, knowing when you're at your best doesn't guarantee you'll be able to achieve it each and every day, but it will give you information you can readily use to change your mind, make new choices, and position yourself to live and work more appropriately, according to what means the most to you. Knowing when you're at your best, and being able, at the end of each day, to compare to that inventory makes it easy to judge your progress more objectively.

Where Else Does Feedback Come From?

Think back to Chapter 2, where you learned about the pacing of goals and milestones, and remind yourself of the objectives, habits, or projects you identified there. Then recall the exercises in Chapter 5, where you identified and scrutinized your social network. Both of these efforts are significant forces that come together to immediately impact the value and power of feedback that comes your way.

Now ask yourself: "How much time have I put toward clarifying my specific goals and anticipated outcomes, and how can I grow my social network to support me in moving from where I am to where I want to be?"

While coaching leaders around the world, I've made note of six sources of high-quality feedback.

1. Results

How are things going relative to what you can remember from a couple of weeks to a couple of months ago? Sure, this is a bit subjective, but you can use your short-term-memory to compare the recent past to this week. For example, what did you start, engage in, or complete yesterday? Last week? Last month?

If, at the end of the day or the week, you can stop and process the results you know you achieved, you may wind up identifying a question or prompt to help you look for valuable feedback, either using one of the feedback loop processes described in this chapter or by asking someone in your social network to provide you with some of his or her ideas.

2. Experience

How do you feel things are going, on a sensory level? If you have completed or achieved something significant lately, pause and reflect on the time leading up to and at completion of the project. All too often, we wind up finishing a task or project and moving directly into the next project, situation, or crisis that needs our attention; it's simply the nature of the personal and professional culture in which we live and work.

By making yourself consciously aware of the process of acknowledging completion of your work, as well as the effort it took to get from where you started to where you ended, you just may find a new way to examine what you've accomplished. This can have the effect of changing your perspective and, subsequently, allowing you to identify a new aspect about the experience.

3. Contribution

Try asking yourself, "Who said thanks?" I know this is a significant question to consider, and for good reason: It's essential to the feedback process. There's something going on, something good, when a person pauses long enough to write a thank you card, or takes the time to call you to say "good job." Such an acknowledgment can act as a force that anchors you to your passions going forward. When people take the time to tell us that what we did mattered to them, we realize how vital our actions are, not just to our own sense of achievement, but to others as well.

4. Measurement

How much money do you have in your savings account right now? How many new clients have you brought in since this date a month ago? How many days of vacation have you taken this year? How many books have you read this month? How many hours have you spent watching TV/movies? How many dinners have you eaten with your entire family sitting around the table?

Answering these kinds of quantity questions are incredibly useful ways to garner objective feedback. One great thing about them is that no one else really needs to know whether you're tracking the answers. Additionally—and you may have found this to be true while reading Chapter 6—the moment you start tracking something, when you get the first objective feedback about exactly what you are doing with your time, energy, or focus, you immediately gain valuable information you need to begin making some significant changes.

5. Service

What has happened to you recently that's directly related to the "So that . . ." statements that you created in Chapter 7? It is essential that you look around from time to time, at least monthly, and preferably weekly, and ask these two service questions:

1. Who have I helped lately?
2. How have I been helped lately, and by whom?

The answers to these two questions can provide very insightful feedback relative to your development as an effective leader, efficient communicator, and practical team player. Effective leaders spend time and use their focus to seek out opportunities to be of service—to their communities, their companies, and their social networks. Efficient communicators are adept at listening for and taking advantage of situations where they can be of service. They use the topics other people are talking, complaining, or bragging about as jumping-off points to make additional contributions to the discussion—often bringing it to another, higher, level of engagement.

Team players look out for one another, encourage each other, and help everyone on the team find ways to get better. Being of service and willing to assist others in areas in which you have experience and expertise is an excellent way to seek out and capitalize on making your own best that much better.

6. *Habits*

In Chapter 10, I will go into more detail about practicing a new behavior until it becomes a habit. For now, I want you to begin thinking about the habits you have created that: (1) have helped you get as far as you've gotten up to now, and (2) may be keeping you from reaching your next level of accomplishment—say, a promotion.

Your habits provide excellent feedback about what you once considered to be acceptable (and, perhaps, in some cases still do). You can examine any habit and learn from it.

Is It Time to Ask for Feedback?

An important question to ask yourself and the people you work with on a daily basis is: "Are the results you're achieving moving the mission forward?" I have used this question over and over again in my coaching sessions and I am consistently surprised by the response I hear (though I suppose I shouldn't be, by now). Many times, I note a discrepancy between the daily tasks in which people are engaged— meetings they attend, e-mails they send, interruptions they manage, and so on—and the overall mission of the team or department and the purpose of the organization.

You know it's time to slow down and ask for feedback when you recognize yourself in the following statement: "I'm busy—*very, very busy*—but the really important things aren't getting done."

Like many people, I'm sure you have experienced days at work, or even on weekends, when you were so busy trying to catch up, managing a crisis, or being distracted by all kinds of things that the days flew by, leaving you without the time to work on your MITs.

Keep in mind that asking for feedback doesn't necessarily indicate that something is wrong; it simply means that you want to fast-track your efforts and maximize your focus, energy, and time to get more of the *right* things done. I've already shared with you my personal definition of productivity, but it bears repeating here: "I am getting the right things done, doing what I said I would do, in the time that I promised to myself and others."

The easiest way to begin soliciting feedback is to consider the areas where you spend a lot of time and do a lot of work.

- Do you frequently speak on the phone?
- Do you attend a lot of meetings?
- Do you travel for work (and/or pleasure)?
- Do other people count on you to get things done?
- Do you manage complex projects?
- Do you interact with customers, vendors, or clients?
- Whom can you ask for feedback on those things you do the most?

By soliciting, accepting, and using the input of others, you'll put yourself on a fast track to make your best even better. I have seen some of the most amazing feats achieved by people who were doing something "pretty well" and then, with a bit of feedback, were able to supersize their productivity and get even more out of their day and their efforts.

Creating Big-Impact Feedback, Quickly

I once worked with a senior executive who asked me during our long-term coaching program, "Jason, what is the one thing you think I could work on that would have the most significant impact on my productivity?" We'd spent several days together over the period of a couple of months, and I knew the feedback she needed would have to be big, and immediately powerful.

The answer to her question, I knew, was a simple one; unfortunately, it was not an easy one to implement. It was something we both knew she had to do; however, it was going to take a major effort to take her beyond knowing what to do and actually *doing* it. Several ideas came to my mind immediately, in the form of organizational tips, technology hacks, behavior changes, workspace improvements, and others. I went first with the one that I intuited would make a big difference for her that week and forever after.

I stood up, walked across her office, and opened my briefcase. Slowly, I took out my laptop computer, a USB cable, and my digital camera. While my computer was booting up, I walked to the other side of her office, as she sat watching me from her desk chair. Standing there, I first took a couple of pictures of her sitting at her desk, then the conference table against the wall, the bookcases, and even the boxes on the side of her work station (which she was still waiting to find time to unpack).

In my mind, to this day, I can see her watching me (remember, she had asked me a question and, I presumed, was waiting for an answer) as I clicked away for a couple of minutes in silence. At the time (and looking back it seems crazy) I was taking a big risk by answering her question not with words, but with silence, space, thoughts, and photographs. After I finished taking pictures, I connected the camera to my computer, downloaded them to my photo library, and opened the file to an image of her desk space. As it filled the screen, I turned my laptop to her so she could see it, and then watched her facial expression change as I told her:

> If I could make a single recommendation, one that to implement may take you hours to set up and many weeks, if not several months of time to get used to, it would be to give yourself some space. There is not one extra bit of space in your office; there are piles on your desk, binders on your shelves from 10 years ago, supplies in drawers that are so full you can't open them—and there are those boxes you said have been waiting to be unpacked for five months.

When I stopped talking she began to look around. Her gaze moved from me to various parts of her office to the picture on my laptop back to me again and then back to her workspace. I reached over to my laptop and she watched me delete the pictures I had just taken. I then moved back to sit at the other side of her desk. I didn't direct her to change anything, nor did I show her how to organize her space; I simply offered her feedback from another perspective.

You know it's time for feedback when you are experiencing a significant difference between what you want and what you are getting.

- Are you bored?
- Do you feel stuck?
- Are you overwhelmed by the amount of work you have to do?
- Is your health being compromised?
- Are you exercising?
- Are you eating right?
- Are you getting enough restful sleep?

I suggest you go back now to review the work you did in Chapter 7, where you studied your efforts and the payoffs from those efforts. Clarifying what is happening is a great way to stumble upon feedback that may be hiding in plain sight!

Finally, one more indication that it's time for feedback is when someone in your social network asks you if you're open to receiving it. As you read in the introduction to this chapter, being open to unsolicited feedback proved very valuable to me along my own journey to making my best better. Because I was open to receiving this feedback, it matched my own measure of inside-out feedback—it didn't hurt that the person who gave it to me was 100 percent correct in her assessment!

Calendar Activity

Remember, in order for feedback to be as valuable to you as possible, you're going to need to compare the advice you get, hear, or see against an objective goal. How will you know if the feedback is on- or off-course unless you have some idea of what you were hoping to accomplish in the first place?

The following describes a way you can begin to establish a system for collecting feedback. It's very simple; it all starts with your calendar.

Whether you use a paper or digital calendar, open it up to today's date and then count 45 days into the future. Within that date space in your calendar, describe in one or two paragraphs where you plan to be on one of your significant work projects at that point in time. Describe in some detail how it is coming along, how you're utilizing resources, what questions you are answering, and how you will complete the project on time.

Now count ahead another 45 days (i.e., 90 days from today) and describe a project more in the realm of your personal life. Here, too, write a paragraph or two on a topic important to you right now—maybe a health, wealth, or travel goal, or a goal related to family or a friend. Write a few lines about how you think you will feel after you've achieved that goal.

Finally, pick a date 365 days from today—yes, an entire year ahead. I encourage you to think really hard about this exercise. Spend a good amount of time on it, perhaps an entire 15-minute block (remember, that's the equivalent of 1 percent of your day), and try to imagine what you think things will look like in your personal life, at work, and in your community one year from today.

In describing this scenario, repeatedly answer the question: "What would *more* look like here?" Whenever I do this, I try to write three or more paragraphs. Yes, it's a lot, and it takes some time, but the experience proves very interesting when I open my calendar and look at what I wrote months later. I've noticed that one of two things happens at this time: Either what I wrote seems like so *little*, because I have surpassed that written goal with the actions I've taken and projects I've completed, or something happened that caused me to fall a bit short of the outcome I was planning. Whatever the outcome or impressions I'm left with, I use these semiobjective formats to give myself a forum from which I can provide internal feedback.

What happens when you anticipate something happening? You start asking questions, a habit that's critical to the goal-setting and goal achievement process. Too often, our friends, coworkers, and we ourselves set an intention that is too ambiguous to achieve, without a real objective marker for when we should be where along the continuum to that outcome. Needless to say, simply writing these paragraphs on your calendar will not do everything you need to achieve the outcome you desire, but I assure you, they will take you one step closer. (I will talk more about focus and achievement in the next chapter.)

Asking the appropriate question at the appropriate time is an essential component in the process of gaining and using effective feedback. Of course, you may have forgotten in 45 or 90 days what you wrote "way back then." Thus, the question to ask when you reread what you wrote is: "How did my actions over the past few weeks get me *closer* to this ideal scenario?" Asking the question in this way allows you to gain perspective, come up with answers, and build momentum for going forward.

What Kinds of Feedback Do You Get?

Typically, you'll receive one of four different kinds of feedback from day to day and year to year. I describe them here, followed by a table listing a few examples of each.

- *Formal feedback* usually comes in the professional arena—the performance-based feedback most of us are familiar with, and which usually takes place in annual goal-setting and review sessions.
- *Informal feedback* comes in-between formal meetings, from clients, coworkers, vendors, and managers.
- *Objective feedback* generally has some kind of metric assigned to it; this is why it's essential to have specified what you were hoping to achieve, so that the feedback has some basis for comparison.
- *Subjective feedback* is the kind of information that is more intuitive in nature; it's typically described more as a feeling or sense.

Four Kinds of Feedback

Formal Feedback	Informal Feedback
Annual performance review with manager	Phone call from a customer to say thanks
Midyear goal achievement review	Lunchtime conversation with friend
Objective Feedback	**Subjective Feedback**
Made 17 phone calls	"Feels like" things are going well at work;
Sent 12 client contact cards	"Seems like" the client is happy

Let's look at each one in detail.

Formal Feedback

If it's still handy, flip forward in your calendar to the week or month of your next formal review session at work. If you work in an organization where these reviews are scheduled events, it should be easy to anticipate when you'll go through this assessment. If you are self-employed or don't have a formal review process at work, choose a date when you think you'll sit down next to focus on your annual goals.

Having worked with individuals in leadership positions worldwide, I often suggest that they begin to consider the areas of focus and attention they want to bring up during their performance reviews anywhere from six to nine months ahead of schedule. The most effective tool I have seen for this is to keep a file (paper or digital) to which you can add ideas, comments, and notes at least once a week, so that you have a mini-portfolio ready to go to support that formal discussion.

Informal Feedback

A conversation with a mentor over coffee in the morning, a lunchtime project debriefing with a coworker, a phone call with a friend on the weekend—all of these are examples of the in-between, informal feedback we receive throughout the year. Sometimes we ask for it and sometimes it comes unsolicited. You can easily initiate informal feedback by asking people simple (though not simplistic) questions like, "How do you see me?" "What did you notice I did during . . . ?" "Is there anything you'd suggest I do about . . . ?" Improving your performance in any area of work or your personal life requires that you remain open to receiving input, at any time, from anyone you think might have information you can use.

You can create your own informal feedback loop by keeping a written or audiotaped record of how things are going for you. Writing about the highs and lows at the end of each day will give you information you can use to your advantage at the end of about four or five weeks. This is a form of informal data gathering because there isn't a structure to it, other than your stopping to write something down. "Journaling the journey," so to speak, can play a major role in helping people to grow as leaders over time.

Objective Feedback

Numbers are crucial when you're gathering or soliciting objective feedback, because you need to know your original goal and/or starting point in order to be able to quantify how, or whether, the effort and focus came together to make it happen as you'd hoped it would. Whether this is feedback you collect on your own or that which someone else does for you and then shares with you, you will need to have very specific metrics in place. I have found that objective feedback is one of the best ways to help my clients achieve very specific, behavior-based changes they are seeking to make.

Objective feedback requires that you answer such questions as:

- How much money do you want in your savings account?
- How many days of vacation do you want to take this year?
- How fast do you want to run your next 10K or marathon distance race?

Start collecting and reviewing your experiences as you get closer to your goals (revisit Chapter 6, on tracking, to help you here). To gather your own objective feedback, it's a good idea to make note of statistical actions. For example, if you work in sales, track how many phone calls you make in a day, how many of these calls per week lead to meetings, how many meetings per week lead to clients.

Subjective Feedback

This feedback is a bit "looser" in form (and, often, function). From the outside in, subjective feedback will be structured in phrases such as, "It seems as if you . . . ," or "I get the feeling that you . . . ." From the inside out, subjective feedback you give yourself might sound like, "I wonder if I should . . . ," or "Does that mean I . . . ?"

■ ■ ■

I want to conclude this section by pointing out that none of these four kinds of feedback is better than any other, in any way. In fact, it's important that they work together and that you be very aware of how they show up in your life, and how to make the most of them. That is precisely why it's vital to determine *why* you are seeking and using feedback in the first place.

Mentor/Mentee Feedback and Review Program

Many years ago another mentor of mine, Kevin Wilde, *author of Dancing with the Talent Stars: 25 Moves That Matter Now*, and I started a feedback process that has matured over the years. We decided to make this quick-coach mentoring program as *objective* and *formal* as possible. Here are the steps you can take to create your own comentoring program.

Bring to mind someone who would be willing to talk to you by phone for *eight meetings of 15 minutes each,* to be scheduled over the next eight weeks. Decide who will "go first" as the mentee.

Schedule your first phone call. The mentee uses those first 15 minutes to discuss the next three to six months of personal and professional projects. During this first phone call, the mentor's role is to listen and ask clarifying coaching questions. These questions typically start with open-ended prompts like: "What kind of support do you need to . . . ?" "How would you like this experience to play out?" "Who would you like to assist you with . . . ?" The purpose of this conversation is to clarify two to three goals toward which to work. Focus both on the direction and the destination. Talk about what life and work would look like, and what accomplishing these goals might feel like.

Let's say you are going first, that you are going to work on your goal-setting and goal achievement strategies. At the conclusion of that first phone call, find a place where you can have about 15 minutes of complete silence. On a blank piece of paper, write down a minimum of 30 questions whose answers will show you how you'll reach the destination you've chosen for yourself. In addition, make note of the people you can talk to, the resources you can use, the places you might go, the information you'll need—anything that pertains to achieving this goal. The objective is to come up with questions and ideas to help move you "from here to there."

It's important to point out that you're not questioning *whether* you can get there, or even if "there" is where you should be going. In other words, you're not trying to figure out if this is the right project to work on or your most important goal; rather, you're questioning the *process* you're going to use to get there. You're determining *how* you'll have to act, what you'll need to do, who you'll need to support you, and where you'll need to go to achieve the objective you've set for yourself.

Once you've generated your list of 30 questions, review them carefully at least once every morning for the next five days. Study them—really scrutinize them—and while doing so, ask: "Are they truly the best, most useful questions I could ask?"

Be sure to add any new questions as they occur to you, either as a result of self-reflection or prompted by suggestions from others on your team (review Chapter 5, if necessary). You'll find, as most people do, that some are more valuable than the others. Throughout the week, begin to narrow the questions down to the 10 most valuable ones. Then, e-mail them to your mentor. These questions will serve as the agenda of your next 15-minute call.

During the next call, use the time to further clarify your goal and discuss the questions you've chosen as your top 10. Your mentor's job here is to, first, listen to you and, second, help you limit your focus, as the purpose of this phone call is to help you narrow down your list even further, to just three. These comprise the "biggies"; they mean business! Using these three questions will allow you to seek the feedback you need most, from the inside out.

Before the conclusion of this second call, schedule the next five meetings; ideally, you want to talk once a week. Block off 15 minutes for each call on your calendars, and make sure that you follow a consistent format for each discussion:

1. After a brief hello and catch-up conversation, your mentor asks you the first question.
2. You give yourself a rating of 1 to 5, with 5 indicating you've made a lot of progress since the previous call.
3. You explain briefly why you gave yourself the rating you did. Your mentor takes notes and listens carefully as you speak. In conclusion, he or she may ask a clarifying question.

As you can imagine, over those five calls, you'll cover a lot of ground. You'll answer these really important questions, and your mentor will be tracking your answers—the score you give yourself, as well as some of the comments you make. After the last call, schedule an assessment call.

The agenda for the final meeting is to debrief the process, as well as acknowledge the progress you made over the previous weeks (or, as the case may be, months). Also use this time to review the scores you gave yourself (which your mentor will have kept track of from each call) and the comments you made that he or she recorded. This information will provide you with an interesting snapshot of the past few months.

Now turn the process around and serve as the mentor to the person who just served as yours. Continue the eight-week process, with your partner calling you, and you tracking his or her answers and asking the what, how, and who coaching questions.

Timing: When You Receive Feedback Is as Important as the Feedback You Receive

After you've completed a large project, given an important presentation, or led a meeting, you may be inclined to drop everything and celebrate. This is certainly true for me! Over years of "taking the stage" for 45 minutes to 2 days at a time, facilitating discussions and off-site leadership meetings, I know how tempting it is to shout "We're done!" and move on. Resist the temptation, for this is a great time to collect valuable feedback.

Formal observation questionnaires are staples of most learning and development departments in the companies I consult with around the world. At the end of seminars, participants are asked to fill out these forms and rate such items as the materials, my presentation style, the length of the seminar, and the room and facilities. But there's much more to feedback than assessing, on a scale of 1 to 10, the quality of the presentation, the food, or the learning environment.

Therefore, I make it a point to talk with the participants personally. Often, a few will stay after a presentation to ask more questions. I listen in particular for those who say, for example, "Jason, that was a great presentation," or, "Thank you so much for the talk." When I hear one of those comments, I stop whatever I am doing, look the person in the eye, and ask, "What one piece of information you learned today will have the greatest impact on your performance, leadership, or productivity?"

After I ask the question, I listen attentively to the answer. The key is to encourage the individual to talk about his or her experience with the information. I find that people make valuable comments at such times, and talking with them about how it will impact their work style solidifies their commitment to making changes in their habits. This is *not* the time to defend or explain myself or argue with their comments. This is a time to listen and receive feedback from another person's perspective. And I always thank the person for sharing with me.

I like to write down what people tell me as soon after I hear it as possible, and then think about it more carefully later, when I get back to my office and begin planning the next presentation.

I also collect anonymous feedback via an online survey tool. Whether I send the link to a survey to 4 or 1,500 people, I find the information I receive shortly after a presentation to be incredibly useful. Even if there are only a handful of people in your network from whom you can ask for timely feedback, doing so in the form of an anonymous survey will make it easier for them to respond to you. It also gives you information you might not hear or see if you simply complete the project and move on.

An important question to ask yourself when it comes to the timing of feedback is, simply, *how?* How would you like to receive the information you've asked for? In person? In a digital format like e-mail or video? In a written document, accompanied by checklists of formula questions? Also, you'll probably want to change when you want to receive feedback depending on the kind (objective or subjective, informal or formal) you're seeking.

Key Ingredients of Effective Feedback

To effectively use the feedback you seek and receive so that you can engage more dynamically in the work you do, and do even more of it, you must do the following:

- *Identify specifics.* Moving from the subjective to the objective and identifying very specifically what you're doing, and could change, will give you feedback that will move you from "nice to know" to information you can use right away. Pay close attention when others offer you feedback. Ask questions, clarify responses and, if possible, brainstorm a plan of action to implement some of their ideas right away.

  One method I recommend to my clients, to help them most effectively specify the feedback they want to receive, is to write responses to the five W's: who, what, when, where, why? Do this and I think you will find the answers serve as prompts for coming up with an additional idea that you can work with in the coming weeks or months.
- *Raise the volume.* That's right, make it "louder." Write things down, track your experiences over time, ask people to give you feedback more than once; in short, do anything you can to heighten your

awareness and garner more useful information. Consider recording, either by writing it down or using a digital recording device, the feedback you receive as you receive it. Also, remind yourself about the feedback you're working with by posting it where you can see it regularly as you work.

Additionally, experiment with a single "focus word." Write it on a note card or sticky note and put it where you can see it while you're working. One of my clients who was working on a long-term project chose the word "pacing." He wrote it on a note card and put it directly above his keyboard on his desk. He said later that seeing that word reminded him that although the project was "far off," he needed to stop regularly and focus on what he could do in the near term so that everything went according to plan and he would complete the project on time (which he *did!*).

- *Clarify what you want.* You've doubtlessly noticed a recurring theme throughout this chapter: The value of the feedback you receive is directly proportional to the clarity of your request for it. To solicit and garner useful feedback, you must know precisely what you're seeking in the first place. Otherwise, any input you receive may be off-course, as the person you're seeking it from may not have understood exactly what you wanted.

There are several tools you can use to gather effective feedback. One is to print out the next 90-day check-in described earlier. Bring it to meetings with colleagues and/or friends, and ask for their insights about what they notice you doing over the past 90 days that is moving you closer to, or farther away from, where you want to be. Take time as well to review your "So that . . ." statements from the previous chapter, and pick one or two that you could work on in a mentor/mentee feedback program. Over a period of just eight phone calls, probably totaling less than a six-hour investment of time, you could have in hand some extremely valuable information you can use to go forward.

One of the most valuable benefits of this process is the change in focus you'll make. And that's the topic of the next chapter.

9

Improvement and Focus
The Resource That Affects All Others

As I SIT at my desk writing this chapter, my wife is in the other room talking with a client about an upcoming event. The sound of her footsteps through the room give away that she's on an important call—she usually paces when she's nervous. The conversation doesn't last that long, and I can tell when she's done because I hear her say aloud, "Phew! That was easier than I thought it was going to be!"

"What was that all about?" I ask. "What was easier than you thought?"

She explained that she had just been talking with the director of events at a local four-star resort. Jodi had called her to inquire if the hotel would be interested in hosting one of her upcoming Women's Business Socials, a monthly networking event she hosts for between 60 and 80 attendees. In the short conversation, Jodi didn't have to do any convincing. After she had detailed the benefits to the venue (e.g., a lot of people ordering from the menu and, subsequently telling others what a great time they had there), they agreed on the space, the date, and the time.

Over the past three years that Jodi has been planning these monthly gatherings to boost local business development among other women business owners, she's had her share of individuals show less interest than the woman she had just talked to. So, naturally, in preparation for this conversation, she had planned several "talking points," just in case she had to convince the manager to make space available on a Tuesday evening after work. "I was," she told me, "ready for just about any objection she could have given. Thing was, I didn't need to talk her into it!"

I smiled as she told me what she thought the conversation *would* be like, for it was exactly what I had been writing about the entire week: the significance of focus as it affects our performance, productivity, and ability to "make more." I've known some people to "focus themselves into a mess," and other people who are adept at using focus to reach ever higher levels of success.

"Why are you smiling like you know something?" Jodi wanted to know.

"Because I'm writing about the importance of staying focused on what we *want* to happen, and this is a perfect example for the book," I replied.

Beyond optimism and pessimism, hopeful and realistic, or glass half-full/half-empty thinking is what I call Directed Thinking. I describe it as *thinking toward what we want to be true.* This isn't simply positive thinking, hoping that something will happen the way you'd like. This is about directing your focus forward, taking action, and making things happen.

Throughout this book, you have read about and focused on several significant aspects of your productivity and workplace performance. Of them all, focus is the single most critical component to address when it comes to success—whether you're setting a pace to reach your goals, thinking about how you manage time, building your social network, or clarifying your "So that . . ." statements.

Focus is the one resource that, when compromised, can radically affect what we get done, how long it takes us to get things done, and how we feel once our day is over. A client once remarked, "Whatever I'm doing is amplified as I'm doing it." The significance, urgency, and scope of our tasks do seem as if they are the most important things *as we're doing them.* But, are they really?

Decide What You'll Do Then, Now

Imagine it is Tuesday morning when the phone on your desk rings. You glance at the clock—it's 9:37—and quickly check caller ID. You pick up and say hello, as it's a coworker you're scheduled to meet with shortly in the conference room. "Good morning," she says, "I just wanted to let you know that the meeting at 10:00 AM has been cancelled. We're not ready yet to make the presentation. I'm calling everyone to cancel, and I'll send a meeting invite as soon as we are ready to present our part of the project. Sorry about the late notice."

You hang up, look around, and immediately three thoughts occur. (I've been in offices large and small around the world and have observed this phenomenon firsthand, and so can say with confidence that these three things occur, in about this order, just about *every time* a meeting gets cancelled.)

1. Your first thought is "Woo hoo!" You indulge in a mini mental celebration as you realize you suddenly have an extra hour.
2. For those who work in a networked office, your second thought most likely is, "Hmm, I'm going to leave that meeting *on my calendar*, so nobody knows I'm free." When everyone can see everyone else's calendar, it is tempting to leave time blocked so that no one can replace a cancelled meeting with another one. (In fact, I have no doubt that some of you reading this have even put a *fake* meeting on your calendar from time to time just to block 30 minutes during the day when you can work on something important!)
3. The third thought, the one that gets you in trouble, and is directly related to the theme of this chapter, is: "Wow, a free hour. What should I do now?" This ambiguous (and, thus, often nonproductive) question jeopardizes your time management.

That third thought and open-ended query compromises your productivity. How? Because the moment you ask yourself such a question, you come up with answers—many of them. Think about the last time you had a free hour: What were the options you immediately came up with? Were any of these on your list?

- I'll go get a cup of coffee.
- I'll grab a bite to eat.

- I'll organize some of the piles on my desk.
- I'll walk over and talk to _____ about that other project we're working on.

  And, the most common one I've heard:
- I know; I'll just check e-mail really quick.

The moment you click on your inbox, your focus goes and your stress grows, as you proceed to delete, respond, forward, and file the messages you find there. You see names and subject lines, and suddenly your mind starts racing; all you can think of are the latest projects, the "loudest" issues, and the high-priority work that shows up. So you try to "clean things up." Before you know it, that extra hour is gone, and you're still running at the same pace you were before the meeting was cancelled. You're barely staying current, and now your focus is compromised, too.

Focusing on Making More

Remember, in Chapter 3, I shared this saying from a mentor of mine: "If you're waiting until you have time to decide what you'll do when you have time, you'll always run behind."

Making more—of whatever it is you'd like to make more of—will come down to your ability to manage, direct, and maximize your focus. Let me show you how.

Start by asking yourself: "What is a typical workday like?"

Can you count on meetings starting late or getting cancelled at the last minute? Do you generally have customers or colleagues requesting help (i.e., interrupting you) throughout the day? Do some of your coworkers seem to be "in it for themselves" when working on group projects? Understanding what is likely to disturb your focus during the day is a very telling way to realize just how fleeting your attention can be. And once you realize how precious your focus is, you can begin to implement ways to keep more of it to, and for, yourself!

- *What do you do during a typical day?* Think back on the activities you completed in Chapter 6. Those tracking exercises helped you realize that your routines and habits were probably established at another point in time, when you were doing different kinds of work. In fact, with all the tools and systems available to you now, there may be tasks you no longer have to think about; that is, you no longer have to focus on them to make them happen. Here and now, review and reflect on those. Your goal while reading this chapter is to be aware throughout the day how much *quality focus time* you have to do deep thinking, get important things done, develop new ideas, and build on the old ones.

If you work in a highly interruptive (e.g., competitive) environment, and you find yourself multitasking often, add just a few longer blocks of focus time to your calendar to block out the distractions and get some important work done. To begin experimenting with this practice, start with smaller chunks of time. Consider blocking just 20 to 30 minutes of the time you "get back" from the next five cancelled meetings, to focus on bigger projects. Get a timer and set aside some work on your desk so that when the next meeting is cancelled, you're ready to go!

- *How long do things* really *take, when you have all day?* Remember Parkinson's law, which I quoted in Chapter 7: "Work expands to fill the time available for its completion." Building on the previous point, try this workflow experiment: Make a plan for having an extended work session on one of your projects tomorrow. Identify an office you can go to and work in (or a conference room you can reserve) and schedule a 30-minute block of uninterrupted time. Be sure to keep that countdown timer nearby. When it's time to work for that block of time, instead of saying you'll work on the project "for a little while," write down, in no uncertain terms, what you will have done by the exact hour and minute of the coming day. Then set the countdown timer and go, Go, GO! Focus on completion—or, as I say in seminars: "Focus to finish."

- *How do you feel about the day, at the end of the day?* Have you noticed that you feel better when you get things done? Think about a day in the recent past when you left the office inspired, when you ended the day feeling just a bit "ahead of the game." I know what happens when I experience completion: I feel a boost in confidence, interest, and energy. I love the feeling of having finished something, whether it's an article, a triathlon, or a seminar. It's part of my own "I'm at my best when . . ."

I once worked with a client (a managing director at a firm in New York City) who had designed a great tracking system for the work she did. About a year after attending my "Mastering Workplace Performance" seminar, she and I met for lunch and talked about what she had implemented. She told me she had set up a weekly reminder on her calendar to help her focus on completion. Specifically, every Thursday afternoon, she stopped for one to two minutes and added her "big accomplishments" from the past week to an ongoing list in her time management system. It was a digital inventory that enabled her to synchronize it between her BlackBerry and Microsoft Outlook. That way, wherever she was, she could add to the inventory. Then, at the end of each month and quarter, she said, she'd stop and look back over what she'd finished, and feel good. The real win, however, was when she sat down at the end of the year to write her annual performance review. "Jason," she said proudly, "I just looked over my list of accomplishments, and I had it all there in one place!"

Your Fleeting Focus

It's probably safe to assume that no matter what you are doing right now, you have several (perhaps even *dozens*) of other ideas, projects, or tasks nagging at and distracting you. If you work in an office, there's always someone "right there" to compromise your focus. If you work at home, then the challenge may be to not distract yourself! Staying busy is becoming easier and easier. But, are you staying busy and focusing on the right things?

As an advisor, I often work with clients over a period of many months, meeting regularly for a day or two each month, to create, implement, and habitualize systems and processes to improve their performance and workflow. In the time we spend together, I am intent upon the "supergoal": to enhance focus and intention on effective workflow management. We work together to build effective habits of performance and productivity. Each habit requires a significant amount of focus and action.

Following are examples of typical activities that require focus during the course of a day. As you read them, consider making your own list of what *you* need to focus on at work (and, what deserves your focus at home).

- Opening a PDF on your computer or ereader.
- Scrolling through e-mails on your mobile device.
- Waiting for others to arrive at a meeting.
- Reviewing a document that was printed out for an upcoming meeting.
- Talking to someone who just walked over and asked, "Do you have a minute?"

And, usually, even while you are working on that *one* thing, there's something else waiting to grab your attention!

Let me give you an example of how fleeting focus can be while you're reading or doing research. Let's say you're at your office and you have a window of time, and you want to read a bit of the document you recently received in preparation for a project you're managing. You settle down in your chair and start to read. At one point, you realize you've gone through several paragraphs of the document and have *no idea* what you just read—nada, zip, zilch, zero return on the time you just invested. Does this sound familiar? This is what I'm talking about when I say that focus is a limited resource.

Think back to the prologue to this book: Did you begin to think about, focus on, what your own Ideal Day would include? Just getting you to focus on that, to encourage you to think deeply and then actually write down what "making more" would look, sound, and feel like to you might be worth the price of this book!

If you still haven't gone through the Ideal Day process, please, do so now. Give yourself the gift of your own attention. Write it down, look at it; ask for help from your friends, coworkers, and mentors to get started. You just might be surprised! A lot can happen when you focus on a direction you want to move in.

Before I talk about focus-to-finish in the next section, I have a quick question for you: "Do you talk to yourself?" Most of us experience the low murmur of a mental monologue constantly going on in our minds. I refer to this as Ping-Pong thinking. On the one hand, you're trying to stay focused on, say, reading this book; on the other, you're simultaneously entertaining random thoughts about all kinds of things that are coming at you and competing for your attention.

You probably already have realized that despite your effort to "manage time," being productive and getting things done is not really about managing *time*. It's not even what you *do* in time that you manage. I believe that what you manage is what you're *thinking about* in the time you have between now and the *next* thing you think about.

Remember: "If you're waiting until you have time to decide what you'll do when you have time, you'll always run behind."

Implementing a Focus-To-Finish Mind-Set

You've arrived home, have eaten dinner, and are about to sit down and _____ [watch TV, read a magazine, talk with your family/roommates, etc.]. But just as you're beginning to relax, you suddenly think, "Oh, wait, let me go to the next room and get the _____ [reading material, thing to show someone, notebook to write in, magazine or stack of bills to review, etc.].

You get up, walk to that other room, and suddenly stop: You can't remember *why* you are there!

Has this happened to you? Lately? Why does this happen? Are you losing your mind? Are you "focus-challenged?" A possible reason you can't remember why you've walked into a room when you just had a thought that took you there is that, on the way from one room to the next, even *more* things came to mind. And, not surprisingly, you don't remember why you got up in the first place—that is until you go back to the place where you had the thought that took you away. Talk about a time-waster!

Another way this plays out is that you'll think of someone to call, because you need to "go over" a few things. You make the call, talk for a while, end the conversation, hang up, and then minutes later remember that you forgot to tell the person something important. So, you wind up calling to interrupt him or her again!

I talk frequently with my executive coaching clients about the difference between *remembering* and *reviewing*. Those two verbs relate to different aspects of productivity and performance. If I force myself to try and remember something later, I may give it extra (too much?) attention. I may think to myself something like, "Don't forget, you need to . . ." Or, I may ask someone else to take responsibility to help me out: "Hey, will you remind me to _____ when _____?" Or, I may forget it altogether until hours or days (or weeks!) later.

If, however, I set up my systems and processes to "stop and think and 'bunch'," then I am able to review that idea, action, or reminder *only* when I can do it. In this way, I move closer to completion. This is why, by the way, I'm just as likely to send an e-mail to myself from my BlackBerry, or even take a picture of something with my digital camera. I'm reminding myself "there" what I was thinking while I was "here."

Now, let me explain what I *don't* do. If, while sitting on my sofa at home, I think about going to my office to get a book, I don't take out my notebook to write, "Get *Triathlon Training Log* from office," then get up, go to my library, and look at the reminder to find the book. But, if I were out to dinner with friends and the topic came up and I had that thought, I most likely would write it down so that I could review it later. This prevents me from wasting thought cycles thinking, remembering, and *rethinking* about that "thing" wherever I am. I operate with as much of a focus-to-finish mind-set as possible, which states:

Do as much as you can, with as much of your focus as you can, toward completion, in the next few minutes.

How much of your day do you spend interacting with other people? Bring to mind the past few meetings, phone calls, and hallway conversations you've had. Have you ended any of those by saying something like, "I'll get that information to you soon"? Walking away, what do you do next? As far as I can tell, there are two options:

1. *Stop and do.* Surely, some of the things you think of to do would take such little time that it just makes sense to complete them now, while you're already in a momentum-building and maintaining state. However, this kind of "think it/do it" approach to productivity makes for a very busy day and often results in getting a lot of the little things done while making minimal progress on the bigger issues. There are, however, days and times when it's appropriate to take this "do it now" approach; just know that it's most effective for smaller, less demanding tasks.

   It becomes a problem, however, when you stop every time you think of one of these quick tasks. I've seen clients justify filling their day, morning to night, working on things they can do in "just a couple of minutes." Then, when they end the day, they realize they didn't have the time they needed to do the deep thinking required to move forward on the important projects.

2. *Stop, think, and bunch, and* then *do.* When it comes to managing projects of any size and scope, be they professional or personal (writing a report, researching an event, planning a trip), it sometimes helps to "go vertical"; that is, focus in on everything having to do with that outcome for a period of time. One activity I ask clients to complete is what I call a "directed freewrite." To do this, take out a lined piece of notebook paper (or open a word processing program on your computer or tablet). Then, write down the first 60 (!) things that come to mind when you focus on that project. That usually takes only about 10 to 30 minutes. Afterward, scan the inventory looking for actions to take.

For example, you might capture 3, 7, or even 12 actions to take relevant to that project throughout the course of a day or week. Consider keeping a single page of your notebook (or a sticky note or a digital document) near where you're working. When you think of something else to do that pertains to a particular aspect of the project, simply add it to the list. Then, whenever you get a chance throughout the day, put a "fence" around your calendar for 30, 60, or 90 minutes when you'll work *only* toward that outcome.

There's a simple but incredibly valuable question you can ask whenever you're about to do something: "Can I finish what I start?" Of course, you might not be able to write the entire report, coordinate all the logistics, or manage all the pieces of a project in a single sitting, so it's important to pick a next milestone. For each piece of work and marker along the way, identify clear and objective goals.

Clear and Objective Goals

If you can't explain it simply, you don't understand it well enough.
—Albert Einstein

Let's take a look at the following definitions:

- *Clear*: Easy to perceive, understand, or interpret.
- *Objective*: Not influenced by personal feelings or opinions in considering and representing facts.

Now is a good time to revisit some of your bigger goals in light of your areas of interest and responsibility. Consider reviewing Chapter 7 on purpose, and the items you listed as your MITs, your Most Important Things.

Imagine the following scenario as an example of how we tend to misdirect our focus relative to our own professional and personal development: Most people spend a few hours toward the end of the year hastily collecting information and entering it into a form that they submit as their Annual Performance Review and/or Individual Development Plan (called different things by different companies). However, when this process is handled this way, and the end-of-the-year report ends up lacking or incomplete, you may experience negative consequences—not earning a promotion, not getting a raise, or failing to be recognized for all the work you did throughout the year.

Creating clear and objective goals requires more than this kind of a "rush job" when we do something once per year that may or may not lead to a personal and/or professional feeling of success. Setting appropriate-for-you goals also demands that you focus on the things that ultimately will make the biggest difference in your life, your work, and your world. Though goal setting is a common practice for many people throughout the world, it doesn't need to be a difficult or painful process—not if you concentrate on and work toward those goals effectively.

Commencing this process can be as simple as starting where you are—right here, right now—and focusing on what is true, what you're doing, and where you'd like to go. Instead of thinking you need to make up new, even bigger goals, begin by recalling your Most Important Things. Clarify ideas and actions for one or two of these that relate to the purpose you established in Chapter 7. Concentrate on an objective you anticipate achieving in the next 90 to 180 days.

I choose this three- to six-month time frame for a couple of reasons: (1) It is near enough that you can anticipate the work you will need to do, despite the fact that other things will clearly emerge during that period that either may help or distract you on your way to the goal; and (2) It is far enough in the future that you will be able to make noticeable progress, chipping away, working a little bit each week to achieve something big.

The following are examples of clear and objective goals I have set for myself:

- "I have published a 55,000-word manuscript that provides leaders with a handbook to improve. This book is designed to initiate thinking and conversations that equip readers with practices to make their best better, both in life and at work."
- "I have completed the September triathlon in Carpinteria, California, finishing in the top two and earning a medal for one of the fastest times in my age group. I raced smart, stayed healthy, and utilized my equipment efficiently and effectively."

Both of these are clear. I know exactly what "finished" looks like for each, and I included a little extra to give the goal some additional focus power. I can easily bring to mind that little extra while I'm writing the book or training for the triathlon, and use it to push further.

It's also important to note that I've written my goals in the past tense, as if I have already accomplished them. I have found this to be the easiest way to anticipate and plan toward successful completion. When I read my goals and see them as "done," I'm compelled to ask myself a few questions, such as:

- What surprised me about reaching that goal?
- Whom do I wish I had talked to sooner about that goal?
- What did I *not* need to do to reach that goal?
- What would I change now that I know what it took to achieve that goal?

When working with clients who are setting their objective goals, I listen to the vocabulary they use. Are they talking about the past, the present, or the future? Do they use more nouns or verbs? By stopping and focusing with all your attention on the clear and objective outcome toward which you are driving, you'll increase your chances of taking actions, meeting people, and finding information that will move you further, faster, toward your goal.

Stop "Should-ing" Yourself

If there's one thing I believe in very strongly, it's that we are better off when we don't constantly "should" ourselves. It's a negative experience that only clouds our focus and pulls us away from thinking about what we could be thinking about right now. I encourage you to start slow; don't go too fast with this philosophy. It can be hard to adjust your outlook and begin overnight to think this way. Consider the following statements, many of which have occurred to most people at one moment or another:

> "I wonder if I *should* read that book that my boss recommended; I really don't have the time."

> "I probably *should* sign up for that professional development program; it will probably take a year or so to earn the credential."

> "I keep seeing that new _____
> [fill in the blank with whatever "it" is]. I think I *should*
> _____ [buy it, borrow it, rent it, etc.]."

I initially started to reduce the amount of should-ing I did simply by taking notice of where and when I did it. In fact, during my years as a high school teacher, one whole page of my quarterly notebook was dedicated to the "shoulds." On the top of each page, I wrote, "I think I should . . ."; and I continued to add to the list over the years I taught. I remember such items as:

I think I should . . .

- Get my doctoral degree.
- Apply for the department chair position.
- Write a new course for business students.
- Ride my bicycle to school more often.

I had written down so many of these statements over time that I remember feeling anxious simply looking over the list. Then I started experimenting with various methods to reduce the "shoulds."

Using the same ideas I share with you in Chapter 3, on time management and working smarter, I began to reign in the number of things

I thought I *should* do—things that I only continued to ponder as time went by. I did this by stopping what I was doing to truly reflect on—not just dance around—one "should" at a time. I paused long enough to attach an action step to it. That was all.

I remember when I was deciding whether to pursue a doctoral degree, I invited a senior mentor in my district to meet for coffee before school one morning (at 6:30!) to talk it over. In the span of 30 minutes, she gave me her attention, asked me questions and, provided me with some feedback to make it easy for me to decide that it wasn't something I wanted to do—at least not *that* decade.

For example, let's say you've been told about a book you should read (or a seminar you should attend, or a new gadget you should buy); before you make a "go/no-go" decision, do a little more research. Here are some ideas:

- *Search the Internet.* I know, it sounds basic; but a few extra search terms help me get some of the information I need easily, quickly, and (generally) for free.
- *Watch a video, listen to a podcast, or read a book* by someone who has experience with the matter you're considering.
- *Invite a friend or mentor* to lunch and ask a direct and meaningful question. Asking honest questions—and receiving the absolute truth in return—saves *so* much time.

These kinds of focus activities make it easier to decide whether to say yes or no, whatever the situation or question. Either way, you'll save time and get engaged faster in making your ideas happen, because you'll be one step closer to moving your focus away from "Should I?" to "How *can* I?"

Distract–ology: Studying What Gets in Your Way

When I was in high school, I asked one of my teachers what an "-ology" was, since we were studying biology and I had other classes like psychology and sociology. I remember the other kids laughing, but I really wanted to know! Her response: "It's the study of something."

I like that, and I think about it often. I also make up words whenever I want. For example, *work-ology*, *meeting-ology*, even *triathlon-ology* are all subjects I've enjoyed studying and learning about. It seems that the more I understand the fundamentals of performance, the easier it is to make the more important things happen. It's kind of like when I'm getting ready for a triathlon: That morning, I always spend time . . .

Oh, wait a minute: I got *distracted*! Back to the topic of this chapter—focus.

See how easy it is to lose it? It can be extremely helpful to discern exactly what it is that gets in the way of your focus. Identify what is blocking your ability to give all of your attention to what needs your attention. Once you have this inventory, you can begin to make subtle changes so that you wind up getting more done, in less time, at a higher level of quality.

Remember, there are 168 hours in a week, and just 96 15-minute blocks of time in a day. Recall what you learned in Chapter 6 on tracking. How you currently use (or misuse, or *don't* use) your time is your *normal*; remember, that's what we call homeostasis. As you can imagine, it's often easier to keep on doing what you're doing. But if you're going to get a different result, you're going to have to—you know what's coming, right?—do something different!

Of course, you don't want to try to change everything at once. I look for what I call the "big two" when I'm coaching clients. Together, we uncover just two common interruptions or distractions that are getting in the way of their getting more important work done each day. My goal is to minimize the kinds of distractions in my clients' work world that can easily pull them away from doing the meaningful, important, prioritized work they need to get done.

These distractions fall into two categories: (1) *visual* and (2) *auditory*. If you can minimize these, you may find that you're using your hours and minutes more effectively—and indeed improving your work while remaining focused on completion. In this way, you'll maximize your focus.

Visual Distractions

What do you see when you look around the area where you're reading this right now? Are there papers piled high on your desk or tacked to your cubicle wall? Do you have sticky notes on your computer monitor? Is the red light on your BlackBerry blinking, reminding you there's a message? Visual distractions can so significantly affect some people's productivity that they resort to tricks and "hacks" to get more work done. (One of my clients actually put a piece of black electrical tape over the blinking light on the phone on his desk!)

During the corporate programs I present for companies, I plan the day accordingly, to take advantage of focus and visual distraction. I use the room, the desk and table setups, the workbook and materials, and the presentation itself to provide changes to the visual stimuli while maintaining a focus on the theme of the program.

While you're working at your desk, sitting in a meeting, or even traveling (by plane or train or car), reflect on the power of visual stimuli and what it does to add to or detract from your productivity. Then, over a period of days, work to minimize the visual distractions and experiment with an increase in focus while you're taking on certain tasks.

Auditory Distractions

What sounds distract your focus when you hear them? Working in an open-plan office on a big floor or in close proximity to other people is especially challenging for people who are easily distracted by sound.

Years ago, Jodi and I realized that whereas I'm an extremely visual worker, she's the opposite; she's very auditory. We know this about each other and work accordingly in our offices: I schedule phone calls while she's away at appointments, and she shows me checklists of what she wants to talk about before we sit down to discuss it. We've come to know extremely well how the other person works best.

■ ■ ■

Distractions and interruptions can fool us into thinking we're being productive. Too often we get to the end of a day and say, "I was busy all day today, but what did I do?" Many times, the answer is "not much!" Now is the time to pick just one of those things that distracts you. Turn off dings, alarms, notification alerts, popups, and the like. Make these seemingly subtle changes, work for a week, and see what happens. If your focus improves, along with the quality of your work, then continue to do more of it!

The Significance of Perspective and Performance

When I lived in Mexico City many years ago, I regularly took weekend trips to the pyramids at Teotihuacan. I'd go out for the day, walk along the main street, eat a picnic lunch, and often, climb to the top of the Pyramid of the Sun. I knew what that pyramid looked like from the perspective of standing at the bottom, climbing the stairs up it, and standing on the top.

Then, one day, my perspective changed; rather, it was changed because of something I saw. Someone sent me a picture taken from a hot air balloon a few hundred feet above the pyramid and, suddenly, I was looking at it in a completely different way. From that viewpoint, I was looking *down* on the pyramid; I could see the line of people climbing to the top, and where the structure was placed along the avenue built hundreds of years ago. I remember thinking, "Wow, there is more to that than I thought." It was a very significant learning experience for me, about understanding the power of focus—and changing focus—on the process and product of workplace performance.

I tell this story to share the significance of perspective relative to focus and productivity. Your point of view—the assumptions, beliefs, and attitudes you bring to your goals—can radically affect the odds of your achieving these goals. It's not just about positive thinking; it's about directing your focus in the direction you want. What you focus on, and choose *not* to focus on, has a direct impact on what you will achieve.

Think back to Chapter 5 on building your social network. Developing your team requires that you assemble a group of people who are going to help you get from "here" to "there." Sharing your ideas, challenges, and opportunities with these individuals invites them to share their viewpoints—and easily add to the perspective from which you view this collection of goals. (A word of caution here: You want to be careful about the people with whom you share your goals, as well as *how much* you share about your plans. Some friends and colleagues can have such a strong perspective about what *cannot* be done that they can cloud your vision of what *can* be.)

Why a Short Memory Is Key to an Elevated Focus

What might keep you from doing something great today? Remembering something you *didn't do* yesterday.

As simple as that thought is, I have seen how people's memories can be strong impediments to their performing well on a particular day. When people are expending all of their energy recalling everything they have to do, they're less apt to focus fully on what's right in front of them. I've had people tell me, "Jason, I can't put any more information into my mind. I already have too much to think about."

Long ago, I realized that using short-term memory is a key to elevating one's focus. I personally support thinking longer thoughts and spending more time—seconds, minutes, even hours—immersed in a single problem, challenge, or opportunity. When I can spend that much time concentrating on one topic, I get more done, at a higher level of quality, and I rarely have to redo my work later on.

In order to maximize this kind of limited mental recall, you'll have to utilize some kind of personal management system. I mean, what happens when (not if!) you think of something for project B while you're working on project A? People use many tools to keep track—to-do lists, personal calendars, note pads, and sticky notes posted on their computer monitor, the refrigerator door, or even, as I've seen several times in my coaching work, stuck in a wallet or a purse. I'm not suggesting you work on a *smaller* number of projects, think of *fewer* ideas, or agree to do *less* than you're currently doing. What I am suggesting is that more ideas come to you every day than you can possibly manage to accomplish. So take them a few at a time: Write these ideas down, reflect upon them, and choose the ones you want to engage in most. In other words, focus on the ones you *can* do, and put aside those you can save for later.

In short, use your mind to create new ideas, develop old ones, and prioritize those you're contemplating right now. Don't use your brain power to constantly remember and remind yourself about what you "need to do."

Three Decisions That Change Your Focus

There are three decisions you need to make, almost simultaneously, about any new piece of information, item in your inbox, or idea that pulls at your focus:

- Me or them
- Now or later
- Track or trust

Me or Them

The first thing you need to decide is whether *you* are the best person to do whatever it is that you're pondering. You might be better off asking someone else to do it for you. Of course, not everyone has someone to whom they can delegate work. If this is the case with you, think about the fact that there's likely a system or tool that can do the work for you, or help you do it. For example, while doing research for this book, I introduced myself to many people, seeking stories, anecdotes, or quotes on making a person's best even better. One way I did this was to send messages via LinkedIn.com. I picked several people in my network to message simultaneously, which saved me a lot of time and effort. I also made use of a news clipping service (Google Alerts) that sends me daily e-mail digests for key words I define that are mentioned in the news, on websites, or in blog posts.

Now or Later

Chances are while reading this book something I wrote made you think, "I could be doing that"—that is, something else. If you did not stop reading, put the book down, and go do that immediately, it means you opted to do it later. My question is: How do you remind yourself about this "thing" that you want to do later? I'm not advocating now over later, or vice versa; I don't believe that one is necessarily better than the other. I'm simply asking you to focus on the decisions you tend to make in terms of particular conflicts.

If you stop *now* to do something—at the very moment it occurs to you—you're likely to break the focus and momentum you set while doing whatever you were doing. If, on the other hand, you stay focused on doing what you were doing, you run the risk of that idea distracting you repeatedly—or, at the other end of the spectrum, escaping your mind completely.

Track or Trust

This leads me to the next question: Do you track the idea—write it down, send yourself an electronic message, insert a bookmark? Or, do you *trust* that you will remember to do it, and therefore decide not to make a note of the idea that crossed your mind?

I have worked on this track-or-trust methodology for over a decade. My clients realize repeatedly that they trust themselves, and those around them, to remember such things too often. Tracking your tasks or projects from formation to completion makes it easier for you to focus on what you're doing *while* you're doing it.

The Real Reason to Focus on Completion

Hint: It's not to achieve the goal.

Try to recall a time when someone asked you, "So, what are your goals?" Maybe it was during your last employee performance appraisal, or during a recent dinner with a good friend. Perhaps it was when you graduated from college, or when you applied for your job.

How did you respond? Did you talk about something you did, were or are doing, or wanted or still want to do? And did you talk about the goal as if reaching it were the most important thing to you? If you believe that reaching that goal is that important, I ask you to sit back, read along, and consider the following.

Goals do more than pull us toward some future reality. They give us more than a target at which to aim. They are more important than giving us a picture of what "there" might look, sound, and feel like.

Goals make us change what we do *today*. With a strong goal, a clear objective, and 10 to 15 minutes of time to focus, you just may be able to move much farther, much faster, than you thought possible.

Think about a current goal. Bring one to mind—better yet, write one down on a piece of paper or whiteboard in your office. Now, consider the 5 or 15 or 85 things you might need to do to make that goal a reality. These may well be single tasks (e.g., send a press release to the local newspaper) or a subproject (e.g., organize catering for the opening party); whatever the case, you'll probably come up with a long list of things to do. Now, let's say the due date (or submission date or event date) is 180 days away. You have just six months to get everything together.

Consider a goal that is clearly and objectively defined, such as: "Present the release of *Your Best Just Got Better* to at least 30 CEOs, founders, and senior executives working in partnership with the

Ventura Ventures Technology Center (V2TC) at a book talk and book signing event by February 1."

Now, if I look at that goal regularly and ask myself a single question, I know that I will automatically shift what I am focusing on that day. The question I ask is: "What small, easy-to-do action can I take today that will get me closer to that goal?" My focus goes from "Wow, there's *so* much to do to make that happen!" to "Well, I could review the flyer used by the last author who spoke at the V2TC and brainstorm ideas for my own."

Goals are good; a change in focus is even better!

Years ago, a mentor of mine said to me, "When you label something, when you give it a name, you can focus on it with more intention." I have found this to be true, especially in regard to goals that are more subjective or ambiguous. I had once set a goal to "get in better shape." Sure, I had an idea in the back of my mind what that might mean (based on the fact that I felt I was "kinda" in shape during my college years). Then, one day, everything changed; I bought a brand-new pair of pants that were just one size smaller than the ones I had recently purchased. I put them in my closet and for several weeks made a point to try them on every Saturday. I had given one aspect of my goal a very clear endpoint; this way, I would know when I reached the milestone of "fitting into a smaller pant size." I worked consistently to achieve that outcome.

And then one day it happened: The pants fit! Since then, I've used this technique to manage our company's product releases, develop new training materials, and acquire new clients. For example, I've printed out e-mails from people that contain messages with notions to which I aspire. My day changes vastly for the better when I see and read and think about them.

What is pulling *you* forward? It's some kind of goal. An outcome. A desire. A wish. Call it what you will; but when we have something we'd like to be true, our focus moves to that place. The trick is to use those thoughts as both magnets that are pulling you toward that future, and filters that help you avoid what gets in the way of achieving that future. A completely defined, clear, and objective goal has one more benefit: In addition to getting you where you want to go, it helps you say no to the things that *keep you from getting there*.

As I've mentioned before, one of the areas I address in my client consultations is "having too much to do and not enough time to do it in." What helps you to say no? How do you know what to say no to?

The easiest way I know to determine when to say no to an incoming opportunity is to weigh it against how much it will help me achieve one of my clear and objective goals. If it doesn't align with my prequalified intentions, I take it off the list! You want to build practices that lead toward success, and that's the topic of Chapter 10.

10

Improvement and Practice

Practice Doesn't Make Perfect, It Makes Comfortable

IN CHAPTER 1, I asked you to think about the Nike slogan, "Just Do It," and then I suggested that when it comes to professional development you instead focus on this idea: "just get started." The approaches to workplace performance and personal improvement I presented throughout the book are designed to answer this question: "How can I *just get started* today?"

I consider the ultimate achievement in "making more" to be identifying, building, and sustaining new practices that will help you make your best even better—better in work, in life, for yourself, and for others.

Recently, someone asked me, "Jason, what is your intention in publishing this book?" I replied, "I sincerely hope that people think about what they have to do, *and* do the things they are thinking about!" I believe *that* is a key to success.

Think.

Do.

Think more.

Do more.

I've been a proponent and practitioner of iterative change for many years. I know that the actions you repeat with purpose and focus will support you in achieving more in life and work; you'll experience more, notice more, give more and enjoy more.

I wrote *Your Best Just Got Better: Work Smarter, Think Bigger, and Make More* for *you*, to support your continued movement toward positive and sustainable change. Now it is time to study the power of practice. As you read this chapter, take the opportunity to think about what you're going to do, and build practices to do the things you're thinking about.

When Do Most People Practice?

When I started studying this topic, I "accidentally" found a book called *Mastery*, by George Leonard. (I put accidentally in quotes because I believe in that old saying "When the student is ready, the teacher appears." That is what happened to me!) Have you ever finished reading a book and immediately returned to page one to start reading it again? That is what I did with this book. I've read it again since then, and every time I think about it I ponder the levels of learning the author describes. Growing—that is, becoming better and better over time—requires that we go through natural cycles of practicing, learning, and getting better at what we do.

When you think of the word "practice," what images come to mind? Are they positive memories? Did you enjoy what you practiced? Maybe you learned to play a sport as a child, and went to after-school practice. Or, perhaps, you took music lessons, and had to repeat scales and chords over and over again until they became part of your "muscle memory." Today, do you still practice the skills you're learning?

In my own professional and personal experiences, I have found that as most people settle into their routines, managing the multiple complexities and priorities of their professional and personal lives, they make less time for practice. Sure, they may learn how to do something, but do they return to the fundamentals and practice them? Without taking this too far, think about the time you spend:

- Practicing typing on your laptop keyboard
- Practicing a foreign language

- Practicing listening while observing communication preferences and nuances
- Practicing writing for impact and action

That list could go on and on; and if you and I were talking right now, I know we'd come up with 5 or 10 things that you might consider practicing. Problem is, you're busy! Who of us takes time to practice something if simply by learning a little bit about it we know we can "get by," get our work done and move on to the next thing? I've had people tell me that typing with two fingers is just as fast for them as typing the "correct" way they were taught in school. I've heard people say, "I learned that language when I was in school, but I just don't use it now so I don't need to practice it."

I'm asking you to practice. Take the opportunity to review the chapters of this book and pick some exercises from them you'd like to practice. For example, take one of the first activities I introduced, way back in Chapter 1. There, you drafted an "I'm at my best when . . ." inventory. Many people I work with tell me it was pretty easy for them to write down a few things. Was it easy for you? Have you practiced looking at that list each morning? Have you practiced doing some things you wrote on it?

I continue to review my own "at my best when" list several times each week:

"I'm at my best when I eat a balanced breakfast in the morning."

"I'm at my best when I end the day reflecting on action and contribution."

"I'm at my best when I acknowledge someone for something he or she did to move the mission forward."

I've always said, "Practice on the small things so you can perform on the big ones." If you're ready to take your productivity to a new level, identify a new practice and incorporate it into your day. Here's how.

Start Where You Are and Grow from There

Start with this question: "What gets in the way of my ability to just get started?"

As you let your mind wander, consider the things that are on your to-do list, your "honey-do" list, or your "bucket" list. Are you waiting to "get around to" some of those things until you know *what* to do? When you practice "practicing," you're admitting that there is room to grow, room to go, and a new level to reach.

In order to build new practices and begin implementing these ideas, you're going to have to back up, all the way to the beginning. You need to be willing to be a beginner again! Recall a time in your life when you learned a new skill; maybe when you learned to ride a bicycle, wrote your first lines of computer code, gave a large-group presentation, or took up a hobby in your free time. What were the efforts you had to make early on in the process in order to get better? What did you need to do to *enjoy* it more?

Practice.

Be wary of your focus and your actions when it comes to practice. Since the beginning of this book I have encouraged you to "just get started." You may recall Yoda, the sage Jedi master of the *Star Wars* movies, saying, "Do or do not. There is no try." You need to be prepared to venture toward a new practice, whether or not you'll ultimately make a habit out of it, in order to *know* whether there is value in incorporating it as a new habit. Trying something new means that you've probably thought about it, researched or planned a bit toward it, and that you're going to be a beginner at whatever this particular endeavor may be.

Seeking out opportunities to be a beginner is one way to practice the small things and get ready to perform on the big ones. When you *do* decide to experiment with something—for example, by utilizing the TeamMap you drew to identify your social network in Chapter 5—it will be most helpful to pick something relatively minor that you can do *and* observe on a daily basis.

A Beginner's Mind-Set

I wrote earlier about my mentor Jim Polk. He's living an incredible life, and he's shared a lot of what he's learned with me through story and example. A few years ago, he invited me and Jodi, and our dog Zuma, to join his family for a visit to their Lake Tahoe property for a few days. He even flew us there in his own private plane! I remember talking with him the day before the journey—I was so excited about *not* having to go through the Los Angeles International Airport security measures to board a plane!

He asked, "Jason, have you been watching the weather throughout central California?" I thought I was prepared for this trip: I knew Jim was flying us to Truckee, and had packed my suitcase for summer on the lake; but, no, I hadn't been watching the weather reports.

He told me that he had been tracking the weather throughout the state over the past week or so. He explained that when he had learned to fly many years ago, his flight instructor told him to keep track of the weather each day of the week before he was going to fly, along the flight path he was planning to take, and at about the same time. This gave him a way to visualize the conditions he might face "up there," as well as prepare him for the next lesson. I was learning from Jim—again. He demonstrated what it is like to hold on to a beginner's mindset, and the value of continuing to practice through time.

Jim continues to practice. Even though now he is a seasoned pilot, and he's logged hundreds of hours in flight, he is still willing to practice those basic lessons he learned a long time ago.

Intuitively, you probably know you need to start practicing something. Use any one of the ideas from the three parts of this book—*Work Smarter*, *Think Bigger*, and *Make More*—to initiate the processes of observation and action. Choose an area in which you'd like to improve, and just get started! Maybe it's the way you use your mental focus, or how you receive feedback. Perhaps you'd like to manage your time better, or track some of the things that are getting in the way of building the career and life you'd like to enjoy. As you read the rest of this chapter, determine what specific actions you can take that will help you get started.

One important note before you get started: You're *not* saying, "From now on, I absolutely commit to do X, Y, or Z, *no matter what*." For every practice you consider, try it out for just five days, and *then* give yourself the freedom to say, "No, that's not working for me right now."

My only request: Please go through an *objective* and *qualified* experimental period for each practice. If you're going to do something daily, do it with full focus and a directed mind-set for those five days. If you're going to try something once a week, schedule it, quantify it, and stick to it for five weeks. Doing something five times won't necessarily make it a habit, but it may provide enough information and experience to let you know whether it *should* become a habit!

Practice Makes . . .

When I was young, as I've said before, my family, teachers, and coaches told me, "Practice makes perfect." Whether I was training with a sports team or learning a musical instrument or foreign language, I remember thinking that I would master it if I could just do it over, and over, and over, and *over* again.

I truly believed that if I practiced "enough," I would get better at it, whatever "it" was at the time. What I discovered, however, was that when I did practice something over and over again, it *did* become perfect; trouble was, I did it "perfectly" right or *wrong*, exactly as I'd practiced it!

For example, do you have a friend who has "perfected" the art of always being late, someone who is so good at rushing through projects and getting things done at the last minute that he or she has established an identity as a "procrastinator"? This person has, essentially, become an expert at putting things off until "later," perfecting an ability to perform only in the stress of the undone.

The easiest way I know to *get started* doing things differently is to begin *slowly*, and practice with incredible intention and deliberate focus. It's far better to take on just one new idea and spend precious energy and focus on it *every day* for a week than to spontaneously decide to make several big changes, only to give up on them in 48 hours. Practice doesn't necessarily make perfect. Practice will, however, make your repeated actions more comfortable.

Practice Makes Familiar

Each year for the past 12, I have presented over 100 live presentations in front of audiences as small as 5 and as large as 2,000. I've facilitated leadership workshops in executive boardrooms, led courses in corporate training rooms, and spoken in more hotel ballrooms than I can count. Whenever possible, I practice certain actions to make those events less complicated and increase the likelihood they'll go well. For example, if I can I like to spend time the day before a presentation walking around the room in which I'll be working. I like to know as much as I can about the physical space I'll be in. I look at how high the ceiling is, and how far away the first and last rows are from the front of the stage. I even practice speaking out loud to hear what my voice will sound like in the space.

Preparing—*practicing*—in this way makes it a little more comfortable for me. This rehearsal also removes some of the complexities of walking into a meeting room for the first time just minutes before I'm scheduled to begin. Often, I will see something I can incorporate later (a plaque with the company's mission statement on the wall, for example) that I may have missed had I walked in the next morning at the same time as the participants.

Another practice of mine is to prepare for triathlons. Race season spans April through October. I race once per month. I train year-round, and I spend a month before each event reviewing the racecourse map and visualizing it daily in detail. If possible, I drive the racecourse, or even bike and run the course in advance of race day. I've competed in some races every year for the past 10 years, and *I still do this rehearsal!* It makes it easier to see useful (and/or important) information when I am there "practicing." It is also a good way to focus on the upcoming event without the added stress brought on by race-day energy.

Reading this book and thinking about all the ways you can make your best better has led you to answer some big questions, in particular *why* and *what* you want to do. Now it's time to answer the question that will enable you to take off and soar: *How?* How are you going to do all of this? How will you take the ideas and match them to actions? Perhaps more importantly, how will you make those ideas and actions stick? How can you sustain these changes once you make them?

It's much easier to know how you're going to do "it all" when you start practicing something small, with your focus at a serious degree of intention. This gives you an opportunity to pay attention to what *has* your attention.

Practice Makes Comfortable

Think back to Chapter 6, on tracking, as those ideas relate to your productivity and practices. When you measure your activities, you can get a very clear and objective view of what's normal for you, what's comfortable, and what you accept as "just the way it is." As I shared earlier, a teacher of mine many years ago taught me that once I named something, I could study it from a different perspective; that once I had built a level of familiarity, I might see it differently.

So let's start by naming the comfortable routines, habits, and actions that most of us have practiced to habit. Do you have a habit of arriving late to meetings? Do you put important projects off until the last minute? To change these kinds of habits, to establish a "new normal," you must start practicing something new.

How? Make the experiment objective, and believable! Here are two examples relevant to the habits just described:

- "I'm going to track the exact time I arrive at the next five meetings."
- "I will take time at the end of each day to write down the action steps I took related to a large project that's due six weeks from now."

It's crucial to remember that the first part of adopting a new practice is to simply notice what you've considered comfortable up to now. Once you see it you can slowly start to change it. Though it may take longer to see actual outward change this way, when you eventually *do* see a different behavior—arriving to meetings on time or early, starting large projects weeks before they are due—chances are high that the changes you make will stand the test of time.

What does it feel like to practice? It feels slow and deliberate, two very important aspects of instituting and maintaining change.

Writing teachers will often ask their students to write an entire scene of a story, including dialogue, description, and narration, with their "nondominant hand." Lucia Capacchione's book, *The Power of Your Other Hand*, is full of writing prompts, scientific explanations, and further resources on this topic. For those of us who have a creative aspect to our jobs (design, coaching, inventing, managing, etc.), one that requires us to evaluate a project's multiple angles at the same time, writing with our *other* hand does something quite important: It slows us down. That's right; and as we write with our opposite hand, we tend to use different words, say things in different ways—and, most important—stop and think *while* we're writing. It's a very different process than seeing the words just seem to appear on a computer monitor, that's for sure.

How do you make a new behavior more comfortable? You experiment. You try it once, and then you reflect upon it. You try it again, and you tweak it. Then, you do it one more time. Again, if you repeat something in a focused state for five days in a row, the chances are high that you'll have the information you need to decide whether or not to continue doing it, whatever "it" is. You make things more comfortable by being more comfortable making those things. Make sense?

Of course, it is inevitable that you'll face outside challenges and internal changes that will affect the practices you incorporate over time.

Practice Makes Habit

Here is my coaching philosophy: "Think about what you have to do, and do something you're thinking about." To me, that sums up the entire process of *practice*. Think, and then go do; and then think again. If practice makes habit—and *you* are the arbiter of that as a working hypothesis—what do you want to start practicing? Which habits would you like to become (more) comfortable, so that they become part of your normal routine?

Once you have named the practices you have already perfected, you'll probably have to admit that they *are* habits. Good or bad, helpful or not, your habits are what got you here. Look around you now; notice that where you're sitting, the sounds you're hearing, and the things you can see were all created as a result of your day-to-day routines—your habits.

Routines are established via repeated action and positive feedback. Your actions *do* speak louder than your goals. Over the course of my coaching programs with clients, which run 10 months, we focus on the actual, describable behaviors these individuals want to improve. Month after month, we identify new actions they can take to significantly change the results they achieve, one habit at a time.

One client told me, "I've got to get better at recognizing when the people on my team are at the edge of being overworked, so that I can step in before they burn out." I was fully aware going into coaching this client that the practices we were going to use would take months to identify, study, implement, and assess. Truth was, he had established some pretty deep-rooted habits that were getting in the way of his stated goals, such as sending e-mails after midnight and on the weekends, and delegating work tasks on Friday afternoons. We addressed these habits by implementing two new practices:

1. We talked about how he could use electronic and paper-based reminder and tracking systems. Because his team was "trained" to keep their mobile messaging devices nearby "at all times," when my client e-mailed his team members late at night, they interpreted it as work. To address this, he created as part of his organizational system a note feature, built in to his smartphone, where he could put down his thoughts and ideas relative to people and projects. Several times a day he would review that inventory and move many things forward, in fewer conversations. Using this technique, he was able to cut down the number of times he and his team members interrupted each other, while improving the quality and timeliness of the more important conversations they had. (I talk about this more, later in this chapter, when I explain how to "maximize interruptions.")
2. My client and I also discussed scheduling 90 minutes of "think time" each week. He opted to put two "meetings" on his calendar, Tuesday midafternoon and Thursday midmorning; each for 45 minutes. The focus for these time blocks was to review two of his main areas of work: the short to midterm product launches he was responsible for managing and the next 7 to 10 days on his calendar. Specifically, I encouraged him to take on a role of "forecaster."

    The goal was to come up with work he could hand off to his team on Tuesdays and Thursdays, and practice getting ahead of the curve. Over time, he was sending out fewer "Friday fire drills" (that's what they were called around his office), and his team was able to spend more focused time working on the events, projects, and products he assigned them.

Practice on the Small Things to Perform on the Big Ones

I repeat this one mantra the most in all of my work: "Practice on the small things." I am confident that working from this mind-set has saved me time, energy, focus, and even money on occasion. I continue to practice on the small things so I'm prepared to perform well on the bigger and more important ones. Whether in my personal life or professional career, I've been able to decide where I'm heading and identify small, repeatable efforts that build comfort and consistency.

By testing the changes I have planned to make on smaller projects and with local clients, for example, I have been able to shorten the learning curve and increase the impact of the practices I've undertaken. Then, I take on larger projects (like this book) and market to bigger clients (like global manufacturing firms).

One area where my practice has become comfortable is with workplace performance technology and professional productivity systems and apps. I commit to testing them before I teach or coach my clients. For example, I presented several live webcast videos to my friends and family before ever using them with clients. I wrote and produced training videos for my friends on topics of interest to me before building a digital learning program for corporations.

When you make the leap to practice something new, you move from a passive state to an active one. You're engaging both attention and intention on a direction, and are willing to declare a destination while knowing that change may occur on your way from here to there.

Where to Begin: Examples of Client Practices

Practicing on the small things is much more than a nice idea; it is a philosophy and methodology that works. Consider some of the habits and routines that affect your productivity and that could (or should!) be different. What would your work and personal life look like, for example, if you said no more often, were interrupted less, presented yourself in meetings more effectively, and improved your overall professional skills? The following are just a few areas where other people have decided to start practicing, along with some ideas of what you can do, starting this week:

1. Saying no
2. Maximizing interruptions
3. Managing meetings
4. Practicing accountability

1. Saying No I worked with a client who had labeled herself "the perpetual yes person." (Her words, not mine.) It was obvious during our time working together that her team and clients were used to hearing yes whenever they asked her to take on more work. It was also obvious that her to-do list was way out of control because of all the things she had agreed to do for other people.

She claimed that the one thing she'd learned since her promotion to manager was that it was important to say no more often, but admitted that she didn't know *how*. As we discussed this idea, it became apparent to me that she had not practiced on the small things yet. She told me she once said no to a meeting request about a project that was months in the making; but when her boss got wind of her refusal, he expressed concern about her willingness to act as a team player.

We decided she should practice saying no to smaller—much smaller—things. We started by updating and collating her to-do lists into one, long master list, and then reevaluated each item, one by one. Her goal: renegotiate and say no to at least 1 out of every 10 items. Next, she wrote out a script that I encouraged her to practice for a week before she used it. Here is what she wrote:

> I understand what you're asking me for, and unfortunately I'm completely booked this week. If you can wait, I'll be able to look at what you're asking me for next week. Or you can ask someone else to help you in the meantime.

Chances are, you're looking at that script and responding to it in one of several ways:

"Yeah, but you don't know my job."

"Yeah, but you don't understand how the people around me work."

"Yeah, but you don't know that I just got my job."

"Yeah, but you haven't met the people I work with."

This is *exactly* why we practice on the small things. After my client had practiced her script (and had let her group know that she was, indeed, working on her "overcommitment" issue), I challenged her to use the statement just once per week. It was a small experiment that gave her complete freedom to choose when to apply this technique.

I will remember the call I got from her for the rest of my life. It was early afternoon when my mobile phone rang; the woman on the other end was speaking quickly and very excitedly. "Jason, it worked. It *worked*! I can't believe it worked."

For a moment, I had to think, "Who *is* this?" but then I recognized her voice and smiled. It had been almost a month since we had started working together, and she wanted to let me know she had just used the script with someone who had asked her for assistance on a project. She knew it was time to experiment, so she explained to this individual that she wasn't able to give any attention to the project that week. She then suggested he ask someone else on the team for assistance, since the deadline was approaching soon.

She paused for a moment, and then said, "And you know what he said, Jason? Do you know what he said? He said, 'Yeah, you're right. I bet John has time for this.' And he turned and walked away. Just like that, I had regained a couple of hours in my schedule that week. This is going to work!"

I was smiling ear to ear as I hung up the phone.

Practicing saying no does not mean that you have to shut your door and make yourself entirely unavailable to your team, friends, or family. It simply means that you become aware of what you commit to, and choose very wisely when you can gently decline to become involved in something else that will pull you away from the important work.

2. Maximizing Interruptions Another negative workplace productivity influence is the constant stream of interruptions that scatter our focus all over the place during any given day. A recent *Harvard Business Review* report estimates that individuals lose an average of 96 minutes of productivity each day to interruptions, which equals roughly 8 hours per week, or 32 hours each month. I know you cannot eliminate *all* interruptions, but you can practice maximizing them.

Yes, I do mean *maximize*. Over the years, you've probably tried to reduce the number of times people interrupt you in a day. Well, now it's time to maximize each interruption. Here's how I do this. When I need to interrupt someone, whether by phone or in person, I:

1. Ask for approximately how much time I think I'm going to need with them. I never ask "Do you have a minute." I know everything takes more than a minute. Instead I ask, "Do you have about 10 minutes for me so I can run something by you?" And then, I keep to the 10 minutes, or less.
2. Follow up in 36 to 72 hours (via e-mail or voicemail) to let the person know how our conversation has helped me move forward on the issue we discussed. I do this as a "transaction" (i.e., not in person) to continue to demonstrate my awareness of the importance of the other person's time.

It's always easiest to pick a practice over which you have 100 percent control. One way to do this is to spend the next five days or so maximizing the amount of time you need to interrupt other people. Say you work side-by-side with a colleague, or you're connected via IM, text messaging, or e-mail. To get the most from the next interruption, save up your questions and prompts and experiment with "bunching" them together.

One of my clients implemented this, with remarkable results. He kept five small note cards on his desk, each one labeled with the name of one person he worked with. Every time he thought of something to ask or tell one of his five teammates that was *not* urgent, he wrote that on the individual's card. Then, twice a day, he'd ask each of them, "Do you have a few minutes to go over some things with me?" He told me he rarely spent more than 10 minutes on these conversations; he explained further that he and a colleague will "plan a 30-minute meeting in a conference room away from our desks if I collect enough to discuss." By his estimates, this practice has cut down his interruptions by 50 percent throughout the day, and has given him back one to two hours *per day!*

Test this idea yourself. Measure the impact it has on your productivity when you interrupt your coworkers as infrequently as possible, by asking them to discuss several items at the same time time, a few times a day, instead of interrupting them several times per day and asking just one question each time. Note: If you decide to conduct this experiment with a larger team, make sure that you explain what you're planning to do beforehand, to identify how you will know when a single-item interruption is appropriate and necessary.

3. Managing Meetings Think back to the last meeting you attended where more than a few people were present, and reflect on how you spent the time in a room with these 5, 10, or even 30 other people. Where did you sit? How did you interact with the information as it was presented? What did the presenter do to engage the audience?

If you act as both participant and observer at meetings you attend, you can pick up subtle clues and ideas you can use to run your own meetings more effectively. A few things I've learned over the years:

1. *Schedule the meeting to begin on the 00:15.* If you're in charge of the next meeting, send out the invitation to it for, say, 10:15 to 11:00 AM. In my experience, most "on-the-hour" meetings wind up starting a few minutes late anyway (and, throughout the day, meetings tend to end 5 to 10 minutes late). Try scheduling 45-minute meetings; you may find those in attendance are more focused for this shorter period of time.
2. *Start the meeting by reviewing PAD—purpose, agenda, duration.* Share the logistics of the meeting again (as you no doubt did in the invitation) so that everyone knows why they are in the room, what the topics of discussion are, and what the scheduled end time is.
3. *Mix the media you use, to engage all types of learners.* Show a chart, tell a story, pass around a handout; and ask for brainstorming ideas in a group discussion. The more you can do to get everyone involved with visual, auditory, kinesthetic interactions, the more successful the meeting will be.

There are many more ways to improve the effectiveness and efficiency of your meetings. To get started, simply *observe* how meetings are generally run in your office over the next week or so. What happens that works? What happens that gets in the way of what *could* work? You shouldn't have any trouble identifying a few ideas to implement at your upcoming meetings. Remember, practice won't necessarily make perfect, but it will make things less complex, and perhaps ingrain good habits for the future.

4. Practicing Accountability Quite some time ago, Jodi, (an entrepreneur who founded www.NoMoreNylons.com, a community-based economic development advocate supporting women in business) created an accountability call-in program with two successful women who also own their own businesses. Depending on the business cycle they are in, they meet at least monthly to talk about goals, areas of concern, new opportunities, and other business-based topics.

These meetings are so powerful that Jodi has begun teaching this technique to other women in business. I've heard her speak over the years in Los Angeles, New York, London, Paris, and Venice about the significance of building an accountability program to staying on course and on purpose. She says the experience of sharing with fellow female professionals gives her a platform to practice describing her products and services, as well as float new ideas and address concerns, all within a focused community.

With some coaching from her, I've practiced with different accountability calls and group meetings over the past few years. Here's what I've learned that works:

1. *Stick to the point.* These are semiregular check-in meetings to update and hear questions from one another on a specific area or project.
2. *Focus, focus, focus.* Even though you may want to share or hear about personal issues, I use these meetings as "let's talk about the project" time, and choose *another* venue to catch up on how the family is doing or how much we enjoyed our last vacation, or discuss other personal projects we're working on.
3. *Show the rest of your team that you're engaged and involved.* Be present when you're on the phone or videoconferencing with this group; ask clarifying questions, listen attentively, and be supportive.
4. BONUS: *Follow up in the days after the call.* I've started doing this after my own meetings, and have enjoyed a positive effect. A few days after a call, I e-mail or send something to someone in the group that connects in some way to a project we discussed. It keeps me engaged and allows me to practice something I do for clients after I talk with *them* on the phone.

When Do You Practice?

I'm sure you know by now what a proponent I am of the process of practice; simply put, I think it's one of the most important ways to help make our best better. When you hear an idea or a suggestion, don't just accept it as is, and don't discount it, either. Test it. Experiment with it. Attend to it with short bursts of focus, and see what this does to help you maximize the time you spend learning and implementing.

I've stated this previously, but I want to repeat it here: It helps immensely to figure out when you're at your best (go back and review Chapter 1). Pick something you're going to practice this week and think about when you'd be the most focused on the activity, and therefore, better able to learn effectively. Some people like to set a timer first thing in the morning and focus 100 percent of their concentration on thinking about, experimenting with, and engaging in one particular new practice. Other clients have found that by scheduling time at work they are better able to be more consistent about what they are doing.

As a client of mine once told me, "I want to practice focusing on just one thing. I feel that from the moment I walk into the office I'm being pulled in a thousand different directions." Now, before I share the experiment I asked him to try, I'd like to think about what you would recommend. What do you suggest people do when they need to practice the skill of focusing on one thing?

Because I had a good understanding of this executive's roles, skills, and routines, I knew that it was important to "practice how he played." That is, we needed to find ways he could undertake his tasks in his actual office space. He was spending anywhere between 9 to 12 hours a day in or near his office, so the practices had to be within that context. This way, when he found something that worked, he: (a) would be able to do it consistently, and (b) could actually use that space to remind him what to do.

The first experiment I assigned him was as follows: "For the next 10 days, when you get to your office, sit down at the small conference table away from your desk. Set a timer for just three minutes, and write what the Ideal Day looks like to you on a piece of paper."

At the end of two weeks, as I learned during our debriefing phone conversation, he had increased the time in the second week to five minutes every morning. For these 300 significant seconds, he "pressed the pause button"— really, before he even got started—to think about the day ahead of him. He told me that he'd been working on strategy more, and focusing on and completing a greater number of his MITs. He also felt he was able to be much more available to his team, because he had given more thought to the projects they all were managing.

Remember, I suggest you "practice on the small things," because I am confident in the carryover effect of this exercise. That is, if you practice focusing for small bursts of time—say, just 3 minutes—on a regular basis, you will eventually find that you're stretching your focus to 5 to 10, or even 15, minutes. And that is going to have a powerful effect on your productivity.

My client preferred to do this in the morning. You may choose a practice, routine, or habit you want to experiment with later in the day or in the evening. But whenever you decide to do this, be consistent. This will allow you to collect information as you go along that will serve you well going forward. As a result of a few practice sessions, you'll be able to look back with some objectivity and ask one of the most important questions of this chapter: "Should I continue this practice for another few days?"

What Is Important to Practice?

Are you ready to get going? Have you chosen something to test and experiment with?

Good!

There are three keys to effective practice: (1) visualization, (2) rehearsal, and (3) the five-day experiment. As you review these three significant aspects of effective practice, plan to apply them soon—perhaps even later today!

1. Visualization: "See It Before You See It."

Remember in Chapter 8, I asked you to think about what you make? Then I asked you to write down what you want to *make more of*, in life and at work. Well, now is the time to focus on exactly what you want. What does your best getting better mean to you?

Let me show you how to get real, to start visualizing, as if what you are working toward is already on the way! Although I can think of many reasons to do this, I'll share my top two with you here:

1. You want to recognize it when you see it.
2. You want to be ready for it, when it shows up!

Here's how to visualize:

1. Think of an event you'll be attending or participating in sometime in the next week or two.
2. Close your eyes and bring to mind some of the people you might see there. If possible, picture their faces in your mind. Are they smiling? Are they serious? Are they speaking? Are they listening?
3. Now think about what you'll do while you're there. Will you sit, stand, or walk around? What kind of clothes will you be wearing?
4. Imagine what you'll talk about while you're there. Bring to mind the other people you'll be with. What will you most likely discuss? What will you want to ask them?
5. When you've completed the first four steps (which might take only one to two minutes), stop and write down one thing you'd like to do now that you've visualized, but have yet to experience the event.

Here's another, more active, visualization technique I've used and taught: Spend time with people who are better, more experienced, and more practiced than you at whatever it is you're preparing for. Simply spending time around experts will lower the amount of stress you might experience as you prepare to perform. If possible, ask them to talk about how they learned to do what you're learning now; and, of course, listen for any special clues they might share with you along the way.

However you choose to visualize, the goal is to get you where you're going; and while you're there, experience a feeling of: "This looks kind of familiar; seems like I've seen something like this before."

2. Rehearsal

Okay, you're mentally prepared; now it's time to "go on stage" by yourself! Here, I use "go on stage" as a metaphor for what I'm asking you to do next, which is to practice, at least once, by yourself. As a professional speaker, I regularly practice parts of my programs—new introductions, new content pieces—long before I "go live." As a triathlete, I practice a lot throughout the year to perform in just six or seven races during the summer. (One year I calculated that I had trained 225 hours to race for fewer than 30!)

There is a group of triathletes I spend a lot of time with in Ojai, California, and we meet at the athletic club by 7:00 on most Saturday mornings. These workouts are scheduled to last 90 minutes: We swim, we bike, then we run. Of course, we can't go all-out, all the time, so I always set a training goal for each Saturday, one that comes as close as possible to at least one of the events I've visualized for race day. For example, if an upcoming race consists of a 1,000-meter swim, during the weekend workout I may get as close to race pace as possible during the swim, but not on the bike or the run. The following Saturday, I'll focus on the bike portion.

For each workout we also pick a part of town in which to run or ride that mimics the course of the actual race: If it's a hilly course, we head toward Santa Paula; if it's flat and fast, along Creek Road we go.

Whatever it is you're visualizing and rehearsing, you do so with one intention: to get to "that day"—to compete in the race, facilitate the meeting, present to the client, whatever the goal—with that one thought in the back of your mind: "This is familiar; I've been here before, and I know what this looks, sounds, and feels like."

3. The Five-Day Experiment

What have you been thinking about changing or trying relative to time management, organization, and productivity as you've been reading this book? One of the lessons I've learned is that if you try something every day with just a little bit of focus, you can decide in about five days whether or not you should continue doing it. There are all kinds of scenarios in which this approach works.

For example, I worked with one client who decided she was going to show up on time to every meeting she had scheduled for the next five days. (This was a *big* deal for her, as she had a habit of always running late.) I coached someone else who claimed he was going to decide the moment e-mails arrived in his inbox whether he would act on them, file them for later action, or simply delete them. When he deleted an e-mail, it was *gone*. When he filed it, he put it in the folder, along the left-hand side of the screen, where it needed to be. And if he needed to act on an e-mail in short order, he filed it in a folder called My Actions. Within days, he was working in a much more focused manner, because he was spending the majority of his day addressing the items in his My Actions folder, getting the important work done.

These are the kinds of experiments people have engaged in over the years I've worked with them. Now, as you well know, because I've been emphasizing it throughout the book, merely doing something five days in a row will not make it a habit. But doing something five days in a row with *intention* and *attention* will signal whether you should continue doing it; whether it's worth it to continue practicing that soon-to-be habit.

Those two "-tion"-suffixed words, intention and attention, are very important. Consider the first: *intention*. That's what I'm thinking about on my way to the office, when I'm making a mental to-do list. "Today, I'm going to . . ." describes my intention. How often do you sit down and actually write a to-do list for the day? Maybe you jot something down on a sticky note and attach it to your computer monitor in the morning. Or perhaps you e-mail yourself while you are out of the office, either from home or a mobile device, to remind you what you need to do when you get to work. You design a five-day experiment to (1) figure out what you need to focus on every day; and then, (2) you follow through with your design. That's your intention.

Your *attention* refers to what you *actually got done*, what you attended to. Many people find that their attention gets compromised in a typical weekday. Colleagues come in and ask for help or information; they tap them on the shoulder and utter that dreaded phrase: "Do you have a minute?"

You can build five-day experiments for both "-tions." For your intention, sit down on the first of the next five days and make a list that has no more than two, or maybe three, "absolute must get-to's" for each day.

As far as your attention is concerned, sit down and decide that, for the next five days, you're going to track the times you get distracted by something or someone from the "outside," whether it's a phone ringing or a colleague walking into your office while you're trying to concentrate. If you can pick one thing with which to experiment, one thing to notice, or one thing to try, chances are you'll be able to look back and decide at the end of five days whether you should continue giving attention to this task or effort, or move on to another five-day experiment.

Questions to Ask While You're Practicing

Now you're ready to get going. You have some ideas, some experiments, and some action steps in mind. There are a few points to remember before you leave this chapter and begin the actual practice of making your best better. Most important: Keep in mind that it took you a long, long time to get to where you are. Many people spend years searching for the tips, tools, systems, and processes they rely on day to day. Since you've made it this far along this journey, I'm going to suggest that you already know what to do. Now it's time to implement what you know.

There are some questions to have at the ready as you move through these practices, and they will sound familiar to you. This list is not exhaustive, by any means, and if you come up with one you think I should add to it, please let me know. I look forward to hearing what works for you!

- What does different look like?
- What do I need to see, read, or do to practice this more?
- Who will get me to think about the next habit to practice?
- Where can I go to practice this?

What Does Different Look Like?

At this stage, you're about to begin the practice you decided to test. It's important to consider the implications of experimenting with this new practice. You must literally stop, sit down, relax, and imagine what your workday and life would look like if you had indeed practiced it enough to make it a habit, one that had become comfortable.

One of the first times I did this was when I started racing triathlons. I worked with an Olympic coach who asked me to visualize the second hand on the clock that hung on the pool deck. "How fast do you want to swim this 100-meter set?" she asked one day. I replied, "Under 1:30, for sure."

"How many seconds is that per 50 meters?" she asked next. As soon as I answered, she said, "And 25?" Again, I gave her a number.

"Now," she said, "imagine the second hand going around, and see yourself where you need to be at each point around the clock." After I did that for just a few moments, she sent me off into the pool.

It was amazing, when my hand touched the wall again, 100 meters later, I looked up to see my coach smiling ear to ear. I'll always remember her saying, "Jason, you did it," as she turned to walk away. Then she glanced back over her shoulder, and added: "1:28. See what happens when you know what it's supposed to look like?"

What Do I Need to See, Read, or Do to Practice This More?

Our brains are designed to answer the questions we ask. My friend and fellow expert speaker Noah St. John travels the world talking about "affirmations," questions we ask ourselves that send our minds searching, reading, listening, and finding answers. You have more resources than ever before available to you to help build the knowledge base of what you can do, starting now, to invite in and practice these new work and life habits.

It might be necessary to take the seemingly simple step of cleaning up first! Do you have some "stuff" around you that is actually pulling you away from your new habit-building practice? Replace it with items that trigger you to engage in the new habit, the new practice—the new you!

Another colleague of mine from New Zealand, Michael Sampson, sent me the most wonderful gift some time ago. Before I had ever written or published a book, he presented me with a wooden, engraved book holder for my desk. Stenciled on the front of the frame are the words "Jason Womack's First Book." Whenever I look at it, I smile and think, "What can I do, today, to keep the writing going?"

Who Will Get Me to Think about the Next Habit to Practice?

Reflect back on the thoughts you had, the notes you wrote, or the highlights you made while reading Chapter 5 on your social network. Those are the people—both the ones you know and the ones you have yet to meet—who are going to introduce you to your next practices. Look around, listen, and be very aware of the influence those people have on what you think about, and do.

While I was writing this book, I started many sessions by envisioning specific people I wanted to read the section I was about to start composing. At times, I would think of a person I'd worked with or knew socially. Other times, I thought of a public figure—a politician or athlete, for example. And, from time to time, I wrote for an entire demographic group—a company, a country, a culture.

Throughout this book I've talked about the proactive experiences I've had with mentoring. Both as a mentor and a mentee, I understand the very substantial value of this kind of mastermind meeting. I believe that power and positive change can occur when people spend time with each other, listening, questioning, and encouraging one another to move forward.

This question, "Who will get me to think about the next habit to practice?" is designed to push you just a little bit. Let your imagination run wild, and then answer the question!

Where Can I Go to Practice This?

Over the past 30 years I have spoken in front of thousands of groups: I've taught in middle and high school; I've spoken at national and international conferences; I've lectured at universities here in America; I've talked to local community groups like Rotary and the Chamber of Commerce. When people see me, they see the "best, current version" of what I have to offer. What they *don't* see is the work that's directly behind my presentation.

I go to my office, to conference rooms, to hotel rooms—anywhere available—to practice. When I identify a new piece of research I want to share, I begin by collecting information I might be able to use. Then, I write. I write in a notebook and on my whiteboard. I write on scraps of paper, in Microsoft Word and using MindJet MindManager (a mind-mapping software on my laptop). All of this effort—consuming information and creating written content—is part of my practice. Then, I say it. I stand up in my office and "talk out my slides." I give a mock presentation to hear how everything is going to sound.

For years, I have video-recorded many of these presentations. Sometimes I do a voice-over recording of the PowerPoint presentation I am preparing. Other times, I turn on the video camera, press record, and "act as if." I have found in both instances that if I "go away to my creative corner," I can practice while the presentation is still "small," make adjustments, see where I'm at, and get ready for when it needs to be big.

By now, you've probably thought of a few things you're ready to take on and practice (or practice anew!). Remember to take it easy; start slow, and check in regularly on your progress. Use all the tips and tricks you now have available, from asking someone to work alongside you to checking in with an accountability buddy on a week-to-week basis to writing down *exactly* what you want to do and posting it in front of you as you work at your desk. In the Conclusion of this book, I'll suggest a few things you can do right away to "just get started!"

Conclusion

Pulling It All Together

Making Your Best Better, a Chapter at a Time

LOOKING BACK OVER this book, it will make sense to you that now it's time to build practices and implement experiments applicable to each. To begin, I offer you some overall comments about Chapters 1 to 10, followed by a practice you can implement for each to *just get started!*

Part 1   Work Smarter

- **Chapter 1, Improvement and You: Identifying Your Role in Making Your Best Better.** Reread something you wrote while you were reading this chapter. Review your "I'm at my best when . . ." statements or your list of MITs. One of the easiest ways to begin to get a sense of what is important to you—what you're focusing on and what is taking up your time—is to go back and read what you wrote. That is how you can "see what you think." And the process is as simple as opening the Sent Items folder in your e-mail system, flipping through the pages of a notebook you used last year, or looking over your current handwritten to-do list.

There, in your own words and your own penmanship, you can see what *is* important to you and begin to practice small changes leading to big differences. Remember, it takes only five days to experiment with a new behavior to discover if you want to continue building that habit!

- **Chapter 2, Improvement and Pacing: Building and Sustaining Habits That Lead to Productivity.** My dad, one of my greatest mentors, taught me a lot about goals, project pacing, and setting milestones. He told me that he looks at himself in the mirror each morning and asks one question: "What can I do today to improve things?" I remember when he told me this; it was a very significant moment. Over the years of asking myself that question, I have found it to be a wonderful prompt to practice pacing. Because I can't do everything at once, I start the morning off by concentrating very specifically on what it is that I *can* do that day.

- **Chapter 3, Improvement and Time: Get the Most from 1 Percent of Your Day!** Use about 15 minutes a day to make your best better. Remember, there are 96 15-minute blocks in a day. As I said repeatedly throughout the book, "If you're waiting until you have time to decide what you're going to do when you have time, you'll always be behind." I believe that to be true. There are really three different kinds of work we do, and that first one, thinking, is more significant than the other two, managing projects and doing tasks.

  Once you know when you work at your best, begin to practice using those precious blocks of time. Start right now by writing down 20 to 30 things you *know* you're going to have to do this week that will take "just about" 15 minutes. Keep that list handy, and next time a meeting gets cancelled or you decide to stay at work a little late, take a look at the list with one question in mind: "What can I do right now?"

Part 2   Think Bigger

- **Chapter 4, Improvement and Self-Efficacy: If You Think You Can, You Probably Can.** One substantial way to build up momentum toward the next big goal is to reflect on a goal you recently achieved. There's something incredibly special and valuable that happens when you stop and direct all your thoughts to what you did the last time you were successful: It gets you ready to "go for it" again. Practice this once a week (even better, every day!). Stop and think about a goal you achieved, somewhere you went, or something you did. Actually recall everything it took to make it happen, and congratulate yourself on a job well done.

When I'm advising founders of start-up companies, I often share with them my Three-Point Business Development Plan. Then, when I debrief a single day or a week later, I go back and reflect on each step along the way:

○ *Show up.* This refers to much more than just "being there." It means to show up on time, prepared, and willing to do my best. It signals to my clients that I've put everything else aside, and for the time we've contracted to spend together, they get all of my attention.

○ *Do good work.* I'm always pleased when a client says, "Jason, you always do what you say you're going to do." More than once someone has said this with a sense of wonder and surprise in their voice. Think about what you can do tomorrow to demonstrate you're "there" for the people you work with and for.

○ *Stay in touch.* In Chapter 5 I wrote about the social network as your gateway to further accomplishment and thinking bigger. As I told you, I regularly handwrite cards, and often send a magazine article or a book, to someone I'm working with, if I think he or she will gain insight or value from that information.

■ **Chapter 5, Improvement and the Social Network: If You Want to Go Far, Fast, Go Together.** Practice introducing yourself; likewise, practice asking for introductions. Build your network intentionally. In today's business environment, people change jobs and locations often. Stay connected to those professionals you meet and work with regularly. Experiment with different routines of writing letters and e-mails, making phone calls, even inviting people to coffee in the morning or to lunch, to catch up over new stories. Continue to stay "looped in" via your online networks, and review your address books on a regular basis. Another great tip: Review your Sent Items in e-mail from a year or so ago; you're bound to remember *someone* to check in with and say hello.

- **Chapter 6, Improvement and Tracking: What Is in the Way, What Is Along the Way?** Over the years I've tracked so many effort/payoff areas of life and work that I'm now used to it; it's a part of my daily routine. Some months I track the hours of sleep I get, other months the minutes of exercise; sometimes the pages of professional books I've read, and other times the number of clients I reach out to per day. Start today, and for the next five days track *something* you do regularly. At the end of those five days, look back and assess the value (both actual and perceived).

  One way to practice tracking is to set a big goal and then find a monthly magazine that matches up with and somehow helps you meet that goal. Whether the topic is business, health, or family life, you can surely find at least one monthly periodical filled with articles, interviews, and even advertisements about that topic. While you're learning all you can to help you reach that new goal, keep track of new information, and review the results of implementing ideas you find.

- **Chapter 7, Improvement and Purpose: Clarify and Promote Your Own "So That . . ."** This is one of the easier ideas to practice. How? Attend a conference. Find an event taking place in the city or state where you live; or travel across the country (or the world!) to put yourself in a position to learn more. Surround yourself with people who share your passion. What happens when you attend a national convention or a statewide conference? For many hours, or even days, you'll meet a variety of individuals, hear countless new ideas, and engage in conversations where you hear real-life examples of how people are making things possible. When I attend these conferences—often as a keynote speaker at large global events—I talk with people in the hallways and go to all the meals and events I can, so that I can dive in deep and practice talking about those MITs, the Most Important Things.

Part 3   Make More

- **Chapter 8, Improvement and Feedback: Knowing How to Ask for It and What to Do with It.** My wife and I end every day at home by asking each other the following question, and then listening to the answer. We call it the Evening Question, and it goes like this: "What did I do really well today?" When Jodi asks me that question, I share with her the things that I saw *her* do well. Because we live, love, *and* work together, it is always possible to find something!

Some days it takes longer than others, especially if we were busy and a lot happened. I have come to really appreciate this time with her, as I get to hear from her perspective what she thought I did well, and why. We take turns thinking, sharing, and hearing one another debrief the day.

- **Chapter 9, Improvement and Focus: The Resource That Affects All Others.** Remember the advice I gave to "practice on the small things, and perform on the big ones"? Well, there's one thing you can do here that just may change the entire game: Buy a countdown timer and bring it to your office. Over the next week or so, schedule several 15-minute work sessions and "single-task." Decide to work on one thing, with as much focus as possible and with as few interruptions as necessary.

  When I do this, I literally walk away from my desk and go to another workspace. It might be easier for you to do this in a conference room or an empty office space across the floor. I set the timer for a period of time to work on one thing, and then do everything I can to "focus to finish" (or at least finish that work session). If I'm working on my laptop computer, I turn off the wireless connection so that I'm not tempted to quickly check a website or review e-mail. Simply having to turn on the connection, wait a moment, connect to the Internet, launch a web browser, and go to a site (all of which might take 60 seconds) is enough to convince me to say, "I'll do that later," add a reminder to my to-do list, and stay focused on the MIT I assigned myself. Try this several times in a week and see how far you get on some of those projects and actions you've been putting off "until you have the time."

- **Chapter 10, Improvement and Practice: Practice Doesn't Make Perfect, It Makes Comfortable.** This is where it all comes together. Improvement comes easily when you identify new habits to practice and focus on them for short periods of time. Remember to experiment with practicing for five days at a time; not because five days will magically turn a practice in to a habit, but because five days is generally long enough to provide you with some objective feedback as to whether or not you should make the practice a habit in the first place. Your competitive advantage derives from what you think about and what you do about what you're thinking. Go now; get started. Pick something small, yet significant and repeatable, and start practicing to make your best better.

Will It Be Worth It?

And now, an important question to ask when you think of the effort it will take to make your best better: "Is it worth it?" That may be the most important question I've asked you in the entire book!

I made a promise to you in the Introduction. How did I do? And how did *you* do? Did you try some things, think about some things, talk about some things, and assess some things?

I dedicate this book to you, the reader, for choosing to think about, read about, and practice ways to make your best better. You're on a new path, toward identifying what could be done; developing ideas and a plan for working on that idea; experimenting, testing, and practicing; and, finally, assessing the value of the time, energy, and focus you spent working on it.

I hope you have found it to be worth it. I always have.

Acknowledgments

Many years ago, an influential writing teacher, Anne Lamott, taught me to say this more: "Thank you, thank you, thank you."

To my friends Quanah Ridenour, Joe Bruzzese, James Ellengold, Nik Chapapas, Mark Rosky, Ben Anderson, and Alden Levy: Thank you for the ideas, advice, and shoulders to lean on.

To the Womack and Rosenthal families: Thank you for encouraging me to think- and be-bigger.

To my mentors, Tim Braheem, Steve Silverman, Marshall Goldsmith, Kevin Wilde, Frances Hesselbein, Larry Chambers, Jim Polk, and Irene Dorner: Thank you for listening when I bring questions to the table; you always share your perspective in a way that builds me up and makes it easy to believe more *is* possible.

To my teacher Rao Machiraju: Thank you for including me on your team; it is my true hope that I can learn and grow and do *half* of what you see me as capable of doing.

To the people who believe in me, and continue to pick up the phone when I call. You always listen when I say, "I have another idea!" Thanks go to David Bailey, Maurice Springer, Mary Dean, Morris Sims, Joshua Millage, Marc Grainger, Dan McHugh, Ron Menning, Tim O'Keefe, Lisa Shalett, Michael Butler, Craig Sieber, Damien Hooper-Campbell, Rob Saucier, Christopher Scott, and Su Zurbin.

There were many people who were there for me early on in my teaching, speaking, and writing careers, and I'm thankful to you for being a part of my life: Steve Bennett, Leslie Ogden, Julie Graham, Gwen Gross, Lu and Tim Setnika, Sandra Lee, Kim and John Hoj, Mark Biallas, Thomson Dawson, Chris Clark, Larry Clark, Gaston Gonzalez, Howard Tucker, Torry Burdick, Russ Stalters, Ron Bezoza, Jim and Debbie Ziegler, Caroline Burnett, Rene Rodriguez, Jen and Ryan Speed, Cico Rodriguez, Kieu Frisby, Randy and Liz Harward, Martha Ringer, Rob Steven, Mark Lloyd, Adrian Trenholm, and Donavon Roberson.

There have been *so* many clients along the way, people I've coached, partnered with, and built organization-wide learning programs for. Thank you: Jon Peters, Steve Daniels, John Robinson, BJ Bedford Miller, Tim Scanlon, Lawrence Carter, Kevin DeNoia, Mary Kline, Mervin Staton, Carrie Randall, Jennifer Piperno, Amy Margolis, Nick Bhuta, Bjorn Blanchard, Emma Pace, Lida Miskiw, Andrea Caldas, Rose Simmons, Rhonda Johnson, Pierre Dobson, Richard McNulty, Erin Karnik, Tanya Macaluso, David Fink, Shaun Branon, Steve Walker, Gary Press, Tracey Dunn, William Johnson, Alison Gavin, and Ilene Bezjian.

To the editors who have "let me play," writing articles and features over the years, thank you Lorri Friefeld, Ken Shelton, Laura Lober, Anne Kallas, and Emily Paulsen.

There are several authors, speakers, and thinkers who sent me on this quest for knowledge, and special thanks go to Napoleon Hill, Dale Carnegie, Stephen Covey, David Allen, John-Roger, John Morton, Don Pink, Steve Jobs, Steven Snyder, Shakti Gawain, Keith Ferrazzi, Lorraine Monroe, Jim Collins, Peter Drucker, Tom Peters, Warren Bennis, and Seth Godin.

It is important to say that this book is in your hands because Pam Slim hosted a panel at SXSW, where I met Matt Holt from John Wiley & Sons, Inc., and working with Lauren Murphy, Christine Moore, Peter Knox, and Susan Moran has been incredible. Thank you *all*!

And, to my dear friend Jodi: Thank you for walking hand in hand with me through this amazing life journey. I love you.

Index